Mastering Graphics

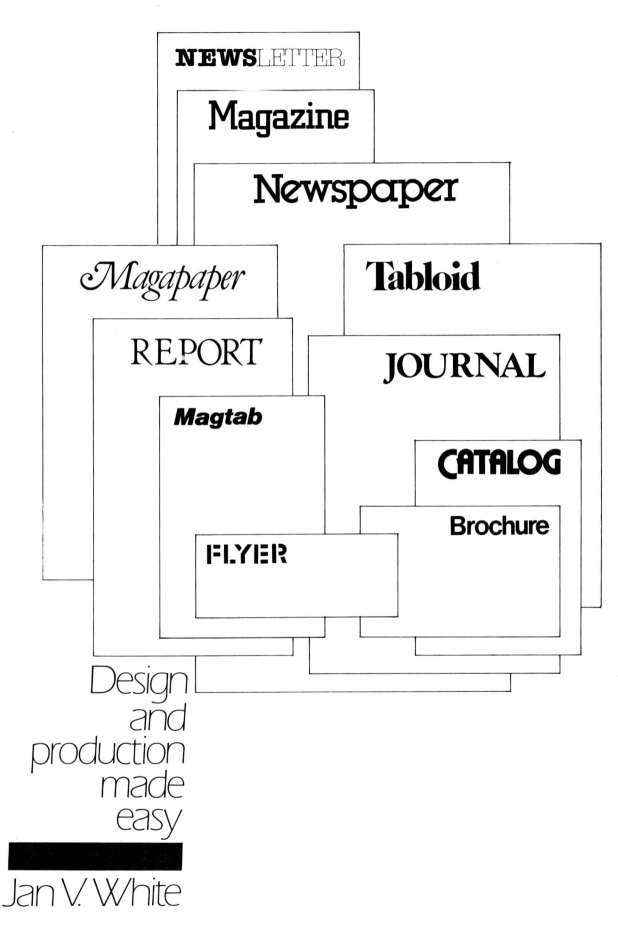

NEWSLETTER

Magazine

Newspaper

Magapaper

Tabloid

REPORT

JOURNAL

Magtab

CATALOG

Brochure

FLYER

Design
and
production
made
easy

Jan V. White

R. R. Bowker Company, New York and London, 1983

Published by R. R. Bowker Company
1180 Avenue of the Americas, New York, N.Y. 10036
Copyright © 1983 by Jan V. White
Printed and bound in the United States of America

Library of Congress Cataloging in Publication Data

White, Jan V., 1928–

Mastering graphics.

Includes index.
1. Graphic arts.   2. Printing, Practical.
3. Newsletters.   4. House organs.   5. Pamphlets—
Design.   I. Title.
Z253.W47   1983   686.2   83-6004
ISBN 0-8352-1704-3

CONTENTS

13 What you absolutely must know about printing, folding, binding, and finishing 168

INTRODUCTION

The title for this book could have been *Graphics Without Fear*, except that it was decided that something a bit more positive was needed—hence *Mastering*. The notion of graphics *without fear* remains operative, however, because graphic design is not a nest of weird secrets revealed only to some wild-eyed practitioners of an occult art. Instead it is a working tool for working editors and their good right hands—their graphic designers, if they are lucky enough to have them.

When graphic design is considered as an end in itself and is done for its own sake, then it is terrifying indeed, for its validity depends entirely on one's subjective "liking," and "liking" is a quality that no one can define and few agree about. All anyone can do is to feel insecure about it and defend one's arbitrary position. Furthermore, such an approach to design is nothing but a quest for superficial beauty: making a publication look good, and pleasing to the eye. It is, of course, possible to develop such cosmetic gloss on any printed product, but that approach was nailed down forever by Oscar Wilde when he referred to the dead fish in the moonlight: "It glistens, but it stinks."

When graphic design is regarded as a means to an end, then it is no longer self-centered art-for-art's-sake, but rather an outward-looking technique-for-communication's-sake—and that is a very different kettle of fish that smells delicious. As such, it becomes accessible to anyone: those who originate the product as well as those who receive it. It is this aspect of design that *Mastering Graphics* deals with. Because the book is based on common sense, you will find that *without fear* is not some bombastic claim but a statement of simple fact.

Graphic design is a functional response to specific, realistic problems that can be simple and quantifiable (such as how to shoehorn too many words into too small a space) or esoteric and hard to define (such as how to give your publication the character appropriate to its purpose and readership). Yet at neither end of the spectrum is graphic design an arcane art. At the simple end, all you need do is count up your total number of characters and do some elementary math. At the esoteric end, finding your ideal solution may take a little longer, but it is no more difficult: all you need do is to break that apparent enormity into its component parts and then proceed to make one small decision for each. In both cases—the simple and the complex—you make your judgments based on facts and options that are accessible to all. The result may look like "art," but you will know perfectly well that your decisions had little to do with your artistic talent or training (or lack thereof). Your decisions had everything to do with sound *editorial thinking:* the capacity to analyze and make judgments based on logic and common sense for the sake of the product and the story.

Graphic design in publications exists on two levels that are interconnected, yet quite separate: (1) the character of *the product as a whole,* and (2) the successful communication of *the ideas inherent in its parts.* The first aspect has to do with what the object looks like and how the stories leap off the page into the reader's mind; or, how you recognize the product from page to page and issue to issue and how memorable or exciting your readers perceive the content to be. The character of the product as a whole is created from the choices you and/or your designer make that fuse into a mix that is particular to your product. It consists of many factors such as: the weight, color, texture, and snap of the stock you use; the page size; the ink color; the proportions of the margins around the page; the column structure in the live area of your page; the texture, color, contrast, and patterning of the type you use for the body copy, display, and other areas of typography; the style of the standing art used for logos and other graphic elements; the format of the many elements recurring from issue to issue such as covers, contents, editorial, and so forth; the style of illustrations; the handling of photos . . . and many more. Such choices are made from a nearly infinite variety of possibilities and are influenced by wholly practical considerations such as what your suppliers can offer in the way of services and materials, press size, number of copies to be printed, method of distribution, as well as the overriding question of budgets . . . and so forth. They are also influenced by criteria that are much harder though no less necessary to define, such as the average age of your readers, the degree of their visual/verbal sophistication, the purpose of the publication . . . and so on.

When you know what your problems are and base your decisions on the right criteria, you can construct a solution that is fitting and elegant. It must be based on a dispassionate analysis of your needs, purposes, and limitations that define the graphic materials you will be using—if you accept as a definition of the word "materials" anything that is visible on the printed page. The resulting mix of those materials will be what makes you "you" . . . your format. You will work with them until you decide to change them.

What you decide to do with graphic materials and how you apply your ingenuity to telling individual stories within the restrictions imposed by these materials will be the challenge of that other aspect of graphic design—the communication of ideas inherent in the parts of the publication. First you must attract the potential reader's attention by whatever means you can devise to make the story appear irresistible. Then you must hold it by making your story fascinating; you must get the information across quickly by efficient presentation, and ensure its being memorable by emphasizing that which is significant. You have to make the value of the product apparent to your reader so that it will be anticipated and welcomed as a trusted friend, by making it both recognizable as well as packed with useful content.

But that is precisely why you have to know what you are doing and why you are doing it the way you are doing it. Flying by the seat of your pants can lead to losing your shirt. That is why this book has been assembled as a compendium of the fundamental practical knowledge you need in order to approach your task fearlessly. It carefully balances the essential technicalities of graphic design and production with suggestions on how to use them effectively. Since it is as dangerous to know too much as too little about any one aspect of the process, the material here has been carefully chosen to give an overview for handling your publication-making responsibly.

The book is the result of the 30 years I have been involved in publishing, the last 20 as consultant and lecturer. The truism that a teacher is taught by his pupils is absolutely unassailable: they asked the questions and needed the answers. I have fielded those questions often enough to have learned what the most common fears and insecurities are, and which gaps in knowledge cause them. It is my hope that the answers to the most frequent questions can be found here. If they are not, perhaps I may do my readers an even greater service by telling you not only where to go to find them, but—more importantly—that it is perfectly all right to ask! Nobody has all the answers, and making publications is an extremely complex procedure. It is no wonder that so many people have technical problems as well as more hard-to-solve, editorial ones. To help at least in the area defined as graphics, this book has been divided into a set of logical areas. Refer to the chapter titles to determine the particular area of interest and then scan the headlines that have been placed on the page to help you close in on a narrower topic. This book intentionally has no glossary in the traditional sense, because people seldom use it. Instead, technical terms and concepts are highlighted in boldface in the text so you can find them quickly—and discover their meaning in the context in which they occur. The index is, of course, a cross-referencing guide.

One last thought: the tasks we do not like tend to be put off until the last possible moment—when we cannot avoid them any more. Too many word-oriented people fall into this trap when they face the task of turning those words and thoughts into marks on paper that communicate to readers. Because they are unsure of themselves, because they do not know what they are doing, and because they are afraid, they postpone it until the task becomes a last-minute overnight nightmare. You cannot avoid doing the layout forever; isn't it wiser to get on with it in good time, so you can develop a solution that will *sing*? When you discover how logical and easy it really is, who knows? You may even become as fascinated by the way your product appears as by its content and writing. At that point you will become a fully rounded communicator.

Now with respect to this book: it has some 480 line illustrations if you count typographic examples as "illustrations." Please don't check up on the number: I made some arbitrary decisions as to what constitutes a separate illustration and what doesn't, in trying to come up with the total. Besides, who cares? Suffice it to say that there are a lot of them. There are also some 80 halftones. And reams of words. Assembling all this stuff would have been a daunting undertaking, had I not been fortunate to have the help of several skilled and indispensable professionals: Mary L. Young transcribed the tape into legible typescript (which must have been some task, given my propensity for disjointed complexity and seemingly endless verbosity). Betty Sun and Iris Topel edited the manuscript with insight and diplomacy: they got rid of the obfuscations and circumlocutions together with most of my funnies. They clarified obscurities and challenged some of my rasher assertions. They did it all with extraordinary patience, for this is a rather unusual book in terms of bookmaking: the author didn't just write and illustrate it, but he also oversaw the typesetting and then assembled the mechanicals himself. So the proper control of consistency, which is a normal part of an editor's responsibilities, gently evaporated. I acknowledge their self-control with such frustrations. You see, I enjoy playing with this marvelously malleable material that typography and illustration and space are to such an extent, that I make decisions about detailing on one page that may be quite different from a similar situation on another page. So when you notice such inconsistencies, blame the author: he was having fun. Blame him also for any mistakes—the editors did their best under unusually trying circumstances.

The typesetting was done by J&J Typesetters in Norwalk, CT. They are a joy to work with. The stills from old movies are used by kind permission of the Still File Collection. Other photos don't deserve crediting: they are supposed to be bad, and I have little difficulty taking such pictures myself. My thanks to Carl Moreus of Norwalk, CT, for the use of his photomechanical conversions on pages 130–131. My thanks, also, to Helen Einhorn for overseeing the excellent production of this book.

Without my Clarissa, I would not have had the courage to tackle this monster. I must also thank my four sons: Charles, with his Caroline, Alexander, Gregory, and Christopher. Each in his own way is cause for paternal pride. I know they want me to dedicate this book to the memory of KW.

Westport, CT
May 1983

Which will you choose:

newsletter magazine magapaper magtab or tabloid?

Let's assume that you are faced with putting out a publication. You are then very likely to have a stack of publications sitting on your desk: big ones, little ones, fat and colorful ones, thin and floppy ones, newspaperlike ones, and flamboyant annual-reportlike ones—and the prospect of making your own is terrifying. How can you possibly do something like that?

Don't be overwhelmed by the quantity or the variety. Instead, go through the mound again and weed out everything that doesn't feel right. Keep those pieces that seem to have the right character for *your* needs and *your* audience and that are, therefore, to *your liking*. Elsewhere in this book, the verb "to like" is seldom used because subjective liking, which is based on an emotional response, must be supplanted by logic, strategic planning, and rational decisions when you put your publication together. You must know what you're doing and why you're doing it that way. But, for now, your intuitive feeling of rightness, expressed in terms of "liking," is a valid and valuable tool to use.

When you've narrowed the field you may well decide that a modest, single-page, typewritten newsletter is what you should be doing—fine! You can forget all about magazine formats and newspaper makeup! Or you may have gravitated toward a more newspaperlike product: a tabloid with all its hard-hitting, newsy flavor—fine! You've taken the first major step in your publication-making process.

Your ultimate choice, however, will need to take three factors into account. It is hard to make intelligent generalizations about these factors because their specifics are so variable, but you should know about them and figure them into your equation before you commit yourself to a final choice of format.

1. The availability of suppliers in your vicinity who have the right machinery to produce the kind of product you'd like.

2. Some idea of the way your product will be distributed, for that may well affect both costs and the physical limitations within which you'll have to work.

3. The availability of enough money to create the very best version of the product you'd like to have. Clearly, some are cheaper to make than others. It is far better to produce a first-rate version of a cheaper kind than a shoddy version of a more expensive kind. Only common sense and

discussions with your suppliers can give you the information you need to base your decisions on.

Those are three practical considerations that must be made. To make your life even more complicated, there are three more fundamentals you must also absorb at this early stage of your publishing career, if you are to succeed. They are not practical, but without them you cannot muster the intellectual freedom you need to do the job right.

1. Forget everything you ever learned about the way reports are supposed to be done. Anyone who has ever submitted a paper to the English teacher in high school had to put his or her name in the top right-hand corner, align the date below it, center the title in all capitals on the page with a line under it, place the bibliography at the end and footnotes on the page where the reference occurs, and so on—you know what I mean. Such patterning is one of the useful disciplines of school and perfectly valid for what it is. It is even useful for doing college papers. But publishing is a broader world where such rules or guidelines don't exist. Clear your mind of those cobwebs.

2. Don't think that there are any correct ways of doing anything. There aren't. There are traditions. There are rules of thumb whose application may or may not be appropriate. There are comfortable ways of doing things that have been developed over the years and that are effective in one product but disastrous in another. There are endless slogans about never setting type in all capitals, about italics in bulk being hard to read, about trapped space being anathema, about big headlines having to go at the top of the page, and so on ad nauseam. Slogans are slogans and embody only a sliver of truth. There are also lots of books that tell you what you must always or never do if you hope to do it right. Nonsense. There is only one right way: Think the problem through, decide on the editorial point you're trying to make, then express it in the appropriate physical format, be it for a single story or an entire publication. If the form grows out of the content, you'll have succeeded in finding the optimal way of communicating your meaning—which is the purpose of this whole business to start with.

3. See beyond the beguiling pictures when you examine other people's publications. Look beyond or behind them to notice the structure of the pages, the rhythms used to assemble the whole piece, the patterning and repetitive elements used, the length of the stories, the way headlines are used, the variety of subjects covered. It is one of the hardest things to learn to do because even bad pictures are so fascinating. And if the samples of publications you have gathered are exciting (which they probably are, otherwise you wouldn't have kept them), chances are the writing and subject matter are equally alluring. It is hard to resist getting involved in these publications, and their very capacity to draw in even those disinterested in the subject is the mark of their excellence. Resist it if you want to become a dispassionate, professional analyzer.

But for now, shelve all the worries about suppliers and finances as well as about not knowing how to begin, and concentrate on the pile of stuff on your desk. To help you analyze the various characteristics of formats, here is a short overview of the three basic types. Obviously there are hybrids as well as unique publications, which attract much attention by virtue of their uniqueness. Doubtless there are several of such types in your pile. There's no reason why you should not depart from the standard formats. Be aware, however, that what looks simple can turn out to be quite tricky to achieve; and every time you do something special, it is likely to cost you both aggravation and money. So here are the fundamentals, if only for comparison.

Newsletters

What a multitude of sins this term encompasses! It is so often misused that it is almost meaningless: it means whatever you want it to mean. It describes a publication of limited circulation that is essentially informative in nature and that is published often or seldom, in a format that varies from the simplest to the most complex. For our purposes, let's return to the original definition: a newsletter is a simple medium that is easy to produce and probably one of the most effective to ever have been invented, because it is forthright and unassuming.

A true newsletter is simple, informal, relaxed. Its effectiveness lies in the illusion it creates of being a person-to-person letter. It should be quick to read and full of news (although what constitutes news is arguable, if it is news to the recipient, then news it is). It should be written in a series of short paragraphs that summarize events and bring out their significance to the recipient. Longer items are, of course, perfectly acceptable, but the longer they are, the less "newsy" the product appears. To be a true newsletter, it needs to look like news and be edited down to the essentials: the who, what, where, how, and when—and why the reader should need to know about it.

It ought also to look informal and inexpensive, unpretentious, not sloppy or messy, but relaxed and unassuming, in order to create that atmosphere of one-to-one personal communication. When typewritten, its informal character and "inside-scoop" feeling can best be communicated.

If it is typewritten, then it ought not to have typeset headings. Otherwise the image that readers typically have in mind of the editor batting out the latest hot news on the typewriter (or word processor) will be destroyed if visual elements obviously not generated on a typewriter are added to the mix. By all means have a logo set in type and run it off in color to create a **letterhead** on which the typescript can then be imposed. That reinforces the personal quality of the newsletter. But inserting headlines in type is something else.

Because it is a "letter," its page size is probably the standard 8½" x 11". The simplest newsletter is, of course, a single sheet. Two sheets stapled together in the top-left corner are the next step. From there you can have several other variations of physical format—but eight pages is about the maximum for a plain newsletter.

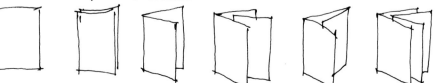

The next step up the scale is when the ambitious editor becomes design conscious and yearns for something more formalized, more expensive looking, more valuable, more "finished."

So the page is split into two columns, and the copy is retyped several times so that columns are made neat on both left- and right-hand edges (**justified**) instead of unaligned, which is the way the machine naturally produces lines of type. An **executive typewriter** may even be used in order to create an aura of sophistication. That soon gives way to rejecting the typewriter's directness and large scale, in favor of **cold-type** typesetting, the rationalization being that you can get more on the page. Soon, instead of a straightforward newsletter, you have the poor cousin of a magazine—set three columns per page, with headlines in contrasting sans-serif type, and—the ultimate development—pictures. At this point, longer stories that are no longer news-oriented but rather analytical or descriptive in nature shoulder their way into the product, and you have a mini-magazine that doesn't quite come off. And it doesn't quite come off because the techniques of one medium have been applied (wrongly) to another medium. Using slick stock and fancy tricks to "catch the reader" is inappropriate to true newsletters, whose entire character is properly predicated on the assumption that their readers are predisposed to reading because they are vitally interested and want to know the latest news. Magazines have to "sell" their stories by bringing out their content through complex headline/deck/text relationships as well as graphic/photographic/layout manipulations. Newsletters don't need such trickery because their readers are already sold on the importance of the content. Therefore such flamboyance is misapplied and turns the newsletter into something else.

Magazines

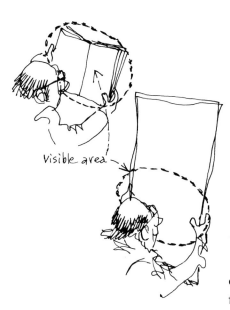

visible area

Although there are small ones made to fit the pocket (6" x 8") and bigger ones (9" wide by up to 12" high), the majority of magazines are becoming standardized to 8¼" x 10⅞" or so. These dimensions are based on the smallest page size one can use to accommodate the standard **7" × 10" ad** and allow a workable margin all around. For economic reasons, paper and press sizes are slowly adjusting to this standard. It is also a size that allows for exciting handling of visual elements as well as pedestrian handling of textual matter, as a visit to your local magazine counter will quickly attest.

The essence of handling a magazine lies in two factors that are peculiar to the medium.

1. It is small enough for each **spread**—two facing pages seen together—to be visible as a total unit. It makes one overall impression per spread.

2. It is made up of many pages and therefore becomes an object in three dimensions with many impressions following each other as the reader turns the pages.

These essential characteristics can offer tremendous advantages: you can create an artifact that has such personality and unity that the reader will find it valuable, useful, and important. How do you achieve that? By making the most of the sequence of impressions the reader develops as he or she turns the pages and perceives the pages in progression. You establish sequence or progression by repetition, by horizontal alignment from page to page and spread to spread, by the use of minimal variety in typography for maximal effects, by consistency in the placement of like elements on the page, and by standardization of everything that can be standardized. Far from making the object dull, such techniques make it strong, while at the same time giving it impact and recognizability.

These are qualities that cannot be built into a newsletter, because eight pages aren't enough to work with. They are also qualities that a newspaper cannot achieve, because its page size is too large.

The magazine is made up of groups of pages printed on a flat sheet of paper (**form**) that is later folded into a **signature** that is then assembled with other signatures to form the final product. Each signature consists of multiples of 4 pages; 16 pages is the most economical, although 8-page and 12-page signatures are possible. Large magazines are printed in 32-page signatures. Black-and-white pages are printed separately from color pages, because single-color presses are cheaper to run than four-color presses; often the paper stock varies. Thus a magazine often consists of several black-and-white signatures interlaced with or surrounded (**wrapped**) by color signatures. You need to understand the fundamentals of the physical makeup of the object, in order to make the most of it within its own limitations.

The way people hold the product is another factor to take into account. Holding it by the **spine** the way we do when we first pick it up to examine it, we flip the pages fast; we only see the outside half of the pages because the inside half is hidden. That outside half of the pages, then, is where we ought to put our attention-grabbing material. Later, when the product is studied for the second time, after the potential reader has decided, "Yes, it looks interesting," that inside half is laid bare because the object is then held differently: on the lap, on the desk, folded backward.

The page of a typical magazine is usually broken into two or three **columns**.

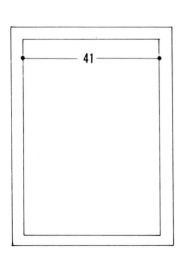

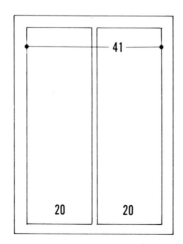

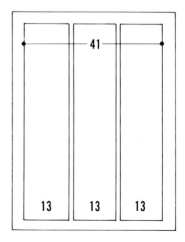

All dimensions shown are in picas.

Some magazines also use a four-column format.

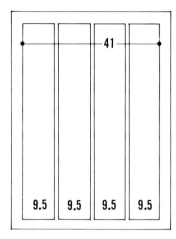

These are by no means the only patterns although they are most often found, for they fit the sizes of advertisements. Publications that do not have to face the problem of accommodating ads need not restrict their thinking. They should develop other patterns, such as these: Narrower columns can be concentrated toward the center of the spread, allowing a wide outer margin; that precious high-visibility area can then be penetrated by headlines or small pictures or can have pictures extend into it.

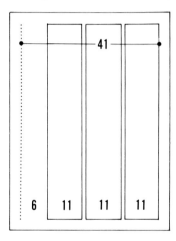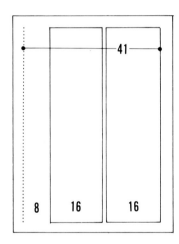

Or how about taking two columns, centering them down the middle of the page, and giving them ample outer margins to create a quiet, elegant, dignified feeling?

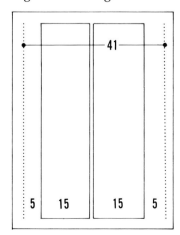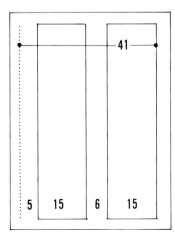

Or consider taking three columns per page but making them narrower than the maximum. You then have the option of placing them in two positions on the page: working outward from the gutter, yielding a wide outer margin; or working inward from the outer edge, yielding a wide gutter margin.

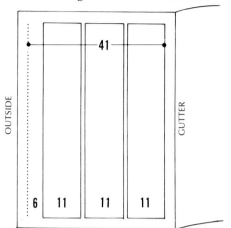
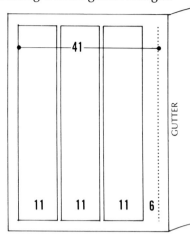

There are, clearly, lots of different ways of organizing the space at your disposal. The advantage of an unusual arrangement is that it makes the product look different. Not only does the type feel different, but the pictures do too. That is because in the usual two- or three-column makeup, there is an expected sameness to the pages, no matter how hard you may try to be original or even to obtain striking photos. The skeleton to which you are attaching your material forces you to size it according to certain proportions. If the skeleton is ordinary, so will your proportions be. If it is unusual, then the result will look unusual.*

If your publication is likely to have a great many photos in it, then it may well be a good idea to work out a column format that encourages a variety of sizes suitable to the variety of pictorial matter you'll want to accommodate. If your page can be so arranged that it remains within a standard, recognizable margin—so the pages hang together clearly—yet allows the live area to be broken into two, three, four, and even five columns, you have a scheme that will be the basis of a product whose interesting expressiveness will be the result of the flexibility of the system.

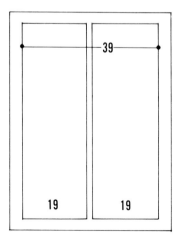
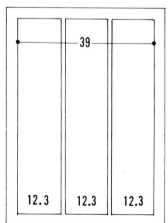
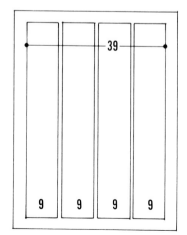
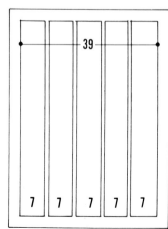

*See Jan V. White, *18 Ready-to-Use Grids* (Arlington, VA: National Composition Association, 1982).

The combinations such a scheme allows—for example, coupling various column widths together to leave empty areas of different proportions—can be both gratifying and enriching. Gratifying, because it lets the material be made to the size the editor deems appropriate for it; enriching, because the journalistic thrust, joined with the visual effect, creates excitement in the product. It says something and says it clearly, at first glance.

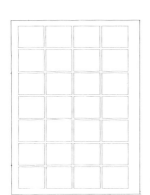

By the way, breaking up the page into component columns is sometimes thought to be a Big Solution to All Our Problems when it is referred to as a **grid**. A grid is nothing but a geometrical pattern that divides the area of the page into vertical shapes (columns) and also into horizontal shapes. The columns have already been discussed. It is the additional horizontal ones that make the true grid. They can be coordinated with type lines—individually or in multiples; or they can break the page's height arbitrarily into equal-sized pieces. If the publication is likely to use a lot of photographs, it is good planning to shape those pieces so they will fit the proportion of the photos: 4 to 5 proportion for 4" x 5" photos, 2 to 3 proportion for 35mm photos. Clearly, any arrangement that helps to define the future page design is feasible. It can be as simple as a few lines that define the edges of things ("text up to this point and down to here but no further . . . headlines in this area, decks in there . . .") or as complex as imagination demands.

The grid is said to embody some kind of magic that makes it easy to produce the publication and makes it an effective vehicle. Alas, it does no such thing. It is a framework that may or may not fit the material, and insofar as it is better to have a framework than not to have one, it helps. But it is no substitute for thinking, journalism, writing good stories, inventing clever graphics, or getting fine photography. All it provides is a set of slots into which to insert all that material.

On the other hand, it is the frame on which the publication's visual character is hung; it helps give identity; it creates consistency from page to page; it speeds work habits; and, of course, it is the forerunner of the coming technology: when page makeup will be done on **video terminals**, the grid will be universally used.

In terms of style, there are four other characteristics that have become essential to true magazine makeup.

1. Space is used actively to create the product's patterns. A newspaper page is expected to be fully packed from side to side, top to bottom. Not so a magazine page (although there are some, such as the newsmagazines, that do fill out the **live-matter rectangle** as a matter of course). Such an informal approach, whereby white space is utilized actively to focus attention onto the matter the editor deems important, is something that magazine makeup encourages. Unfortunately, this valuable capacity is often unused, because the boss objects to "wasted paper," and because many editors, trained as they are in newspaper journalism, cannot purge themselves of the rigidities imposed on them by newspaper traditions. Interestingly enough, as papers evolve, many magazine techniques are invading the supplements—and that includes the utilization of space as an active element in presentation, instead of as just the passive white background on which the words and pictures get printed.

2. Newsletters plunge right into their contents on the first page. Newspapers run their most important story atop page 1, often above the flag. But magazines are packaged like cornflakes: in a box—between covers. The picture and **cover lines** become shills and are made irresistibly enticing in order to pull the reader into the product. Obviously, **covers** also exist to create recognition for the product from issue to issue, so they have to express the publication's personality and be consistent with its policy. The picture that is run on the cover usually has something to do with the major story. Artwork or typographic covers are also sometimes used, and they can be highly successful as sales tools if they are well executed. It is much easier and safer to use a good photo, though.

3. Magazine pages have their center of importance at the top; that's where the eye goes to find the important matter. The foot of the page is much less important. It follows, then, that it is not necessary to make the bottom of the page always precisely squared off and neat. True, filling columns down to the bottom margin makes it look tidier, but so few people become aware of that area of the page that you can get away with inaccuracies without worry. Certainly it is foolish to insert space between paragraphs in order to fill out the columns, for that destroys the flow of the typography—and to what end? Perhaps some theoretical principle of which few are aware. Certainly a newspaper page made up in the traditional, full arrangement has to have a neat outline, and there the lack of alignment across the foot of the page looks noticeably messy. But newspapers are a different case altogether, and it is unwise to transfer the necessities of one medium to another.

It is much wiser to make a virtue of necessity—for example, by making the foot of the page deliberately staggered or **scalloped**, as long as the inequalities are sufficiently large to make it quite evident that this is what you intended to do and that it is not a mistake.

4. In general, the most successful presentation is one whose spreads are devoted entirely to one story. There the medium's proportions are used optimally and concentrate the reader's attention most effectively. The page size evidently coordinates comfortably with longer stories. A newspaper page could not be as successful because it is far too large; the scale would be wrong. By the same token, magazines that crowd a lot of small items onto a page newspaper style can never succeed to the degree that newspapers can, simply because of the smallness of the page they are working with.

Magapapers, magtabs, and tabloids

Here we are dealing with a much larger object. The normal dimension is 11" wide and anywhere from 14" to 17" high. Usually it is run on newsprint (to get the newspaper feel as well as to make it less expensive to produce), although the format can be used on heavy, white, fine stock too. The tabloid is the basic format. What makes the tabloid into a magtab or magapaper is that it has one more fold and, because of that fold, a smaller cover. That sounds complicated, so here it is in diagrammatic form.

The back page of the tabloid becomes the cover for the folded piece; the upper part is the front cover, the lower part the back cover. The reader sees three sequential elements upon receipt of the publication: first, the small front cover; second, the back cover; third, opening it all up, the full tabloid-size first page.

The word *magtab* comes from *mag*azine (when folded) and *tab*loid (when opened up). (Nobody calls it a tabzine, thank goodness.) *Magapaper*, similarly, is *maga*zine and news*paper*.

Inside, they are all basically the same. Assembled newspaper style in rigid columns, they fill out every square inch of available space; or assembled in magazine style, they have greater freedom of placement and sizing, and often weave ample white space into startling graphic arrangements. Clearly the contents should determine the choice of presentation style: news stories in a news section can and should be presented in a style natural to them; on the other hand, long, analytical stories that are not news-oriented deserve a different handling. There is no reason why there cannot be a variety of handling within the same issue; such variety helps to enrich the product visually, and it can help the reader realize the variety of matter packed in the issue. This kind of variety (in form as in content) grows out of the inner needs of the material. It is an organic, natural development, and as such it must fit the stories—and the vehicle—much more believably than the sort of extraneous variety that one finds injected into a product for its own sake: fashionable headline type; peculiar text block treatments; fussy details that no one notices except the people who put the product out, such as differences in treatment of subheads in copy; and so forth.

Magazine-style layouts work best when a dominant element becomes noticeable at first glance. It is usually a large photo, but it can be anything else appropriate to the story: a large headline, an important chart or map. What deserves prominence for editorial reasons is given that visibility in order to create immediate communication.

Newspaper-style layouts imply putting several comparatively short but unrelated items on the same page. Since the newspaper page—full size or tabloid size—is much larger than a magazine page, it is seldom seen as a totality. The two-page spread of a newspaper is practically never seen that way: it cannot be done without standing back too far. Instead, the page is examined by the reader in a series of jumps. Therefore newspaper design needs to be contemplated from a very different point of view. Its composition is much more complex. Unfortunately, because it is organized in columns, the usual approach is to weave the material through from column to column so that the stories meld into each other; only by reading and concentration can we determine where one ends and the next one begins.

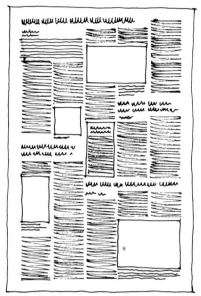 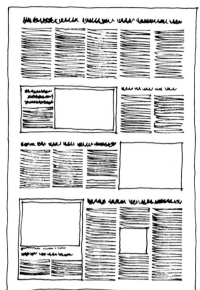

It would be wiser to think of each story as a self-contained rectangle or building block of which the page is built. That way the clarity with which the stories are divided from each other is greater: at first glance the reader can determine the lengths of the stories, where they begin and end, what belongs with what, which pictures go with what text—and which article they ought to get involved in reading.

Another fundamental difference between magazine-style makeup and newspaper-style makeup is the approach to the utilization of pictures. In a newspaper, the story is accompanied by pictures that show what the subject looked like, or that prove the veracity of the report. Seldom does the story depend on the pictures. In fact, the essence of a newspaper news story is straight **verbal reportage**, and the story could happily stand on its own unadorned feet; any pictures are just extra added attractions. They're just raisins tossed in the cake to make it less stodgy.

In magazines (at least in those that make the most of their potential rather than those that are assembled like miniature newspaper pages, as is too often the case) the story grows out of a **blend of the pictorial and the verbal**. The two are inextricably intertwined in meaning: the words cannot exist without the visuals, and the visuals would make no sense without the accompanying words. This is a more sophisticated communication technique and much more difficult to produce than the comparatively simple-minded newspaper story. It makes the difference, however, between a product whose contents are glossed over and fast forgotten (unless the subject is crucially important) and a product that creates such an impact on the viewer-reader that its message is imprinted on the consciousness because of its vivid power.

The standard **tabloid makeup** is based on a 56-pica live-matter area. The height varies with the page size, of course. The 56 picas allow margins of 5 picas or thereabouts, but in its own arithmetic it is a very flexible measurement, much as 41 picas and 39 picas are the key dimensions on magazine-size pages. The page can be broken into:

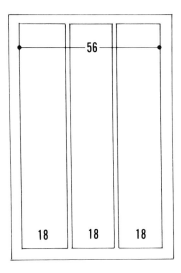 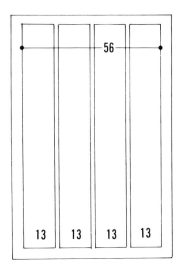 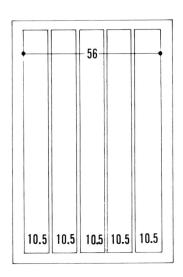

3 columns per page

The overall scale is a bit large, pictures tend to become oversized, and text lines are a trifle long for easy reading, unless you use a large type size. People pictures need to be set into the text or arranged in clusters.

4 columns per page

This yields an excellent copy width for a reasonable type size and better variety of picture sizes; doubling up two mug shots per column accommodates that perennial problem neatly.

5 columns per page

The column width is a bit narrow, resulting in too many word breaks. The use of a condensed typeface can overcome bad setting. A great variety of picture sizes is possible.

Mixing column widths on the same page is an excellent way to create variety in look and scale as well as in emphasis. Furthermore, a change in pattern also helps to segment the large page into its component parts at first glance. Such segmentation, however, depends on horizontal **building-block makeup**: instead of intertwining stories from column to column, each story takes up a clear rectangle of space on the page. The vertical edges are, of course, defined by the columns themselves. The top and bottom edges are defined by alignment of the type (which has to be precise, or it doesn't work) and by the headline that is placed across the top of each story. The space between such rectangles acts as a separating moat, if its edges are precise and straight and therefore appear deliberate. You can always add horizontal **cut-off rules**, if you feel the need for them. But a combination of change of column widths and neat horizontal alignment of type lines makes them unnecessary.

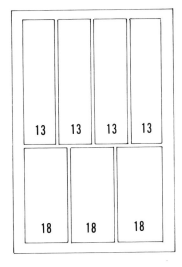 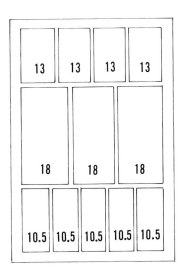

Odd-width columns are also perfectly feasible, and they embody the most useful possibilities if the width is custom-tailored to a specific sort of material. Many tabloids are faced with running numerous short items, endless mug shots, large official pronouncements, lists of anniversaries, winners of awards, and so forth. Fitting that kind of material into the normal column widths often squeezes the matter too tight, or worse, inflates it undeservedly. A specially sized column might just do the trick. Here are four examples. Anything is possible, if the material and typography are made to fit it.

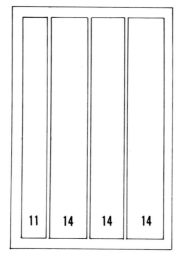

Headlines and capsules can be run in the narrow column at left.

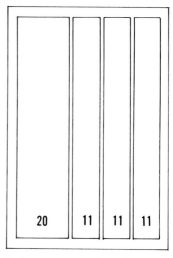

Policy statements from the CEO can be set in large type in an extra-wide column.

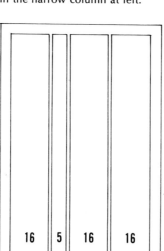

Anniversary celebrants' pictures and names fit in the narrow column.

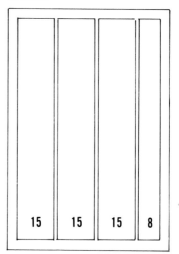

Mug shots line up on the outside of the page.

Horizontal modules are an aspect of grids that are much under discussion nowadays (see page 7). Many attempts have lately been made to organize the page into bands running across the page from left to right, the same way that columns run top to bottom. Theoretically, such a modular system is worthwhile because it can simplify the process of makeup (by predetermining sizing of pictures) and copyfitting (by organizing the page into multiples of lines of type). Such coordination appears to be helpful because it shows you where to put things and how big they ought to be. In practice, unfortunately,

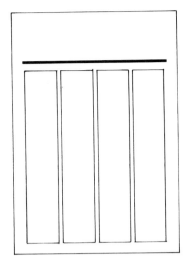

things never seem to work out so neatly: the copy is invariably too long or too short, the photos refuse to crop right, and after struggling for a while you tend to give up on the grid's restrictions. Unfortunately, you either have a grid or you don't; there's no compromise. If you depart from the grid's rigidities, you aren't left with much.

There is one horizontal modular element, however, that appears to make good sense: to have a band of space, about 2″ deep or so, running across the tops of all the pages. You can leave it empty and thus lighten the heavy effect that a tabloid page creates, but you'll be accused of wasting space. Or you can use it as an area in which to insert short, amusing bits and pieces—those usually used as **fillers** that get such high readership. People love to read items that are short enough not to demand effort; they postpone longer stories until they are ready for them. A frieze across the top can be a useful repository for such odds and ends, and can help cajole the readers into reading the big stories by pulling their attention onto the page with small ones.

Sidebars are substories related to the story they appear with, but of lesser importance. They are, in fact, boxes. Their graphic expression can vary from the hackneyed, ruled, outlined box or a tint of black ink over the whole area to a much more imaginative and witty presentation that may help the flavor of the subject with graphic expression. Two factors need to be understood about them.

1. It is necessary to set text narrower than the regular column width, because you have to leave room for the graphic surrounding that encloses it. Such measurements need to be coordinated properly to the column structure. Parallel handling of headlines is also needed: there has to be a relationship between the headline type and the miniaturized version that is used in the sidebar.

2. Because sidebars are peculiar elements inserted into the column structure and appear different from their surroundings, they are disturbing elements. One can even think of them as illustrations—nonpictorial, to be sure, but pattern-breakers nonetheless. Anything that breaks a pattern attracts our attention. So, to get some mileage from this, it might be a good idea to use a typeface of contrasting size, color, and texture, so that the sidebars really are different.

If the basic makeup pattern follows the horizontal layer or building-block approach, then sidebars that are handled as though they were pictures can help enrich the product visually at very little cost.

Make the publication's name its hallmark

Your name is your trademark. It is the major symbol by which you are recognized, and it must become a familiar friend to the recipient of your publication so that every issue is newly welcomed. It ought to be as individual and special to you as possible without becoming exaggerated or illegible. This problem of character and personalization is the most difficult to tackle, since it reflects so much subjective interpretation. What looks technical to one person is seen to be cold and dull by another; what's just contemporary design to someone may well be the epitome of aggressiveness to someone else; what's decorative and amusing to one may be seen as bad taste by another. That's why more intramural battles are waged about logos than anything else. That's why, in spite of the temptation to do it first, it is wisest to leave the logo until last, when you are working on a new format or a new product. Let the logo grow naturally out of the spirit and atmosphere of the entire piece. If you have the discipline to work out the background first, you will have solved so many basic questions that the logo will evolve organically from the decisions already reached. If you do the logo first, it may well become an albatross around your neck.

The difference between logo, nameplate, flag, and masthead

Logo is short for logotype. *Logos* in Greek means word. In the days when each letter was cast separately on a piece of metal and words had to be assembled letter by letter into lines, commonly used short words were made into units to save the compositor's time. Such ready-made words were called logotypes. The name was then transferred to any words that were specially prepared and repeated in that peculiar form, such as company or trade names. (As a company name or trademark a logo is also often called an "adcut.") This usage was then, inevitably, applied to the name of the publication, although, strictly speaking, this is incorrect. The correct name for a publication's title is **nameplate**, or you can call it a **flag**, or a **banner**. The kind of publication you have determines the correct nomenclature, although such pedantic correctness, like beauty, is in the eye of the beholder. *Logo* is commonly used for magazines, *nameplate* for newsletters, while *banner* or *flag* is reserved for newspapers and tabloids (though *nameplate* will also be understood there). All this does not matter very much, but you might as well know the proper terminology.

One caveat: Do not call the name of the publication the **masthead** (*mast* for short) because that term is used for the list of individuals responsible for the publication, the date and volume number, publishing information, where to write for change of address, various pieces of legal information, and all the rest of that small print that nobody ever reads except to check his or her name's correct spelling. Often appended to masthead material, by the way, is information required by the Post Office to qualify the publication for special postage classification, which must appear somewhere within the first five pages following the cover. This legal material is also called the **indicia.**

Where to put your name on the page

The normal or expected position of the logo is somewhere on top of the front page. This expectation on the part of the recipient is the major factor in favor of putting it there, because one of the reasons you have it at all is to tell the reader at first glance which publication he or she is looking at. It is the first and most vital reference point for your product, and traditional placement is probably the easiest to live with.

It is, of course, perfectly possible to position the logo elsewhere on the front page: in the middle (**waist high**), at the bottom (at the **foot of the page**), or sideways, reading upward or downward (**on its ear**). Such unexpected handling can become important as a recognition factor in itself, as long as you repeat it from issue to issue, exactly the way you started out.

Remember to consider how your product will be received: flat or folded? In either case, the logo ought to be the first thing the recipient sees. If the publication is flat, then the graphic strength of the logo will ensure its being seen first, no matter where it is. But if the publication is folded, then the logo ought to be positioned so as not to be hidden by the fold. Such a consideration as folding is another reason why it is essential that you perceive the product as an object held by the recipient in the hands, to be unfolded, uncrinkled, and seen in successive steps as it is opened. It is necessary that you avoid falling into the trap of designing the product as a flat object, even though it is made up flat in order to print and produce it. Remember that there are areas on the page that will be affected by the folding.

One more element to consider: Many publications are mailed out with the **address labels** attached to the front cover. Clearly, the size of the piece, as well as the machinery used to attach the label, affects the placement of that label. But you had better find out about that before you design the front page, for it must be accommodated in the design. It is far better to know ahead of time than to be unpleasantly surprised that the logo you have fussed over with such meticulous care has been overlaid by some loathsome address label.

How to make the name impossible to miss

Seven factors must be taken into account here. But, before we discuss them, you must make sure that the underlying premise is understood: we need to make the logo visible because we are proud of it and because it represents us. It is the image of ourselves that we want to project, and the character and atmosphere of that image affects the mood of the potential reader. So we should show it off clearly, assuming, of course, that it is worthy of such treatment. But let us make a positive rather than a negative assumption on *that* score and analyze the seven factors that must be combined and balanced in order to give the logo its requisite visibility.

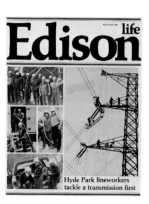

By size

Make it big enough so it overwhelms everything else. How big is that? That depends on the size of the page, the scale of surrounding materials, and the size of the headline typography near it. It is impossible to devise a formula. Use your common sense, but be courageous, and err on the side of bigness.

By blackness

Making letters large but using thin lines just tends to make the logo look scrawny and pale. The purpose is to make your name *visible*. That means giving it ample ink so it will read in bold contrast to the paper background. Boldface type run tightly together or type with "shadows" that add extra ink, good, fat ruled lines—anything to add color and darkness:

Drop shadow type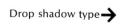

By clarity

The single most important element is the name itself. Alas, usually it needs to be accompanied by several other pieces of information: a line indicating the purpose of the piece, as well as all the essential publishing information such as the name of the publishing organization, the location, the date of issue, the volume and number, and so forth. All this ancillary information needs to be placed in relation to the logo. Regrettably, the normal practice is to surround the logo with itsy-bitsy odds and ends that crackle like visual static all around and only reduce the clarity, and thus the impact, of the precious logo itself. The logo must be allowed to remain dominant. All the additional information should be arrayed inconspicuously alongside or beneath it.

By contrast

The size and blackness of the logo will appear stronger when set off by the smallness and paleness of ancillary information. Such graphic trickery can work magic, because if the secondary matter will be tiny, you can reduce the size of the logo and take up less of your precious front-page space, yet retain the visual impact you seek.

JORNAL DA ABRIL

Publicação interna do Grupo Abril   Ano V   Primeira quinzena de junho — **109**

JORNAL DA ABRIL

Publicação interna do Grupo Abril
Ano 5- N.º 119
Primeira quinzena de novembro de 1978

By isolation

To achieve maximum visibility and impact, it is wise to enclose the logo (with its ancillary material) in a self-contained bubble of space. The area of the page can be demarcated by an edge of some sort: a line of type, a moat of empty space, a box, or even just an implied line that is injected there in the imagination of the viewer. The easiest, and probably most effective, device is to have a ruled line separating the logo area from the rest of the page.

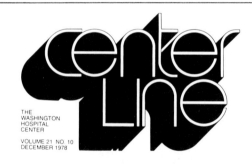

center line

THE
WASHINGTON
HOSPITAL
CENTER

VOLUME 21 NO. 10
DECEMBER 1978

THE DONNELLEY
RECORD
1981 · NUMBER 1

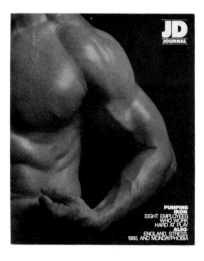

JD
JOURNAL

PUMPING
IRON
EIGHT EMPLOYEES
WHO WORK
HARD AT PLAY
ALSO
ENGLAND, STRESS
1980, AND MONDAYPHOBIA

By juxtaposition

This is just a bombastic way of bringing your attention to a simple but vital concept—that of contrasting fullness to emptiness, printed area to blank area, type to white space. To achieve startling visibility for the logo, allow it to be seen against a large, clear, uncluttered, and geometrically shaped area of empty surrounding space. And "empty" *means* empty. No matter how small or insignificant a word, phrase, or date may be, if it is printed in that valuable white space, it will spoil the whiteness by its presence.

The Gaffer

8/82

The Gaffer is a publication of Corning Glass Works

Summer, 1982

VOLUME 1 NUMBER 7 NOV. 1978

AEA PROGRESS

NEWSLETTER OF THE ARTS, EDUCATION AND AMERICANS, INC.

VOLUME 2 / NUMBER 1

FALL 1981

By separation

No amount of careful logo design—balance against white space, contrast with tiny type, definition of space, and other desirable factors—will be any good if the effect is undercut by competition from the headline below. Obviously, the best story is the first one on page 1. Equally obvious, the space on page 1 is the most valuable. Therefore, the temptation is to cram as much onto that page as possible. It is wise to resist such temptation and retain sufficient space between the logo area and that first headline to allow each to be seen as separate elements, rather than as a mass of matter fighting for the reader's attention and achieving little but confusion.

Your name/your self: why you ought to personalize it

Before thinking about how to make the logo "different," let's just agree on the fundamental need for restraint, because the logo should represent your product in a dependable, dignified manner for a number of years. It must, therefore, be decorous and fit your image; it ought not to be startlingly trendy, because fashions change so quickly; and it ought to be legible—although the distinction between *legibility as type* and *recognition as graphic symbol* is a subtle one indeed to draw. The context, the specific wording, the audience, and the planned image, as well as your own instinctive feeling for rightness, must be the determining factors.

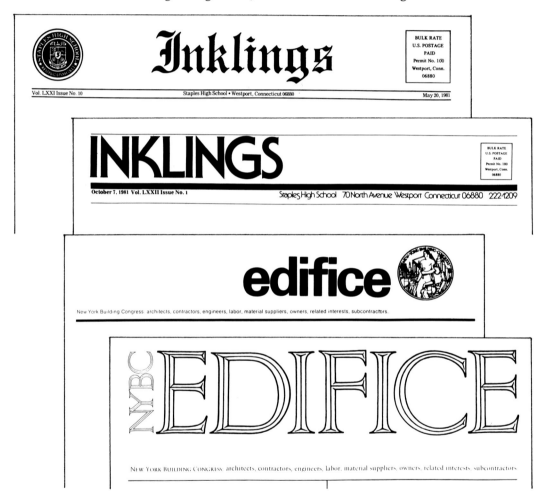

Given the importance of the logo as the symbol of your identity, it is highly advisable to turn its design over to a professional designer. But do be careful about whom you choose, for being a "professional" is no guarantee of capability in this rather arcane field. **Designers** specialize in various aspects of their profession, the same way that lawyers or doctors do in theirs. Design has many branches, and competence in one is not necessarily a guarantee of the same in all the others. Be especially wary of entrusting such crucial problems to too youthful a designer. There is much more to logo design than appears at first glance. Mature judgment as to appropriateness comes only with experience—and this is a quality you must be able to rely upon in your designer. However bright, promising, and exciting a newcomer to the profession may be, entrusting your precious trademark/symbol to him or her may well be gambling with the wrong material at the wrong time. As in all things, you get what you pay for, and what you are paying for is not merely clever design, but *right* design. A good logo is an investment whose cost is amortized over a long period of time; it is therefore wise to pay a little more to be sure of getting the best.

How to make the name look different

Essentially, there are two graphic areas under consideration: typographic amendment and pictorial imaging. They can be used individually or in combination. They are also seriously affected by the surroundings in which they will be observed. All of this sounds awesome and occult, but please don't be put off. They are just a couple of techniques that are given recondite names to raise them to the level of intellectual concepts. Read on—in short order they will become totally demystified and bafflingly clear to you.

By amending the typography

What do we mean by "typographic amendment"? Quite simply: playing with the type—fooling around with the shapes of the letters, slurring them, overlapping them, changing bits and pieces of them to make a fun monogram, pulling at a line and elongating it and wriggling it around; interweaving letters, bumping them up close to each other—in short, using the words and letters as malleable material.

Clearly, how far to go is where the problem lies. Equally clear, if you want a personalized version of a word, you have to do something to it that will change the way it looks in plain type. The straight type you receive from the typesetter or make yourself from transfer lettering is just the very beginning. If you use calligraphic type or a typeface that is sufficiently

VISION

EFLA Bulletin

newsletter of the Educational Film Library Association, 43 W. 61 St., New York, NY 10023. 212-246-4533.

Mobil

unusual in itself, perhaps you should leave it alone and avoid painting the lily.* But if it is an unexceptional typeface, then some tampering may well prove to be called for. Think of the Mobil sign: plain, simple, dignified type with the *o* picked out in red. That is tampering in terms of color. Think of the Exxon sign: the double X combined into one **ligature** with the legs extended beneath the bottom of the word. That is tampering in terms of letter form. Think of Coca Cola: the wave beneath the word remains even when the words are in Arabic! That is tampering with the words by adding an external element to them. Here, for the fun of it, is an arbitrary collection of logos to show the rich variety of which plain old type is capable. Is it any wonder that restraint and judgment are needed to produce the kind that is exactly right for *you*?

*Incidentally, did you realize that "gilding the lily" is a misquotation besides being a cliché?

"To gild refined gold,
   to paint the lily,
to throw perfume on the violet,
to smooth the ice
   or add another hue
unto the rainbow,
   or with taper-light
to seek the beauteous eye
   of heaven to garnish,
is wasteful and ridiculous excess."

(Shakespeare, *King John*, Act IV, Scene 2.)

And here you thought this was just a how-to book!

By pictorial imagery

You can make your symbol unique by adding pictures, drawings, pictograms, visual symbols, coats-of-arms, company trademarks, maps, buildings, and such assorted graphic material to the name. But what a terrifying minefield that is to cross, with booby traps on all sides. First common-sense rule: *When in doubt, don't.* Second common-sense rule: *If you must, then get a competent guide.* Third common-sense rule: *Make it small.* Fourth common-sense rule: *Make the words dominant.* That about says it all, because to try to generalize about this totally subjective and individual set of conditions is not likely to be helpful, except in the most elementary way. Perhaps it is worthwhile showing a few examples.

Enriching the name's effectiveness with color

The visual effect of color may well enrich the physical product—and the cost may well impoverish the coffers. It is worth considering nonetheless, because it is a simple procedure that can pay rich dividends. The logo is an element that is likely to be constant from issue to issue. The date may change, but the logo itself won't. You are, therefore, dealing with the one element that is a known quantity in the future. In printing, as in all manufacturing, unit cost decreases as volume increases. If you have a longer pressrun, if you print more at one time, your individual pieces will cost you less. That might well make it cheaper to do peculiar things like printing your logo in purple or green. In fact, if you run off enough of them, the price may even go down far enough to be economical. Your regular print order is, let us say, 5,000 pieces a month, yet you order 60,000. That way you have a full year's worth of logos in readiness, printed at volume prices, based on today's cost of paper and production. True, your added cost is that of the storage of your **overrun** (the extras you don't need for this upcoming issue). But what is it that you have? Stacks and stacks of your publication's paper **preprinted** with the logo in color, like blank letterheads. Those blanks will then go through the press a second time using normal-color ink (most probably black) to print the actual issue's content.

There are presses that can print two colors in one "pass," of course. They have two sets of rollers that touch the paper in succession, one bearing ink of one color, the other ink of another color. Obviously, such a complex press costs more to use than a single-color press. If you are already using such equipment, you are probably utilizing its capabilities for more than merely running the logo in color anyway. But if you are restricted to a one-color press, you should not rule out using more than one color, if you want it, in a second pass.

Now, take it a step further: How about printing color on something other than white paper? **Color-on-color**—the variety and effects are limitless. Aaah! Yes, money: well, perhaps it might be worth looking into the actual costs. They may not be prohibitive, and the benefit of improved quality and personality may well be worth that added cost.

Colorfulness achieved by running the logo in a "second" color: the panel is in mustard brown, the name dropped out in white and the word "letter" surprinted in black. All on tan-colored stock. At right, colorfulness reaches maximum: the photo (in color, of course) continues up into the logo against a pale yellow background.

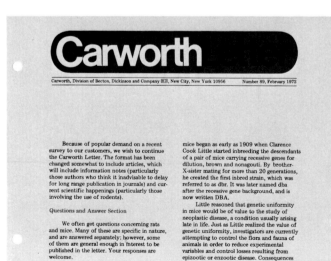

24

How to make your own special logo

By lettering it yourself or commissioning a calligrapher

This is liable to result in the most personalized image of all, if it is well executed. If, however, it is not masterfully drawn, the result can bring down the tone of the product undeservedly. It depends on the character you are trying to achieve: For an informal, unpretentious "family style" effect, comparatively unsophisticated lettering may be just right. But it is always wise to err on the side of well-crafted styling, if only for the dignity that it helps to impart.

By using ready-made lettering

Ready-made lettering comes in two basic varieties (both available at your local art supply dealer): type imprinted on adhesive acetate sheets from which you cut each letter and attach it to your paper; and type imprinted on sheets from which it is transferred to your paper by rubbing. The cut-out kind is easier to control because each letter is movable until you are happy with its position (and you can shift it around afterward, unless you have burnished it down tight). Transfer lettering stays where you put it, unless you physically remove it* and rub down another letter in its place.

The wisest procedure is to do a **rough**—no, *several* roughs—which you then copy in the final, because the lettering sheets are fairly expensive. A rough is simply a piece of tracing paper (transparent, smooth paper specifically made for tracing) that you place over the lettering sheet and on which you *lightly* draw your word letter by letter. The shapes of the letters will suggest amendments to you once you see them strung on to each other. Clearly, the bigger the letters, the easier it is to handle them. Working with type any smaller than 60 points gets to be tricky indeed.

Each manufacturer of ready-made lettering sets has a different system to help you with the spacing of the letters and clean alignment. Most sets have

a horizontal line below each letter, which you place directly over the guideline you have drawn on your own paper. (Each manufacturer also publishes a catalog of its full line of materials, in which clear instructions on how to use the sheets as well as useful tips and shortcuts are included. Most of these catalogs are free.) It is a very simple procedure to produce a word or two with transfer lettering, provided you work accurately, cleanly, and carefully, and use the right tools (the same as are needed for making mechanicals; see page 148).

*To remove transfer lettering cleanly, simply pick it up with adhesive tape.

By having it set in type

In the past, **printers** supplied typesetting as one of their basic services, and they continue to do so. However, since **typesetting** is a highly specialized branch of the graphic arts, many independent suppliers have set up shop. They are likely to have a more interesting selection of faces available, as well as a variety of machinery to generate them. (The richness of their stock-in-trade is their reason for being—added to quality workmanship and service, of course.) You must get their sample book to determine what is

Helvetica Thin	*Helvetica Condensed Italic*	**Helvetica Black Condensed**
Helvetica Thin Italic	Helvetica Extended	***Helvetica Black Condensed Italic***
Helvetica Light	**Helvetica Bold**	**Helvetica Black Extended**
Helvetica Light Italic	***Helvetica Bold Italic***	**Helvetica Compressed**
Helvetica Light Condensed	**Helvetica Bold Condensed**	**Helvetica Extra Compressed**
Helvetica Light Condensed Italic	***Helvetica Bold Condensed Italic***	**Helvetica Ultra Compressed**
Helvetica Light Extended	**Helvetica Bold Extended**	Helvetica Bold Outline
Helvetica	**Helvetica Heavy**	**Helvetica Rounded Bold**
Helvetica Italic	***Helvetica Heavy Italic***	***Helvetica Rounded Bold Italic***
Helvetica Condensed	**Helvetica Black**	Helvetica Rounded Bold Outline

available to you. Then you take your word and specify it. You must tell them the name of the face, the size (in points or a dimension of the capital letter), the case (upper or lower) you want, the weight (bold, extra bold, regular, light, etc.), the style (roman or italic), as well as any other peculiarities you may wish. Many special faces come with alternate characters, such as two versions of e, which you need to specify. You must also specify spacing between letters, for given today's flexibility of photographic output, typesetting machines can give you spacing that is "normal," "tight," or "extra wide" between letters, according to your preference. The terminology you use for such specification varies according to the technology, but common-sense nomenclature in plain English, such as "set normal spacing" or "tight but not touching" is translatable into machine speech by the operator. (See more on typesetting and specifying on page 47) The typesetter will provide you with a **printout** if it is photographically generated, or a **reproduction proof** (repro proof in the vernacular) if it was printed on a press.

normal abcdefghijklmnopqrstuvwxyz

tight abcdefghijklmnopqrstuvwxyz

very tight abcdefghijklmnopqrstuvwxyz

touching abcdefghijklmnopqrstuvwxyz

How to achieve the personalized look once the name is in type

Once you have your word in final, clean typographic form (whether it be hand-lettered, do-it-yourself, or typeset), you may wish to amend some of the letters in order to personalize them, make them more into a trademark form.

Illustrated 1

Illustrated 2

Illustrated 3

Above: this is about the smallest size you can work with accurately and comfortably to achieve the precision the subject demands. The size also helps you to *notice* what needs doing.

First step in tampering with the type is shown in (1): the horizontal stroke of the "t" on the left was removed to close up the space between the "st," but it was left alone in the second "t," because it tucks into the space created by the lower serif of the "a." The "ra" was also tightened and overlapped, as were the "ll."

Second step: addition of the horizontal bar (2).

Third step: shortening the "ll" to allow the bar to extend across the entire word. Enlarging the initial "I" to create a space into which the underscoring bar can be inserted.

Still to be improved: the irritating gap in the "r."

You should never tamper with the original, but have an enlargement made (a "PMT"; see page 130) to much larger scale. Three-inch-tall capital letters are ideal, although if you have a word like "Antidisestablishmentarianism," you might prefer type a wee bit smaller. *That* is the version you monkey with. When you have perfected it, you will then reduce it to the final size needed for your publication. Why do you need to have it so large? Because only when it is large can you discern details and control amendments that are needed. Not only does it make the work easier, but it also protects you, since minor errors of workmanship will disappear in the subsequent reduction.

How do you do the amending? Before doing anything else you must draw a fine horizontal line under the word. That will ensure your getting the letters vertical and properly aligned if you cut them apart for later reassembly. Next, you apply wax to the back of the paper, which will allow the letters to adhere to a surface and worked with until you are finally satisfied with the result and can burnish them down permanently. Then you cut the letters apart with scissors or a blade of some sort and start the tightening, overlapping, and expanding process. Once you have the type the way you want it, you add the art symbols to it, if you plan to use any. The more cleanly you work, the better the final result. Use fine pen and black india ink for making lines. For wider lines you can get broader nibs, or you can affix ready-made lines that you cut from acetate sheets or transfer to the paper from rub-off sheets. Experiment with the techniques involved first; don't expect to reach perfection at first try; go back and start again if the result looks too messy. And, if it looks hopeless, get help. These skills are not easy to acquire. Check with your high school art teacher or get recommendations from the printer, reproduction supplier, or art supply store, or go to the local ad agency or graphic design studio—it is remarkable how widespread the availability of specialized help actually is, if only one looks for it. And quality doesn't ever come cheap, so expect to pay a fair fee for the work involved. Trying to do it yourself first, though, will make you realize what a designer has to do to earn that fee!

3

How to make the most of typewriter "typography"

Many producers of printed communications tend to be apologetic about the type they use—or rather don't use. They feel that a piece is makeshift, second rate, and shoddy unless it has been set in type by a typesetter. This is a grave error, for even the most primitive typewriter image can be handsome, legible, and inviting if used in a fashion that makes the most of its qualities. Typewriter type can be effective if it is appropriate to the writing style, subject matter, format, paper stock, method of distribution, scale of page size, and so on—if, in other words, the reader's expectation is fulfilled by a well-balanced product.

Clearly, attempts at producing a sophisticated image with a typewriter will look unsatisfactory: aping an expensive appearance without simultaneously conforming the content to that appearance creates insurmountable problems. On the other hand, understanding the advantages, as well as the limitations, of a specific medium can result in a product that has vigor, immediacy, intimacy of information, and, yes, the good handsome look of something that is "right" for what it is.

So get rid of that chip on the shoulder and start your fingers pounding those typewriter keys. And, in order to make the most of the technology at your disposal—with all its limitations—restrain your desire for fanciness and dressing things up. Instead, work within the restrictions imposed by the machinery. Write the items as short newsy pieces, have an insider's attitude and tone of voice (to make recipients think they're in on the latest inside information). Think of the product as a hot-tip sheet, be informal in language, make it as person-to-person as is sensible—use the word *you* often. Don't print the piece on slick stock, but use paper that is reminiscent of letterhead: Preprint your logo in a second color, and then impose your contents on that paper as though it were a letter typed on a letterhead. Don't write articles with headlines and subheads in the typical magazine format, but organize the piece into smaller units, each of which is signaled by an underscored start to the paragraph, perhaps; or use boldface or all cap lead-ins or hanging indents. Don't try to "catch the reader": You must work with the assumption that the very fact the recipient is on your mailing list indicates that he or she is already vitally interested in what you have to say. Therefore, saying it straightforwardly and making it appear simple is perfectly satisfactory. The essence of typewritten material is that it is such valuable, timely information that the producers haven't had the time or the need to gussy it up.

The visual success of typewritten pieces lies in the composition of the material on the page, in its simplicity, consistency, and imaginative use of space. Some examples of this approach can be seen throughout this chapter. First, it is necessary to discuss some of the more matter-of-fact technicalities before getting into how to assemble an overall project.

Typewriter type, strike-on type, cold type: what they are

Basically, they are the same thing. They produce little black marks on paper as a result of a key being depressed, which in turn triggers a mechanism that transfers black carbon or ink onto paper. The machine used can be as simple as an old mechanical typewriter, or as up to date as a word processor—but all produce a product without having had recourse to hot metal (as in traditional typesetting) or photographic exposure of the characters (as in phototypesetting). **Cold type** used in reference to phototype is a confusing misnomer. The essence of cold type—just like **strike-on** or typewriter type—is that it is the result of a direct impression on the paper. The machinery that can generate this kind of result is comparatively cheap and easy to use, although, of course, its capabilities vary with the sophistication of the processor. The limitations of what can and cannot be done are built into the machinery. Because of the simplicity of typewriter type, the cost of producing usable typescript, ready for reproduction, is low. But just because it is economical to produce doesn't mean that the final result has to look cheap.

It is difficult indeed to generalize, since there are so many variations of machinery available: their features differ and therefore, too, the resultant output. However, it can be said about all of them that there is some rigidity in the shape of each character and the space each takes, as well as the spacing between characters. Amendments have indeed been attempted to reduce the rigidity of a normal typewriter, where a narrow letter such as a lowercase *i* must be made to take the same space as a wide letter like a capital *M*. On "executive" typewriters, the letters have been given shapes and spaces more appropriate to their characteristics. Nevertheless, the subtleties of spacing between letters, the coloration, and the flexibility that have been developed over centuries of tradition and innovation to improve legibility in typeset material cannot possibly be produced on the typewriter.

Typewriter faces are available in several basic styles. The most common is the **square serif style**: this is the most expected and, therefore, the most innocuous and unpretentious. It is probably the easiest to read, too, if only because the reader pays no attention to it since it is so expected. Therefore, it doesn't interpose itself between the reader and the message as a much more self-consciously designed **script style** does. That has appropriate usage for short or specialized messages, but its use for entire publications is questionable. The **sans-serif** or **gothic style** is bolder, heavier, and larger and thus perfect for headlines. It is less perfect for solid text, although the situation's specific needs as well as your judgment must be the final arbiter, as always. The **roman** or **executive style**, which has thick and thin strokes in the letters themselves, a variety of widths of letters, as well as proportional spacing, is probably the easiest to read since it comes closest to proper typeset proportioning. Typewriter type can also be in **italic style**, a useful complement to the square serif. The examples shown here are from the IBM catalog.

Mixing type styles can yield a piece with great visual variety, and this may well be good, if the type styles chosen help to convey the sense of different kinds of material or messages through their visual differences. A

For lengthy forms, general

For executive, personal uses

For forms, correspondence

For classic strength

For scientific, legal work

meaningless fancy-dress party where variety is used for its own sake tends to look like a formless jumble and confuses readers more than it helps them through the piece. As in all editorial presentation (the "art" end of editing), *what matters is the content and not the form.* If your type can help to communicate that content to the reader, then go ahead and do what your instincts tell you to do and have fun. But avoid being different for the sake of being different.

Some of the newest computers produce printouts that are ideal for reading by machine but are probably the worse offenders with respect to legibility by people, because their wide spacing disintegrates the fabric of the letter group by which we read or recognize complete words. Machines "read" letter by letter, and for them such travesty of typesetting is essential—but let us not attempt to foist off what is made for machines onto people.

We have known many
interviewed scores
we've found there is
employed by the most

How long should typewritten lines be?

Given the standard 8½" x 11" page, you have two basic choices: setting your lines to full-page width in one column about 7" wide, or in two columns about 3½" wide each. In **pica** type, at 10 characters to the inch, you have 70 characters in a line the width of the full page (which is a bit much if there are many lines to face), and you have 35 characters in each half-page-wide column. In **elite** type, at 12 characters per inch, those numbers grow to 84 and 42 characters respectively. If you reduce the scale of your type photographically (see page 31 for how and why) your numbers will grow accordingly.

What is the ideal line length? It varies, depending on the kind of subject matter, size of type, spacing between lines, number of lines, amount of breakup (subheads and the like), color of ink and paper, excellence of printing, size of page, number of pages, and so forth. It is folly to pretend that one single formula can cover all these contingencies, especially if it is a guess to start with. The best decision can be reached only through observation of others' products whose results you admire, and by experimenting with your own publication to see how it comes out most satisfactorily. Clearly, such experimentation should be done before you commit yourself to a standardized format. It is always better to go through a dry run or two than to do your gambling with the first real issue.

The advantage of a single column on the page is that it makes the publication look like a *letter:* a personal communication, inside information. That character is very appropriate for a newsletter; it is enhanced by the title being preprinted in a second color so it looks like a letterhead (see page 24 for logos in color).

A two-column page structure is easier to read because the lines are shorter. But it is much more difficult to compose neatly and clearly, and the resultant confusion may reduce the full page's legibility.

One variation on the single-column format might be considered seriously: Leave an extra-deep **indent** at left to allow space for headings to be inserted. The type lines are shorter. Heads are visible, and generous white space acts as a foil to the type and adds lightness to the overall effect. You do, indeed, need more pages to accommodate your material. Consider this, though: Isn't it better to be read (even if it costs a page or two more) than to be cast aside as unattractive (having saved that extra paper)?

Should you use ragged-right or justified typewriter typing?

Justified setting means that all the lines in the column are of the same length, yielding a clean left-hand edge and a clean right-hand edge—except, of course, for the last line of a paragraph, which is necessarily shorter, and the first line of a paragraph, which is usually indented. In order to achieve the desired alignment of the outside edges, you have to manipulate the lines of text inside the column. You have to **space out** between words or, in some regrettable instances, even between the letters of the word in order to make the line come out to the right length. This undoubtedly helps the page to look neat at first glance, but it disturbs the legibility of the type because we recognize words by letter groups. Making unexpected, random, artificial gaps between the words, or even between the letters, dislocates the rhythm with which we scan the text. That, in turn, makes us conscious of the act of reading, disturbs our concentration, and thus is detrimental to our comprehension of the message.

Ragged-right setting trades off a neat right-hand edge for ease of reading. By removing the need to open up space between words, it ensures a steady flow of typographic images in their optimal relationship to each other and, thus, improves legibility.

In typewritten copy, where the machine itself already compromises the quality of legibility by tampering with the shapes of the characters themselves (by making them fit into spaces of equal width or a small number of subunits), it would be folly to decrease the legibility by yet one more degree. We *expect* to see typewritten matter set ragged on the right, for that is the natural output of the machinery. Forcing it to justify (by typing it a second time and enlarging the holes between words) is an inappropriate mode of expression for the mechanics of typewriting that leads to an unaesthetic visual result. In other words: Sure, you can do it, but it's likely to look awful!

How to reduce the scale of typewriter type

A letter typewritten on a normal letterhead has an image that we expect to see: It looks and feels right. It is in line with our expectations of what we consider to be in scale with the page. The 8½" x 11" page size—that is, normal U.S. letter size—is somewhat larger (yes, larger!) than the standard magazine page. If you count up the number of words* on the typical page of typewritten copy and compare it to the total on a page from, say, *Time* magazine, you'll be amazed at the difference. *Time* crowds in close to 300% more in the same space. Yet, in spite of its smallness, the type is clearly

*About counting words: An average of 5 characters is assumed for each word. In highly specialized texts, you might be more accurate if you counted 5.5 characters per word; and for children's books, perhaps 4 or 4.5 characters per word.

legible. That is because the reader's expectation of a magazine page is quite different from that of a typewritten letter page. The concentration and focusing are automatically adjusted to correspond to the product held in the hand.

To make typewriter type palatable, it is highly advisable to reduce its scale from the normal letter size to something a little smaller. If, as is most likely, you are printing by offset, the printer will have to turn the camera-ready copy you supply into a printing plate that is made from a photographic negative. Any time a photographic process comes into play, an opportunity for enlargement or reduction of the size is at hand. If you submit an original that is a smidgen larger than the final product, the camera can make the needed adjustment for you, probably at no extra charge. Here is a perfect opportunity to improve the scale and look of your piece with very little effort. But it is not quite so easy—You must know two things: How will the type look and read when it is reduced? How much more material will you have to prepare for the page if you reduce the scale of the type? If you reduce the size by, say, 10%, you make room for 10% more material to fill the same space, don't you? To determine the answer to the second question, you must first figure out the mathematics of the first question.

To help you make up your mind as to how type is likely to read when reduced photographically, here is a table of reductions of a sample block

```
This is a sample of several lines of typing using
a typing element called Elite, twelve-pitch, on an
electric typewriter. This is the size the machine
produces. It looks well in its own context, on a
letterhead, but it appears enormous in a book -- and
so it is! That's why it needs to be reduced:
```

```
focus 96.0  This is a sample of several lines of typing using
            a typing element called Elite, twelve-pitch, on an
            electric typewriter. The number of characters per
            line is about fifty -- which is perhaps a good,
            round number for easy legibility in this material
```

```
      94.0  This is a sample of several lines of typing using
            a typing element called Elite, twelve-pitch, on an
            electric typewriter. The number of characters per
            line is about fifty -- which is perhaps a good,
            round number for easy legibility in this material
```

```
      92.0  This is a sample of several lines of typing using
            a typing element called Elite, twelve-pitch, on an
            electric typewriter. The number of characters per
            line is about fifty -- which is perhaps a good,
            round number for easy legibility in this material
```

```
      90.0  This is a sample of several lines of typing using
            a typing element called Elite, twelve-pitch, on an
            electric typewriter. The number of characters per
            line is about fifty -- which is perhaps a good,
            round number for easy legibility in this material
```

of typewriting done on my well-worn IBM Selectric 12 pitch.* The typing has been reduced to a series of decreasing sizes expressed as percentages of the original, because that's how printers and cameramen communicate: 100%, or **focus 100.0,** is **SS** or same size, that is, original size; 90%, or "focus 90.0," is nine-tenths of the original size or 10% smaller; and so on. Use this table as a rough guide. Having determined what looks about right to you, experiment with the printout from your own machine, but don't be surprised if the effect looks very different. The larger the sample you reduce down to the size you guess might be about right, the safer will be your final decision.

Remember one other important factor. What you see here is just a short snippet of five lines. Anybody can buckle down and decipher a few lines' worth of material, no matter how small or illegible. But extend those few lines to a full page, and you have a totally different situation. What may be acceptable, or even attractive, in a small sample may well turn out to be a repulsive mass as a full page. So before committing yourself to a whole issue's worth of disasters, get a reduction of a full page to see if it works.

---

*Ordinary typewriters have either pica type (10 characters to the inch or **10 pitch**) or elite type (12 characters to the inch or **12 pitch**). Obviously, the 12-to-the-inch characters appear a little smaller. Both pica and elite typewriters have the same spacing vertically, yielding 6 lines to the vertical inch (pica is equivalent to ⅙ inch: 6 picas per inch). Pica and elite type differ only in the number of characters they pack in per inch *horizontally.* "Executive" typewriters have **variable pitch**: to get an accurate count, you have to count all the characters in several lines and calculate the average per inch. Other word processors have other counts, of course.

88.0
This is a sample of several lines of typing using a typing element called Elite, twelve-pitch, on an electric typewriter. The number of characters per line is about fifty -- which is perhaps a good, round number for easy legibility in this material

86.0
This is a sample of several lines of typing using a typing element called Elite, twelve-pitch, on an electric typewriter. The number of characters per line is about fifty -- which is perhaps a good, round number for easy legibility in this material

84.0
This is a sample of several lines of typing using a typing element called Elite, twelve-pitch, on an electric typewriter. The number of characters per line is about fifty -- which is perhaps a good, round number for easy legibility in this material

82.0
This is a sample of several lines of typing using a typing element called Elite, twelve-pitch, on an electric typewriter. The number of characters per line is about fifty -- which is perhaps a good, round number for easy legibility in this material

80.0
This is a sample of several lines of typing using a typing element called Elite, twelve-pitch, on an electric typewriter. The number of characters per line is about fifty -- which is perhaps a good, round number for easy legibility in this material

78.0
This is a sample of several lines of typing using a typing element called Elite, twelve-pitch, on an electric typewriter. The number of characters per line is about fifty -- which is perhaps a good, round number for easy legibility in this material

76.0
This is a sample of several lines of typing using a typing element called Elite, twelve-pitch, on an electric typewriter. The number of characters per line is about fifty -- which is perhaps a good, round number for easy legibility in this material

74.0
This is a sample of several lines of typing using a typing element called Elite, twelve-pitch, on an electric typewriter. The number of characters per line is about fifty -- which is perhaps a good, round number for easy legibility in this material

Enlarging the paste-up to accommodate reduced typewriting

You can handle the production one of two ways if you intend to reduce your type photographically: (1) Get every piece of type reduced to the desired size before you begin the paste-up, or (2) paste up the original typescript on a larger sheet of paper, which is later reduced as a whole.

Doing it in little pieces can run into money because it requires a freshly reduced piece to be inserted every time you need to make a change. The second option requires a larger **dummy sheet** to paste up on. How much larger should it be? Obviously it must be larger in proportion to the reduction you desire. Such a ratio is not easy to calculate. For instance, let's assume that you want to reduce your type to 90% of original size, and that you want your printed page to measure the standard 8½" x 11". How much bigger must your dummy sheet be to yield this result? In the table of reductions you'll discover that it has to be 11% bigger than 8½" x 11" (focus 111.0) and that it must therefore measure $9\frac{7}{16}$" x 12¼". (The dimensions in the table have been brought to the nearest $\frac{1}{16}$th of an inch—that's tolerance close enough.)

To reduce typewriter type to this percentage or "focus" of its original size . . .	. . . the page must be enlarged from the original $8\frac{1}{2}$" x 11" by this percentage or "focus". . .	. . . so that it measures this size, to the nearest $\frac{1}{16}$"
98% or 98.0	102.5% or 102.5	$8\frac{11}{16}$" x $11\frac{1}{4}$"
96% or 96.0	104% or 104.0	$8\frac{13}{16}$" x $11\frac{7}{16}$"
94% or 94.0	107% or 107.0	$9\frac{1}{16}$" x $11\frac{3}{4}$"
92% or 92.0	109% or 109.0	$9\frac{1}{4}$" x $11\frac{15}{16}$"
90% or 90.0	111% or 111.0	$9\frac{7}{16}$" x $12\frac{1}{4}$"
88% or 88.0	113% or 113.0	$9\frac{5}{8}$" x $12\frac{1}{2}$"
86% or 86.0	116% or 116.0	$9\frac{7}{8}$" x $12\frac{3}{4}$"
84% or 84.0	119% or 119.0	$10\frac{1}{8}$" x $13\frac{1}{8}$"
82% or 82.0	122% or 122.0	$10\frac{3}{8}$" x $13\frac{7}{16}$"
80% or 80.0	125% or 125.0	$10\frac{5}{8}$" x $13\frac{3}{4}$"
78% or 78.0	129% or 129.0	$10\frac{15}{16}$" x $14\frac{1}{8}$"
76% or 76.0	132% or 132.0	$11\frac{3}{16}$" x $14\frac{1}{2}$"
74% or 74.0	135% or 135.0	$11\frac{1}{2}$" x $14\frac{7}{8}$"

The problem of creating emphasis in typewritten copy

Signaling the start of something new is the major problem in pieces that are made of typewritten copy. Two major areas need exploring: how to separate stories with space, and how to give headlines, or their equivalent, visibility so they pop out from their background. In typeset products you can use boldness and blackness in **display type** such as headlines to create attention-getting contrast. In typewritten pieces, you are limited to what the keyboard can provide, unless you add extraneous material.

If you intend to run lines across the full page—acceptable in a letter, but somewhat dangerous in a publication—hedge your bets by breaking your typewritten mass into units that look smaller. The easiest way to do that is to insert space between paragraphs: a full line if the machine you are using cannot deliver a half-line, but a half-line is as good from the point of view of apparent breakup as a full line, and it uses up less paper. It might be a good idea to accompany this extra space with extra-deep **paragraph indents**; up to, perhaps, a quarter of the way into the line is not excessive.

The problem is that the space needed *between* stories has to be even more generous than the space between paragraphs, if each story is to become noticeable, and that eats up your paper very quickly.

If you intend running two columns per page, you don't need a full line of space between the paragraphs: A deep indent for each paragraph ought to be enough. Furthermore, don't leave too much space between the two columns (the **alley**) because the ragged-right setting of your typewritten copy adds to the visual impression of separation between columns. Too much emptiness on the page may signal the wrong interpretation to the reader— not enough value for your money, perhaps? So, at a two-column-per-page or narrower setting, tighten up; if you feel the need to open up spaces, make the paragraph indents deeper.

How to make headlines using your typewriter

You need a combination of several factors in order to make your headlines visible. You have to have color—more darkness, more ink on the page. You also need a thicker texture of type or greater concentration of type. And, most of all, you need a clearly edged area of space within which the headline is to be perceived. Such **white space** need not be large or excessive. It does, however, need to be clearly, geometrically demarcated, so that it appears as a deliberate ploy. One important factor to bear in mind: If you repeat any technique more than once, you create the impression of deliberateness. So repeat, because it accumulates in the reader's subconscious and adds to the strength and personality of your overall product.

These two lines represent the end of the text piece that precedes the start of a new story; here follows the new headline...

THIS IS AN IRRESISTIBLY INTERESTING HEADLINE

Type your headline all in capitals in a single line, underscoring and overscoring it flush with the last character on the right, but extending the rules a couple of characters over farther to the left. Two lines of space above the head and one beneath it yield the requisite breakup on the page.

Here is the start of the text, which the reader will be intrigued into reading by the cleverness of the language in the headline. Note that the first paragraph following the headline is typed flush left without an indent; that is done deliberately, to make the space in which the headline is seen geometric and clean.

The regular paragraphing indention can be dramatically deep, as in this example, where ten spaces were left for the eye to travel into.

THIS IS A HEADLINE
TYPED IN ALL-CAPITALS

Here starts the text of this article and it is indented the same number of characters from the left for a total of four lines of type; this trick allows the space within which the headline is placed to be clearly visible and pop out from the surrounding text matter. Here is another line of dummy type to illustrate this simple idea. Another minor variation might be the following illustration. Allow 2 lines of space, then...

THIS IS ANOTHER HEADLINE
TYPED IN TWO LINES

Here starts the text of the next article, below the overscore that extends all the way across the page, thus separating stories from each other most obviously and effectively...*Then continue as above*

Break every headline into two lines, type them all in capitals, flush left, with no extra space between the lines. Break the lines according to phrases that make sense. The all-cap lines give the maximum ink coverage except for one other possibility: underscoring. By adding underscoring beneath each line, as well as above the line of typing, you create a dark, triple-decker sandwich. But if you go beyond the obvious and extend the underscores to a width of, say, 24 characters, you add a graphic trademark to your product in all your headlines.

Start the text a couple of characters farther to the right and indent four lines the same way; that will then leave a two-line hole below the headline that acts as a good contrast to the display type.

This is the end of a normal text piece, typed at a fairly narrow measure. The advantage of narrowness is that it allows the left-hand margin of the page to be much wider than is customary, and thus yields a useful space for placement of the display headline at left.

THIS IS THE
FIRST LINE
OF A NICE LONG
HEADLINE THAT
READS INTO THE TEXT, THUS:

Here starts the text of the succeeding story. Note that there are two lines of space skipped between the two stories. The headline can have any number of short, stacked lines in the left-hand margin, as long as the last of those lines reads into the first line of the text.

Type your text to a width narrower than the full-page maximum, say, 55 or so elite characters. Impose the text on the page in such a way that as much space is available in the left-hand margin as possible. Insert your headlines into that space. However, in order to avoid wasting space between stories, skip merely two lines there. The last line of the headline should read into the first line of the new story—perhaps even bumping into the text a little. Then stack the rest of the short lines of the headline flush left above it; underscore them to add color.

Ultimately, there are only a few simple things one can do with a typewriter. *Beyond this, individual good sense and subjective taste take over. It boils down to a matter of mixing and matching gimmicks and tricks to produce the best recipe for the project at hand.*

Here you thought you were reading some philosophy and it is nothing of the sort. It is padding, woffling, humbug, twaddle, prattle, blather, piffle, gobbledygook, gibberish, rodomontade, balderdash, inanity, bushwa! But what an amusing, fresh technique to tuck a lot of stuff in a page, and make each unit appear self-contained and separate from the others below and above it. The change in faces is a great help.

Here's a solution similar to one suggested above but applied to a narrower column setting. It is particularly useful for a collection of short pieces, and may even feature an extra added wrinkle: varying typefaces—easy to achieve on some machines.

Here is another technique for short headlines, shown in a two-column page format; it would be perfectly possible to apply this to a one-column width, of course. You get the necessary details if you read the words.

THE NUMBER OF OPTIONS FOR DESIGNING with a
          typewriter is very limited. It becomes
          an exercise in ingenuity and mathematics,
          how much to indent, where, and with what.
          Hanging the heads out into the space
          at left is a most effective means of
          letting our attention focus on the
          starts of things. But we must add as
          much color (i.e., blackness) to those
          points as possible. Hence the additional
          underscoring and overscoring.
HERE IS ANOTHER SUCH HEADLINE, which inter-
          rupts the flow of the text very ef-
          fectively. But it is not very strong
          in signaling something NEW. A line
          of space preceding it would add to
          its headline quality:

THIS STARTS SOMETHING DIFFERENT: and a colon
          helps the idea of the start along...
          see how that line of extra space makes
          the headline look that much more im-
          portant?

How to make sideheads on your typewriter

Sideheads are headlines placed at the left-hand edge of the page, or flush left with the column, or they may run into the text at left. They are, however, secondary headlines, less important than the main headline, and they are therefore categorized as **subheads** in terms of their functional ranking. The definition of a subhead is simply that it is a headline that starts a subdivision of the text and helps to show the organization of the material, as well as break up the grayness of the type. (In newspaper parlance, a subhead is a short line set bold in the typeface of the body copy, usually all capitals, centered on the column. But that is a highly specialized usage of the term.)

Trying to gain visibility on the typewriter is not easy. As with headlines, it is necessary to create such visibility by manipulating the space and color, by indenting, and by general composition, as well as by using the underscore or other repeated marks of which the machine is capable. One trap to avoid: the habit of centering the line on the column or page. Such a placement doesn't help pop the words out clearly enough, unless there are at least two lines of space left free above and below such a subhead. Furthermore, the white space left over after the subhead is placed has been split into two small pieces, one at each end of the head—obviously, or the words wouldn't be centered, would they? Experience shows that tiny bits of white space don't carry nearly as much impact as larger ones: They aren't noticeable. It is much wiser to combine the two little pieces into a big hunk by sliding the subhead over to the left (thus turning it into a sidehead).

     Sidehead words: The sidehead is indented five characters; the
underscore beneath it is extended four characters beyond the end of
the sidehead, and the first initial of the text is typed in atop the
last stroke of the underscoring. The fact that this block of text is
"justified" at right is purely coincidental and unintentional.

<u>Another sidehead version</u>   This is a variation on the same theme and you can go on playing this way ad infinitum. The variations that are possible are almost endless, and you can figure out the one that will be most appropriate to your content and format.

This is copy that precedes a freestanding sidehead. Two lines of space should be left to separate such a sidehead from the last line of the copy that precedes it, like this.

THIS IS A FREESTANDING SIDEHEAD

After leaving a line of space, the text continues with a fresh direction of its content. The sidehead was typed flush left. The text that follows it was typed flush left also, without indention, to make the space within which the sidehead will be viewed as crisp and clearly defined as possible.

    However, normal paragraphing is encouraged in such page formatting. Here a four-space indent was used to illustrate the principle.

    What follows is another handling of a sidehead: After leaving two lines of space as separator, the sidehead will be typed flush left and in all-capitals. However, the wording of it will be the start of a sentence:

A LEAD-IN SIDEHEAD is one which is integral with the text, for it is made of the first words of a fresh paragraph. Those words must be carefully chosen to be important and interesting, or the subject will be unworthy of the technique!

How to make lists on your typewriter

In typeset type, we would be able to use bullets, triangles, boldface numerals, or all sorts of other symbolic spots to signal a series of material that's different from its surrounding context. On the typewriter, we are restricted to numerals, space, horizontal rules, and punctuation marks. Numerals are too weak to stand alone, except if they are placed on the page as **hanging indents** , i.e., outside the left-hand margin of the list. Here are a few ways of handling numerals.

1	1.	1/	1)	(1)	1-	<u>1</u>	1:	1....
2	2.	2/	2)	(2)	2-	<u>2</u>	2:	2....
3	3.	3/	3)	(3)	3-	<u>3</u>	3:	3....
4	4.	4/	4)	(4)	4-	<u>4</u>	4:	4....
5	5.	5/	5)	(5)	5-	<u>5</u>	5:	5....

It is advisable to build numerals up visually with a little embellishment. Here is a good example, which places them flush left, then skips **four** characters before starting the text. To formalize the arrangement, you underscore the numerals, the four empty spaces, and the initial capital of the text. That adds a touch of color and creates an unexpected surprise to the thus-defined empty space. Placing the numerals flush left retains the precision of the left-hand margin of the text, makes them look neater by contrast to the ragged right-hand edge, and is also very easy to produce.

    The problem with **numbered lists** (1, 2, 3, 4) or lettered lists (a, b, c, d) is that they can be misinterpreted as implying ranking of some kind. To dispel such misapprehensions, it is necessary to introduce a numbered list with an explanatory statement such as, "Here are seven examples of such-and-such." On the other hand, if you want to imply a logical sequence, start it out with something like "The Seven Steps to Happiness."

This is an example of handling lists within the body of the text. Although it is not too wise to allow full lines of space between items normally, it helps the legibility of lists to do so:

1   On the sixth character start the first word of the copy; then continue flush left in the second line. Underscore the numeral, the empty spaces, and the first letter of the text.

2   Repeat the pattern precisely -- and you have a well-working trick to emphasize your list makeup.

These are the last two lines of text preceding a list. Here is a numbered list:

1. *The first item is shown thus.*
2. *The second item is also easily accommodated.*
3. *The third item gets to be tricky because it needs a second line.*
4. *The fourth item is nice and short again.*
5. *How many more do we have to type?*

And this is the start of the text again, set flush left without an indent, to help to define crisply the space in which the list is placed.

---

these two lines of type represent the last two lines of the text that precedes the list:

-- Use dash-dash for short, one-line items.
-- Single space between them.
-- Double space above and below the list.

This represents the first line of the text that follows the list...

o Preceding each item in the list, just tap the lowercase o on your keyboard.

o Depending on the column width and your tastes, indent or type flush left.

o Double space between entries.

o You'll find this method especially suited for entries with two or more lines and multi-sentence entries.

---

a somewhat elementary trick to play to gain variety on the typewritten page is illustrated here:
        Type ten characters' worth of underscoring lines. Then start the sentence which begins the new paragraph. Complete the entire paragraph, and when it is finished, start over.
        Those ten lines of underscoring give an unusual effect in the texture of the column. It is not necessary to leave a line of space between paragraphs when using this trick. The ten-space indents made visible by the underscore are more than enough as signals.
        Here we go again...

        here is a variant on the same trick used in reverse pattern. Instead of poking the starts of paragraphs into the body of the surrounding text, why not
Poke the headline or start OUT at the left-hand margin in some fashion such as this one? Each line of regular type starts with six characters' worth of underscore. New paragraphs do not.
This is a new paragraph starting out at far left followed by the normal or abnormal typing method, whichever way you wish to characterize it...
The advantage of this trick is the very clean left-hand edge that your type columns get

Big initials added to typewritten copy

Inserting an **initial** (a large-sized letter) is a simple way to achieve visual accent on the page, even when there is no strictly functional need for such a signal. In theory, it is unwise to accentuate something that is unworthy of attention. You shouldn't insert a symbol that is interpreted as a break in sense when there is no such change of direction to the flow of thoughts in the text. Not only is it cheating the reader, but it blunts your graphic weapons for the times they will be used correctly for their intended purpose. However, it would be foolish to pretend that such misuse does not exist, or that one ought not to bend the rules a bit when the situation warrants. Initials are innocuous elements in that they have no inherent meaning. It is a far greater mistake to utilize subheads for phony breakup because they are made up of words, and, therefore, they need to *say something*. Initials are just bigger letters, and it is hard to read any meaning into such elements other than their strategic placement in the flow of the story.

However, assuming that your conscience is clear because you have solved the ethical problems, how do you make initials in typewritten material when the typewriter doesn't provide them? You leave a space where the initial is to go, and when the typescript is finished, you add the initial from any of the transfer lettering sheets available. You can select any size and type style you can possibly dream of, and for an initial investment (pun intended) of some $8 you will have enough letters to do a dozen articles—if you can dream up a few words that start with Q, X, and Z! Here are a few examples of handling initials in typewritten copy. The words in the copy describe the variations.

With the exception of initials, which are merely a decorative accent on the page, it is unwise to mix typeset type with typewriter type. Why? Because the two are not compatible: typeset type is so much more sophisticated a material than typewritten type that it makes the latter look crude and shoddy by comparison. It is so much better to accept the limitations of the originating machinery and work within them. That simplifies the production process and gives the product a genuine simplicity that is the first step toward true elegance.

Here are some ideas on using big initials added to the typescript after the typing has been completed. They are simply transfer lettering rubbed on from sheets purchased from the art supply store in an incredible variety of sizes and styles.

Another way to do the same sort of thing is this. It appears just about irresistible on a page. How can the reader NOT be beguiled into reading?

Nobody would accuse these solutions of brilliance or subtlety or even originality. They are completely obvious, once you begin thinking along these lines...

You see how interesting this could be made to look when the particular trick is repeated? The white spaces surrounding each solution, the contrast of color, the precision of the ruled underscore, the startling incongruity of the initial itself, all add up to character-creation with the simplest of means.

What you happen to be looking at is American Typewriter type from sheet LG2803 of Letraset, 48pt caps. I've used it here for two reasons. (1) I believe in using appropriate faces wherever possible; here we use typewriter for body copy, why not a variant thereof for the display? (2) I happen to have lots of it handy. Could there be a better reason?

This is an initial cap hanging at left, outside the left-hand margin, whose great advantage is that it adds lots of white space all around, obviously at the expense of space used for body copy. But you can't have it both ways: If you want drama, you've got to give something up to achieve it. Space is the easiest sacrifice to make.

How to handle standing art with typewriters

In magazine parlance **departments** are sections of the publication that recur in each issue and specialize in a clearly defined area of interest. Subdivisions of such departments are **columns**, which are written by outside authorities under their own names. All such departments are signaled to the reader by a **department slug**, or heading, giving the title of the section (usually its subject) or the title of the column (usually a pun with the name and mug shot of its writer). If the headings are embellished typographically or with additional artwork that is repeated every time, these regularly added features are called **standing art.***

What is the purpose of this digression, where we are dealing with the limited technology of typewritten pieces? The inescapable fact is that in such pieces, too, the need for the equivalent of standing art has to be faced, because any periodical, whatever its nature, is likely to carry recurrent elements that call for special handling.

Here, to prime the thinking pump, is an array of headings easily replicated on the typewriter. They look colorful and perfectly appropriate to the technology: unlimited repetition or patterning of a limited group of symbols. You are encouraged to dream up your own.

```
LOGO


LOGO----------------


LOGO--- --- --- --- --- --- --- ---


::::::::::: LOGO


           LOGO
mmmmmmmmmmmmmmmmmmmmmmmmmmmmmmmmmmmmmmmmmmmm


****************** LOGO ******************
```

```
++++++++++++++++++++++++++++++++++++++++++++
              O B I T S


$$$$$$$$$$$$$$$$$$$$$$$$$$$$$$$$$$$$$$$$$$$$$

THE ECONOMY
????????????????????????????????????????????


%%%%%%%%%%%%%%%%%%%%%%%%%%%%%%%%%%%%%%%%%%%%%

e m p l o y e e   b e n e f i t s


============================================


vvvvvvvvvvvvvvvvvvvvvvvvvvvvvvvvvvvvvvvvvvvv

    L*O*G*O
```

*"Pick up from page 000 in date of issue" are the instructions you give to the printer to have these features repeated.

4

Using type effectively

There is no magic about typography. It is a discipline, a craft, an art that requires considerable technical knowledge and experience, but whose basis is common sense. The best typography is that which is unseen. Typography is a means to an end: having the message read and absorbed. The faster, easier, and smoother that process of reading can be made to be, the more effectively the typographic skills are being applied. If the reader becomes conscious of the act of reading or of the type itself, then the typography has not been used to good effort, for it interposes itself between the message and the reader.

Your aim is to invite the reader to continue reading to the end of the piece. The character of the product you are working on will determine the mix of typographic and graphic materials you use on the page. It can be said, however, that simplicity, discipline, clarity of first impression, limiting the number of typefaces you mix, an evenness of gray color of the type as a mass printed on the white background, and a coherent structure are all elements that attract and retain the reader's attention.

The typography is the fabric of the publication. It is seen on all the pages and, as such, it is a fundamental raw material you can control. Pictures, charts, headlines, logos, and all the rest of the embellishments are additional to the typography. You can have a product without any of the aforementioned elements, but you cannot publish without words, and that means type.

Tone-of-voice typography

If, as the philosopher Hegel said, "architecture is frozen music," then typography is crystallized speech. Or it can be. If you listen to a monotonous speaker, you have to concentrate and work to find the nuggets of useful information that may be hidden in that droning, dull delivery. Translating such a speech into type, you would expect to see it as an unbroken column of gray type—and you have to concentrate and work to find those nuggets hidden on that droning, dull page that you're looking at.

A good speaker adds loudness for emphasis, or allows the pitch of the voice to modulate up and down the scale. Loudness translates into **size** in type: when you shout, you represent such shouting by large letters. Change of pitch can be translated into a variety of **boldness**: lightface for high notes, extra-bold for low ones. This analogy could be carried a little far. It is perfectly logical, however, to think of typography as being nearly as flexible as the human voice. If you think of the material that way, you will be able to decide on typography that is expressive and functionally responsive to your editorial purpose. The whole thing boils down to editorial judgment: what is important deserves emphasis, and what is unimportant, or background, or ordinary can be played down. Precisely how you do that depends on the specifics of the subject, its context, and the courage of your own conviction. Too much printed matter is composed the way it is because we have always done it that way. We seem to be living happily in straitjackets not necessarily of our own making: three columns per page, with two columns as a possible variant for important stuff. "Ten on 11 by 12 pi" ad infinitum. An unquestioning traditionalism robs us of our capacity for meaningful, clear, crisp, obvious communication. Knowingly or not, we tend to drone on and on. Just by being aware of tonalities inherent in typography, we can break out of that monotony and excite our readers.

How? By **contrast of size and color**. What is important ought to be given prominence, so you make it bigger and use bolder type. Conversely, you make the subservient matter smaller than expected, or set it in a lighter face. You mustn't think of the solution as being isolated or limited to one element; in fact, you must realize that any one element on the page reacts with all others. Typography is just like using colors: you can pick a lovely red from **the** swatch book, and it will look hideous when run in conjunction with the green, although by itself the green you picked was also a pretty color. The secret lies in grasping the relationship between the two. Just so with **contrast in type**. Those contrasts are made by varying size and color. They can also be made by varying styles of type—for example, by mixing decorative faces that express the flavor of an unusual subject with workaday type for regular features. But watch out! Too much spice in your stew will ruin the taste.

Today's film-based type fonts are more flexible than the old hot-metal ones used to be. Not only can the spacing between characters be controlled— so much so that some equipment allows you to tighten the setting (by **kerning**) until the letters touch or even overlap—but there are also specially designed **ligatures** that overcome the problem of ugly gaps between some letter forms. Where such special alternate characters are not available, the phototypesetting equipment can tuck letters into each other so that, for instance, an o tucks under the roof of the top stroke of a *T*, which makes it neater and more legible.

We are also fortunate for another reason today: in hot-metal linotype days a font of type (in just one size, but encompassing the full range of faces: roman, italic, and boldface) was a serious investment that had to be amortized over a long period of usage. Today's typesetting equipment is far more sophisticated, and it can produce its output from a master font that is either a film negative or an electronic imaging source. To make such master negatives is infinitely cheaper than it used to be to produce a font of linotype matrices. The investment, at both the production end and the user end, is much more modest. That is why we have such an outpouring of new faces available. To be sure, some of them are probably not going to last very long, but others will prove worthy of longevity. Furthermore, the old, proven faces are being transferred to the new machinery, and their range of sizes and weights are being enlarged and filled out so that the usual type-faces are now available in full ranges from extra-light to extra-bold. Many of these faces have added condensed and extended versions so that a single

foto-typography
foto-typography
foto-typography
foto-typography
foto-typography

fl fi

To To

Light	*Light Italic*	Light Condensed	*Light Condensed Italic*	Outline
Book	*Book Italic*	**Book Condensed**	***Book Condensed Italic***	Outline Shadow
Bold	***Bold Italic***	**Bold Condensed**	***Bold Condensed Italic***	**Contour**
Ultra	***Ultra Italic***	**Ultra Condensed**	***Ultra Condensed Italic***	ITC Cheltenham

family of type can be used to achieve all the variety a publication needs in terms of its graphic expression with a uniform type style. Due to the comparative cheapness of the new materials, and the fact that they can be applied to most typesetting equipment, you are no longer shackled to one supplier, but can demand your particular face from the competition as well. The freedom and riches now generally available allow for more expressive and thus more effective use of type. This flexibility must be used for worthy ends: *not to make things pretty, but to make things work—to tell the story*.

What face to use?

The choice of typeface(s) depends on the nature of the material to be set. If it is body copy, then the tried-and-true standards are probably the safest and best, although they are certainly the most boring. If it is display material, then your search for attention-getting, startling type ought to take precedence over anything else. Yet you must always balance the specific needs of each kind of type with the overall look or design of the product as a whole—as a package. So your choice must take at least two factors into consideration: the specific function of each column, department, or piece and the overall character of the publication.

If you need to create a special mood with your typography, one that reflects the subject matter, you can choose faces that have such special flavor. They are available as display type more readily than as body copy, of course, although certain allusions or impressions can be subtly suggested even in body-copy typefaces. A good catalog of what is available from your supplier, as well as in do-it-yourself lettering, is what you need to study in order to make your selection.

The confusion about names of typefaces

When old Baskerville, Caslon, Granjon, Bodoni, and all the other great type designer/printers designed the faces that bear their names, they gave a distinctive shape to each character of the alphabet. Those shapes remained unaltered over the years because they were physically cut from metal punches—each letter separate. There was little reason or need to change them until the industrial and communications revolution in the mid-nineteenth century. Suddenly a variety of machines came into use that supplanted letter-by-letter handset typography, allowed for the introduction of totally new faces, and led to the adaptation of old ones to the new technology. The great original faces were, therefore, amended to fit the machines. Then, when phototypesetting was introduced in the mid-twentieth century, to be followed by the computer and electronic type-generating equipment, the problem was multiplied. We are living amid an explosion of typefaces. Many of them are fresh, new, and contemporary. Many are amendments of the good old traditional ones. Many are returns to the true originals. That is perfectly logical. Equally logical is the fact that the producers of equipment (each with its own roster of typefaces) compete in the marketplace in terms of the mechanical quality, flexibility, and excellence of typographic result they offer. What is maddening to the user of type is that each manufacturer names the faces, even the derivative ones, differently. As a result, the typeface that Miedinger designed and named Helvetica is obtainable on Alpha type as Claro, on Autologic as Newton, on Compugraphic as Helios, on Star/Photon as Helvet Star, on Graphic Systems as Geneva, on Harris as Vega, on Mergenthaler as the Original Helvetica, and on Varityper as Megaron. They are all a tiny bit different, but all unquestionably the same basic design. What makes life even more difficult is that many typesetters list the face by its original name, such as Helvetica, in their catalogs, but actually give you the version that their particular machinery produces. The fact that you are not getting *the* Helvetica, but Megaron, let's say, could well make a difference in the overall color of the type, its apparent size, and certainly the **character count*** per line. The only way to avoid disaster is to work only with information that your supplier gives you about the specific faces available at that shop. The National Composition Association, 1730 North Lynn Street, Arlington, VA 22209, is the clearinghouse for information on all aspects of typesetting, and will be glad to help.

Preparing copy for setting in type

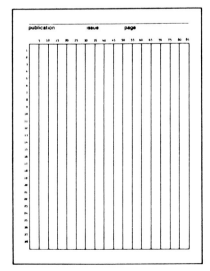

If you want to do a job professionally, efficiently, and economically, the first secret is to be meticulous in the preparation of the final copy. The opportunity for better quality at lower cost is found in the handling of the details. It makes no difference whether the copy is to be set in type by an outside supplier, or by someone on a keyboard in-house. Whether it is to be set in hot metal or by any of the cold-type composers, if the copy is carefully prepared, it will cost less to have typeset.

Type the manuscript on white paper 8½" x 11" double spaced, with generous margins on both sides. Use one side of the paper only. If you generate a great deal of copy for setting, then it might be a good idea to use specially prepared **copy paper** that can be bought ready-made, with or without carbon copies attached. Each sheet tabulates the story name, author name, publication name, issue date, and manuscript page number across the top, and it has markings for character count across the page as well as line count down the page, like the one shown here.

The usefulness of such forms is that they force you to be organized, whereas blank paper requires you to remember to do all that labeling. And, clearly, organization of your work is of the essence. It is so easy to lose bits of paper if they aren't identified, and then you have to waste time trying to recognize the material by its sense—and it is remarkable how fast one forgets.

*Average number of characters or letters in a given length of line. See page 33.

The manuscript need not be typed faultlessly; its beauty will win you no awards. Its legibility will get you thanks from the typesetter, and that is all that matters. So some erasures, crossings out, and the like are fine, so long as they are clearly done. It is wise to make these notations in ink, which will pick up on the xerographic copy that you make for yourself as a backup and checking copy before you give the original to the typesetter. It is wise to avoid splitting words at ends of lines to avoid confusing the typesetter, who then has to decide whether such hyphenation is supposed to be included (set in type) or whether it is merely a word break in the manuscript. It is also wise to make all your setting instructions as close to the place they occur in the text as possible, so the setter sees them during the process of scanning the copy line by line. Such instructions are given in the standard proofreader's marks, although they are not being used for corrections. These marks consist of two sets of signals: graphic signs and verbal abbreviations to explain them. The verbal part is written in the margin at the same level as the line or word referred to. The graphic signs are drawn on the line of text itself. Instructions are circled.

TO INDICATE	MARK WORDS WITH	WRITE IN MARGIN
CAPITALS	word	caps
LOWERCASE (one letter)	woRd	l.c.
LOWERCASE (several letters)	/ORD	l.c.
ITALICS	word	ital
BOLDFACE	word	bf
PARAGRAPH	/First words	¶ ¶ ¶
INSERT (caret)	Missin∧letter	g
ADD BETWEEN LINES	<	< needed words
MOVE LEFT OR RIGHT	⌐ mmmmmm ssssss⌐ nnnnnnn ttttttt	flush left
CENTER	⌐vvvv⌐	center
TRANSPOSE	(second first)	tr.
ADD SPACE	add space add#space	Add space
CLOSE	clo⌢se up	close up
FIX AND CLOSE UP	imp⌢prove sp∧lling	∂/e
SPELL OUT	the (NY) subway	Spell out
DELETE	unwanted word word	ℓ

When you want to kill some words, indicate such deletion with a single neat, horizontal line (but leave the words legible in case you decide to reinstate them later, in which case all you will need to do is put dots under them, which cancels out [stets] the cancellation).

THIS WORD IS ~~NOT~~ NOT NEEDED.

THIS WORD IS ~~NOT~~ NOT NEEDED.

THIS WORD IS NOT NOT NEEDED.

PUNCTUATION	COMMA	✦	PERIOD	⊙	COLON	⦂
	SEMICOLON	⦂	ONE EM DASH	|M	HYPHEN	=
	SLASH	/	QUOTE	∨∨	APOSTROPHE	∨

All the manuscript pages must be numbered consecutively. It is perfectly logical to add pages to an existing set and number them a, b, and so on (3a, 3b, if they follow page 3).

You should try to cut down the typesetter's effort to a minimum in order to save money. You must cross-reference insertions clearly if you cannot squeeze them onto the original typescript. Add a separate piece of paper, numbered page 27a, let's say, and mark the insertion "Copy A, insert on page 27." Then, on page 27 itself, where the insert belongs, write in the margin in large visible letters—perhaps even in red—"Insert Copy A from page 27a." Never staple or tape a slip of paper to the original manuscript and hope that the typesetter will figure out where it belongs. He can't, even if that slip of paper has not fallen off.

It is a good idea to separate your headlines from the body copy if they are to be set in a different typeface. It makes the process of typesetting much easier and faster. Equally, captions could well be bunched together for setting separately.

Specifying type: how to instruct the typesetter

Your instructions must be clear (you must know what you want, and say so), complete (leaving nothing for the typesetter to decide), and concise (expressed in the standard manner understood by typesetters). It goes without saying that the instructions should be legible and intelligible.

Instructing the typesetter is also called **marking the copy** or **specing the type** (short for specifying). The following information is what the typesetter needs to know, although most of it is not actually written down because in practice many assumptions are made based on what is considered to be normal. (That normalness, then, goes without saying.)

1. Type size (in points, or for large headlines, in the measurement of the height of the capital letter in inches or even centimeters).

Swash characters

2. Type **family** (by name—for example, Times Roman, Helvetica).

3. Branch of type family (light, medium, semi-bold, bold, ultra-bold, extra-bold, as far as **weight** is concerned; condensed, extended, extra-wide, as far as **width** of the lettering is concerned).

4. **Posture** of the letters (roman, italic, oblique, slanted).

5. Kind of letters (upper- and lowercase, all capitals, lowercase, **small caps, swash** letters, special characters).

6. **Leading**, also sometimes spelled ledding (space between the lines).

7. Column structure (**justified** or unjustified, or **ragged** right or ragged left).

8. Line length (width of the column or **measure**).

9. **Kerning** (for larger type sizes, it is possible to control the spacing between characters, to make it tight, normal or loose. Each typesetting machine expresses its capabilities in a different set of units, so you need to determine the language or measurement system first).

10. Indentation (in **ems**, which are indicated by squares; one em space is normal) for first or any other lines of a paragraph.

11. Special handling of punctuation (regular or **hanging**, i.e., quotation marks or other punctuation to be placed outside the margin of the type).

12. Spacing between words (**French** spacing, in which the same space follows a period as is placed between words; or **regular** spacing, which is wider).

This list is not meant to frighten you. It merely illustrates the possible complexities of typesetting. The spec you will probably be using consists of a shorthand that looks like this:

$$^{10}/_{12} \, TR \times 15$$

This tells the typesetter that you want to use a 10-point type size with 2 points of leading or space between the lines (that's what the 12 is). The slash is short for the words "set on." *TR* is short for Times Roman, and since it is not followed by any other word, it implies the normal roman version of a regular weight. The *X* means "across" or "line length" or **measure**. And *15* means 15 picas; again, since there is no other instruction, justified or flush-right setting is implied. The paragraph indents will be one em if you don't ask for anything unusual. This will be the type specification that the setter will follow for as many pages of manuscript as do not bear a different specification. So all you need do is write it once at the start. If your manuscript has headlines or subheads interrupting it, you mark those individually; the setter will know to return to the basic body copy specification without your repeating it after each such interruption.

Frequently used terms are abbreviated:

	B F	stands for *boldface*
Bodoni	*U& l.c.*	stands for *upper-* *and lowercase*
	u.c.	stands for *uppercase* or capitals
BODONI	*cApς*	calls for setting in *capitals only*
	C.& L.c.	calls for setting in lowercase with the initial letters of important words capitalized
14 PT. Bodoni SMALL CAPS	*S.Cαpς*	stands for *small capitals* (known as small caps; specially made characters looking like capitals, but whose height is that of the "x-height" of the lowercase)
	C.S.C.	calls for setting in capitals with small capitals
	Stet	stands for the Latin word for "let it stand" and you use it every time you want to return to whatever the condition was before you started to tamper with it, or the *status quo ante.*

Type measurement

When handling type, the printer doesn't work with inches and feet, or even centimeters, but with **picas** and **points**. (Where the metric system is used, instead of picas and points they use ciceros and points. In fact, some machinery is calibrated in the metric system, and that is probably in all our futures.) For all practical purposes, however, you can concentrate on the traditional picas and points. To give you a sense of scale, there are six picas to the inch, and each pica is broken down into twelve points. There are, therefore, 72 points to the inch. Do remember this.

1 pt. = $\frac{1}{12}$ pica or $\frac{1}{72}$ inch
6 pts. = $\frac{1}{2}$ pica or $\frac{1}{12}$ inch
12 pts. = 1 pica   or $\frac{1}{6}$ inch
72 pts. = 6 picas or 1 inch

1 inch = 6 picas, 0 points
$\frac{7}{8}$ inch = 5 picas, 3 points
$\frac{3}{4}$ inch = 4 picas, 6 points
$\frac{5}{8}$ inch = 3 picas, 9 points
$\frac{1}{2}$ inch = 3 picas, 0 points
$\frac{3}{8}$ inch = 2 picas, 3 points
$\frac{1}{4}$ inch = 1 pica, 6 points
$\frac{1}{8}$ inch = 0 picas, 9 points

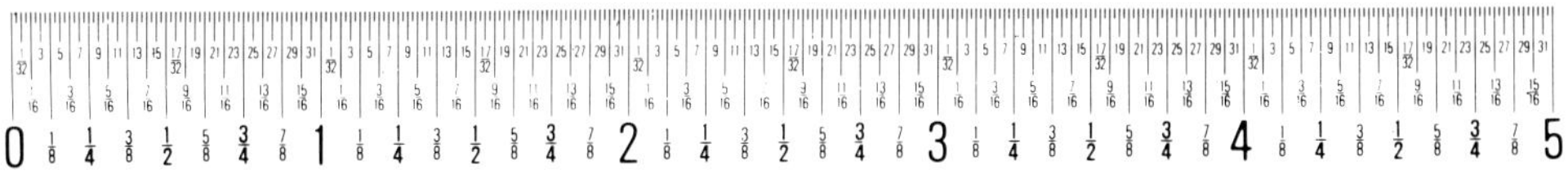

inches

picas and points

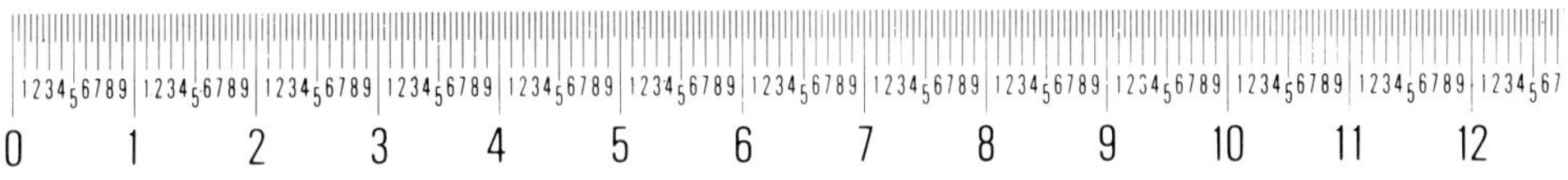

centimeters

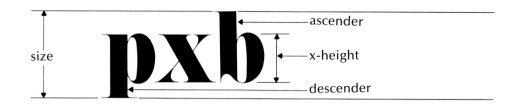

size | ascender | x-height | descender

pxb

abcdefghijklmnopqrstuvwxyz
6 ABCDEFGHIJKLMNOPQR:

abcdefghijklmnopqrstuvw
7 ABCDEFGHIJKLMNOP

abcdefghijklmnopqrstt
8 ABCDEFGHIJKLMN

abcdefghijklmnopqr
9 ABCDEFGHIJKLM

abcdefghijklmnop
10 ABCDEFGHIJKL

abcdefghijklmnc
11 ABCDEFGHIJK

abcdefghijklmr
12 ABCDEFGHIJ

abcdefghijkln
14 ABCDEFGH

abcdefghij
18 ABCDEF(

abcdefg
24 ABCDE

abcdef
30 ABCD

abcde
36 ABC

Type size is measured in points. That measurement is taken from the top of the **ascender** to the bottom of the **descender**. The sizes for type have traditionally been as follows: 5½, 6, 7, 8, 9, 10, 12, 14, 18, 24, 30, 36, 42, 48, 60, 72, and 96 points. Sizes in between were not made, because each set of molds for making them was an expensive investment and such minor differences in sizing would not be economically feasible. Now some of the new phototypesetting technology allows all sizes to be set in half-point increments. But there is a trap here: the design of the face itself. The type may, indeed, measure precisely what it says, 36 points for example. Yet it may look enormous in one kind of typeface and tiny in another. Why is that? It is due to the proportion of the **x-height** to the ascenders and descenders.

abcdefghijklm — Garamond **X**

abcdefghijklm — Century **X**

abcdefghijklm — Helvetica **X**

If the x-height is very large (as it tends to be in contemporary typeface design) then the ascenders and descenders are short, and the type appears very large. That makes it easier to read. If the x-height is very small, then the type, in bulk, looks small and is harder to read. Often, you need to use a larger size for easy legibility. By enlarging the x-height, you can save space overall because you can use a smaller type size, and thereby squeeze more words into the same space on your page without sacrificing legibility. You must, therefore, always know what typeface you are talking about when you say "Ten-point type is easy to read, so let's use that size for our body copy." Ten-point Baskerville is tiny, yet 10-point Helvetica is enormous, and 10-point Times Roman is just right; yet they all measure 10 points from the top of their ascender to the bottom of their descender.

Close upon the hour of noon the whol need of the as-yet-undreamed-of telegr from house to house, with little less than for that afternoon; the town would hav

A gory knife had been found close to tl as belonging to Muff Potter—so the stor Potter washing himself in the "branch" a at once sneaked off—suspicious circum Potter. It was also said that the town had in the matter of sifting evidence and arri

Close upon the hour of noon the w news. No need of the as-yet-undrea from group to group, from house to course, the schoolmaster gave holid strangely of him if he had not.

A gory knife had been found close by somebody as belonging to Muff Po citizen had come upon Potter washi in the morning, and that Potter had at cially the washing, which was not a

Close upon the hour of noon the whole need of the as-yet-undreamed-of telegrap house to house, with little less than teleg that afternoon; the town would have tho

A gory knife had been found close to tl as belonging to Muff Potter—so the stor Potter washing himself in the "branch" a at once sneaked off—suspicious circums Potter. It was also said that the town had l in the matter of sifting evidence and arriv

While discussing measurement systems, it is essential that you also understand an aspect of the printer's measurement that seems a difficult concept to absorb: quadding. The **em quad** is a measurement that is the square of the type's height in points, which sounds complicated, but is very

■Making ■Making ■Making mechanicals

simple. If you are using 12-point type, the em quad is 12 points high (the same height as the type) and 12 points wide. If your type is 10 points high, then the em quad would measure 10 points high by 10 points wide. Eight points? Eight by eight, and so on.

Inescapable

A 2-em quad retains its original height, but doubles the width: a 2-em quad in 12-point type measures the same old 12 points high, but is 24 points wide. A 3-em quad in 12-point type would be 12 points high and 36 points wide.

Make publications

Half an em quad is called an **en quad**. In the 12-point type that we have used before, it would indeed measure 12 points high, but only 6 points wide.

Since it is easy to confuse the difference between em and en, printers refer to em quads as **muts** and en quads as **nuts**. You need to know about muts and nuts because paragraph indenting is so described (indenting one em is the norm) and because horizontal spacing within type is so designated. The handwritten sign for em is □ and for en is ⧄.

Inches. Yes, printers do indeed measure with inches also. They use them to size pictures and to specify paper size or column-inches of type (see below). There is great difficulty when picas and inches have to be coordinated to fit a page together. The confusion will only be resolved when our present patched-up, antiquated, traditional system is replaced by computerized, full-page make-up systems that will appear on the terminal at our desk.

Column-inches are used to express the length of a text once it has been set in type. One speaks of a "6-inch story," meaning that the text measures 6 inches in length. In technical newspaper parlance, the column-inch is a much more specific concept, referring to space one inch deep and a column of type wide. But in terms of advertising space sales, it means 14 inches of agate (i.e., 5½ point) type, which happen to add up to precisely one inch. You can buy column-inch space in a newspaper to fill it with any size of type you wish. On the other hand, if you buy a "line," you get the space that one agate line would take up: 14 of them per inch. So far, so easy: The problem is that the width of the column can vary!

Copyfitting: how much space will the words take in type?

Copyfitting or **copycasting** or **casting off** is the process of determining the space that typewritten copy will occupy when it is turned into typeset type. You have to know that in order to avoid having too much, in which case you have to cut; or too little, in which case you have to add. Cutting hurts—and adding usually means padding. Both are a waste of money. So you have to bite the bullet, and add up your total number of characters and divide them in a proportion that will correspond to the type you'll be using or the space you need to fit into. This may sound frightfully complicated and even looks it, but it is child's play once you master the two simple steps involved.

Step one: counting up your words

No matter whether you are typing the copy on an ancient Royal or the latest electric self-correcting typewriter, or even using electronic magic on the word processor, the first thing you've got to know is how much you've written. You can either count the words (which is boring and inaccurate) and multiply by 5 to get the total number of characters, or you can count the characters (which is even more boring, but a bit more accurate).* You don't have to sit there counting each one individually. Instead, you count the average number per line.

Let's assume that you're not using an executive typewriter (which gives you characters of different widths just like type does), but an ordinary one that makes each letter the same width: **pica** gives you 10 characters per line, **elite** gives you 12. That regularity makes the calculation much easier. Take a sheet of your manuscript and draw a light pencil line down the right-hand edge of the typewritten area. Draw it so that it hits the ends of most of the lines, with the exception of the short lines at the ends of paragraphs. That means that there will be some lines that spill over to the right beyond the pencil line, because typewritten copy is typed **ragged right**. (We'll come to those bits in a moment.) Now, count the number of characters between the left-hand margin and your vertical pencil line. Obviously, each empty space, as well as each punctuation mark, must be counted as though it was a full character. Let's assume that your total number is 50 characters per line (*cpl*). Now add up the number of lines on your paper: If you've been typing double-spaced (which is the norm) you'll probably have 25. Each short line at the end of a paragraph should be counted as a full line because you'll be getting an equivalent paragraph in the future typeset version and relative numbers seem to work out just about the same.

Now, multiply the number of characters by the number of lines (50 × 25) and you've practically finished. You now know that there are 1,250 characters on the sheet of manuscript, plus those excess bits to the right of your vertical pencil line. Those you have to guesstimate, unless you want to count them individually. You'll probably find that four or five such pokeouts add up to a full line. But if you want to be superaccurate and do it quickly,

---

*Although that sounds similar to the way greenhorn cowpokes were taught to count cattle (adding up the legs and dividing by four), it makes sense in copy because dividing the characters by five gives you an accurate word count. Fortunately, typed characters don't move like cows' legs do.

measure with a ruler; add up the inches of pokeouts and multiply that total by 10 if your typewriter is a pica, or by 12 if it is an elite, and add that figure to your 1,250.

If your typewriter is an **executive**, which varies the width of characters, you will have another step to go through: you'll have to find the average number of characters per line by counting ten normal lines and dividing that total number by ten. That's the figure you multiply by the number of lines on the page. The likelihood that there will be very long pokeouts at the right is rather small, since such adjusting typewriters are intended to prevent such unevenness. So you can probably ignore the excess on the right, and your averaging of ten lines ought to give you an accurate enough answer.

Now multiply the number of characters per page by the number of pages in the typescript, and you will have a complete **character count**.

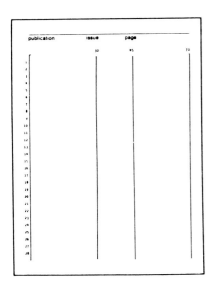

Blank spaces between paragraphs should, of course, be subtracted from the total number of typed lines, as should any deleted paragraphs. Insertions, short lines, and other exceptions to the average must be calculated separately and added to the total. You want to be accurate—within reason.

For regular periodical production, you'll probably know how many characters you need for a given typeset line under normal conditions. If you know that, you can take a shortcut that bypasses all this calculation. You can mark your **copy paper** (on which you do your typing) with the average character count, and then type within it; then all you need do is to count the number of lines that you have written. You need not print the average character count on the paper. You can set your typewriting machine itself to that width. The trouble with doing that, though, is that one tends to forget to reset it until it is too late. If your typeset lines are narrow, you can save typing paper by writing two typeset lines' worth of text on one single line of typewritten copy (80 characters per line or thereabouts). Then, in your quick calculation, you count the number of lines and multiply by two to convert the total to typeset estimates.

Step two: determining the ratio of space to type

Commonsense observation 1. You can accommodate more characters in a longer line than you can in a shorter line of type. From this brilliant insight grows the next, equally scintillating . . .

Commonsense observation 2. For a given amount of copy, you'll need fewer long lines than you will short lines. So far, so good, but the plot thickens.

Commonsense observation 3. If you use type that is small, you can fit in more characters than you could if you were using bigger type in a line of equal length. And further:

Commonsense observation 4. The spacing between your lines is flexible, so you can space them out or tighten them up pretty much at will.

That all adds up to a truth that can be a little frightening: Typography is extremely flexible. So, where do you start?

You make two assumptions, see if they work, and if they don't—you make different assumptions. In other words, you reach a workable result by

Point Size	Pica Width						
	10	**12**	**14**	**16**	**18**	**20**	**22**
6	38	46	54	61	69	77	85
7	33	40	47	53	60	66	73
8	29	35	41	46	52	58	64
9	25	30	35	40	45	51	56
10	23	28	32	37	42	47	51
11	21	25	29	33	38	42	46
12	19	23	27	31	35	39	42
14	17	20	23	26	30	33	36

Characters per pica

Point size	
6	4.89
7	4.48
8	4.14
9	3.84
10	3.58
11	3.16
12	2.99

trial and error. You can also, of course, blindly copy what has been done before, "because that's the way we've always done it," or "because the printer said to do it that way," or "because _____ does it that way" (fill in the name of your favorite publication).

The two assumptions are: (1) the size of the typeface you'll be using and (2) the length of your lines, i.e., the width of your columns.

You need to know the size of the type in order to find the character count that it yields, and you need to know the line length so you can figure out how many characters your line will accommodate.

There are two common ways to arrive at a character count for typeset type. (1) You can use a table that is usually printed on the same sheet as the **showing** or specimen of the typeface you intend to use. Normally, the table is read vertically for type sizes and horizontally for pica widths. You start with the appropriate type size and work your way across to the column nearest to your expected pica width. That number is what you need. (2) You can find out the number of characters per pica. To do this, you use a table that shows how many characters of a particular typeface can be expected to average in a pica, ranked by ascending order of size. You find the number that corresponds to the type size you plan to use, multiply by the expected number of picas in your line, and there is your character count per line. Armed with the character count, you can then quickly compute the number of lines of typeset type your text might require. You already know the number of characters your original text contains from your previous foray into Higher Mathematics (see page 52). You divide the total number of characters by the characters per line that you just found out, and that gives you the number of lines of type to that particular length you can expect.

Now a new factor must come into the equation: the problem of leading or spacing between lines. Its effect needs to be known so that you can determine whether your type-size/line-length ratio is going to work in terms of the space you have at your disposal. You have already assumed the type size—let's say 12 point. If it is **set solid**, it will be 12 on 12 (written as 12/12), which means there will be no extra leading or space placed between the lines, and you'll be able to measure 12 points from the bottom of one line of type to the bottom of the next. The bottom of the type, by the way, is appropriately called the **baseline** (see diagram on page 59). If you add a point of space, so that your spec says 12/13, every line of type will then measure 13 points from the baseline of the first to the baseline of the second. If you add two points of space, it will measure 14 points, and so on. If there are a lot of lines, that little sliver of space can accumulate to quite a sizable chunk. Anyway: you multiply the number of lines that you just calculated by this factor of points. Let's say you'd like to use 12/14. You take your lines, multiply by 14, and get a number in points (because that 14 is 14 *points*). You must now turn that number into picas by dividing by 12, because there are 12 points to the pica. Your result is the depth in picas that your text will need. If you remember what was said about column-inches (see page 51), then you will know that you can convert your picas into column-inches simply by dividing by six, because there are six picas to the inch.

You now have knowledge of the size of type, the column width, and the length of your text block. Does it fit? Probably not. So you change things. If it is too long, you can reduce the type size, or you can take out that extra spacing between the lines. Your column widths—or line lengths—are likely to remain constant, because you are probably working to predetermined page patterns anyway. But if you have freedom there too, you can reproportion the entire thing by altering the column width (however, if you do change only that one element, the overall area required by the type will remain the same as it was before, except that it will have a flatter shape).

If you are not filling the space you need to, you can add to the spacing between the lines, or enlarge the type size, or both. Increasing the leading between lines is easy to calculate—everything remains the same as it was before, except for that point or two of space that you add, which you just multiply by the number of lines involved. Reducing or increasing the type size requires recalculation of everything from scratch.

One other option open to you, of course, is to pick another typeface that is either more **condensed** (yielding more characters per pica and per line) so that you can squeeze more into the space at your disposal, or one that is wider or more **extended** so that it eats up any excess space you have.

It is absolutely essential that the numbers you get from the table correspond to the typeface that your typesetter will use on his equipment. There is considerable variation in the many versions of the same-named face that are available from the different manufacturers.

If your total comes out with a fraction at the end, remember to go up to the next full number when lines are being counted. There is no such thing as one-sixth of a line sliced horizontally! But, if your computation comes out with 45.7 characters per line, for instance, then that 0.7 character is not very significant; you can ignore it, unless your copy is very long. In such situations, all those minor fractions can total enough to affect the overall accuracy of your result.

Copyfitting large-size type

Here again trial and error are your best friends. In single-line headlines, calculating the average number of characters, a method that tends to work out so conveniently in body copy, cannot be depended upon for accuracy. Rather, you have to be more conscious of the width of the specific letters that you are using. Obviously, if you have a lot of m's and w's, you'll be able to squeeze fewer characters into the same line length than if your copy consists of lots of i's, j's, and l's. Furthermore, if you have lots of capital letters, you also reduce your total character count, because they occupy about 50% more space than lowercase letters do. As a result, the character counts in typeface specimen tables are to be seen merely as rough averages. A much safer method is to find a real headline set in the face and size and to the length that you intend to use, and type it on your paper as a guide. Then you compose your own headline to a corresponding length beneath it, and, barring hailstorms, earthquakes, or tidal waves, your headline should fit. If that looks unnecessarily complicated, there is good reason for it: you'll probably want to rewrite your headline several times to make it fit and polish the wording just so. It is easier to do it in a tabulated fashion on your typewriter than to have to count each line separately, character by character, as you write and change them.

Proofs

The typesetter or compositor will return your marked manuscript together with a set of proofs of the type as set. If you are using word-processing equipment, the equivalent of such proofs is a **read-out** on the screen, or **hard-copy** paper printout. The exact form and finish depend on the equipment you are using. But let us deal here with the traditional way of doing things: whether they are true **galley proofs** pulled from hot metal that is placed on a tray called a galley, or whether they are xerographic copies of type that has been set on photographic typesetting equipment makes no difference. You usually receive two sets of proofs for reading, one set or two of reproduction proofs, and a set of proofs on translucent paper. The reproduction or **repro proofs** and the translucent ones may not accompany the first set of proofs you receive, because you may want to make changes in the copy before the final proofs are **pulled**. The sequence of proofs you will get should be decided on before the typesetting is started.

In any case, one set of **reader's proofs** becomes your file copy and should be so marked, dated, and kept safe. The other copy is proofread and marked for corrections and changes, as well as any additions and deletions that you may want, and is returned to the typesetter. You should duplicate those marks on your own master set, so that you keep the stages of production carefully on hand for future reference: the original manuscript; the first proof showing needed changes; and later the final proof on which the changes are reflected. There may be several sets of such changes—but you ought to avoid them if you possibly can, because any changes you make are charged as **author's alterations** (AAs) at a higher rate, and you would be amazed at how expensive they are. Mistakes made by the typesetter should not, of course, be charged to the customer, and when you come across them, be sure to mark them with a PE in the margin, for **printer's error.** Be sure to make a record of any changes that you may be calling in on the telephone.

Proofs are **slugged** at the top of each sheet with the name of the publication, a job or envelope number, and a galley number, as well as any other information that the typesetter may need to have. When phoning in corrections or changes, always refer to the job and galley number so that your typesetter can find what you're referring to quickly.

Reproduction proofs are fragile, sacred, expensive, and final. Avoid marking or damaging them in any way. Protect them. Keep them in the envelope in which they came and stash them away from harm's way in a predetermined place where they can be stored until the final mechanical-making step. If you must mark notes on them, do so with nonreproducing blue pencil or ball-point pen available at the art supply shop. Never fold or crease them, and protect them from being scratched by paper clips or staples. No rubber bands or sticky tape should be anywhere near them either.

How long should the l

If
th
le___
th
in
ey
w
cl
a

This is t
four poir
four-colu
ters per

This is ten point trump leaded five poi
of forty-seven picas, which is the width
two-column, three-column, four-colun
characters in every line of type and the

w
a
B
h
a
c

[

[

[

[

[

|

Proofs pulled from hot metal smudge easily until the ink has had a chance to dry and harden thoroughly. It is possible to protect them by spraying them with a light coat of plastic or fixative. Proofs from photoset equipment may not be well developed and may literally turn green around the edges. They also smell of chemicals. The paper they are printed on is razor sharp, so keep some Band-Aids handy. They don't smudge, but their surface can be scratched quite easily. Hot metal proofs automatically come in three copies; photoset proofs can come singly and you have to fight to get dupes—even at extra cost.

Body copy or text faces

Avoid fashionable faces for **body copy** (the text); their fashionableness is based on exaggeration in some aspect of their design. That very exaggeration, be it in shape, weight, detailing, angle, or whatever, is detrimental to reading type *in bulk*—even though it may be just right for a paragraph or two of advertising copy or for eyecatching display use. It is also wise to avoid faces that are very contrasty in their own line weight. Such strong contrasts create a dazzling effect that tires the eye. That dazzling can also be created by using shiny ink on shiny paper. So be aware of the physical materials of your publication and respond to them. Some faces are better on dull stock than on shiny stock; others are better on newsprint than on offset stock. The rule of thumb is that the better the stock and the printing, the finer and lighter your typeface can be; conversely, the closer to newsprint you get, the bolder, stronger, rounder, and more open your type ought to be, in order to print and read well.

This body-copy type size is 10 point

In general, body-copy type size seems to be growing. Editors complain that their readership is getting older, and therefore requires a larger-size type for ease of reading. Ten points seems to be the magic number. Remember that it is not just the size that matters; the typeface you use makes all the difference. Some appear smaller than others although they may all measure 10 points.

If you are going to be setting type that is to be **reversed** or **dropped out** (white type on a black background, or in a picture) or that is to be **surprinted** on a tint or a color, then you should pick a special typeface. It should be a little larger than the type size you use for normal body copy, and it should be a little bolder, too. That will ensure its integrity when it is printed—the thin lines won't close up with ink, and the type will not be as difficult to read. Also, the face you pick ought to have simple shapes and even strokes rather than fancy ones and heavy contrast of thicks and thins. A sans serif would probably be the safest.

This is seven on nine optima which leaded one point. This is seven on seven point optima leaded one point. which means it is seven point optima on nine optima which means it point. This is seven on nine optima optima leaded one point. This is it is seven point optima leaded one optima which means it is seven point

This is seven on nine optima semibold means it is seven point optima one point. This is seven on nine bold which means it is seven point bold leaded one point. This is seven optima semibold which means point optima semibold leaded is seven on nine optima semibold means it is seven point optima

**The life of Giambattista Bodo
often been told. He was born at
zo, Piedmont, in the year 1740
on of a printer. He had the good
ne of being apprenticed to the
ot printing office of the Congre
e Propaganda Fide at Rome. It
re that he learned not only the
which was his father's, but also
troduced into the art and secre
utting punches as soon as his t**

The life of Giambattista Bodoni has
en told. He was born at Saluzzo, Pie
n the year 1740, the son of a printer.
the good fortune of being apprentice
polyglot printing office of the Congre
Propaganda Fide at Rome. It was her
e learned not only the craft which wa
her's but also was introduced into the
secrets of cutting punches as soon as

The effect of leading on comfort and
ease of reading illustrated in two
examples: Franklin Gothic (top) and
Bookman—both set in 8 point.
The left-hand samples are set solid,
the center ones leaded one point, th
ones at right leaded two points.
Incidentally, these showings are cut
from an old hot-metal typesetting
sample book.

☐ How big is the page? How daunting does the text look?

☐ How much breakup is there? How many stopping points or changes in subject are signaled by subheads, initials, or the like so that each block of type appears short and easy to take?

Such a litany may not be terribly helpful to you, so you should use a rule of thumb. Nine or ten words per line is a comfortable length if you are using serif faces. Sans serif type should be set a trifle narrower—eight to nine words per line, perhaps—because most readers aren't as used to sans serif faces and because the serifs themselves help guide the eye horizontally and thus increase legibility.

Another formula that has been with us for centuries prescribes one-and-a-half alphabets, or 39 characters per line. Another suggests eight words, each reckoned at five characters on an average.

Two other points need to be made: narrow columns tend to break up the structure of sentences and force a lot of word breaks and hyphenation, both of which tend to interfere with smooth readability and comprehension. On the other hand, wide columns tire the eye and make it difficult to find the start of the next line. You have to try to find the comfortable mean.

Should type be set justified or ragged?

Justified typesetting means that all lines in the column are set to the same length, so that you have a neat right-hand margin as well as a neat left-hand margin. **Ragged** means having lines of varying length so the margins are not neat. It is assumed that "set ragged" implies ragged on the right edge of the column rather than the left-hand edge of the column, although ragged left is feasible and is often done in picture captions (see page 70). In long blocks of type, however, it is unwise to use ragged left setting, because a neat left-hand margin is a far easier reference point to which the eye can return in the process of reading; as a result, there is minimal confusion in the transition from one line of type to the next. In ragged-left setting, confusion can easily be caused by its apparent disorderliness.

This disorderliness is not a problem at the right-hand edge of the column, where raggedness does not affect ease of reading. In fact, it has two valuable advantages.

1. Ragged right looks different. It can be interpreted in many ways—as poetry, as informality, as a different visual treatment for emphasis, or even as a deliberate departure from the rigidities of precise, square, hard-edged alignment, which is ordinary. There is no reason why ragged right cannot be used throughout the publication (to give it a visual character of its own), or in parts of the publication (to separate those portions from the rest), or in small bits here and there (as visual relief and contrast). It is particularly useful for major pronouncements (be they by the chief executive officer, the editor, or any other Important Person) that are set in larger type to a wider measure; for commentary on segments such as answers to questions; and for **decks** (the sentence that explains or qualifies the headline) and quotations, and so on.

2. *Ragged right reads better.* We just aren't quite used to it because the tradition of justified setting has been so strongly adhered to. It still looks a little unusual at first glance, but it is coming into wider, more accepted usage, and ultimately that will be a boon to faster reading. Why or how it will do so is, like everything else, a matter of common sense.

   People don't read letter by letter the way optical character recognition (OCR) robots do, but rather recognize words *as words*, as unified letter groups. The word *groups* is not perceived as g r o u p s, but as groups. From this follows the fundamental principle of typographic design: it isn't just the shapes of the letters themselves that matter, but the *relationships of the letters to each other*, i.e., the spaces between the letters, are equally vital for legibility.

   In order to set justified copy, you often have to spread out the spaces between words and, sometimes, even between the characters in order to have those lines come out to the same length. This problem becomes especially serious in narrow columns where the lines are very short. Because the text varies from one line to the next and word breaks at the ends of lines often create problems, there is an unevenness in the spacing that affects the visual rhythm of each line and disturbs one's reading: it makes the eye stumble; it makes the eye work to compensate for these imbalances. In short, it makes reading tiring and more like work.

Identical copy set three ways:

justified x 14 picas	justified x 9 picas	ragged right max x 9 picas no word breaks
In order to set justified copy, you often have to spread out the spaces between words and, sometimes, even between the characters in order to have those lines come out to the same length. The problem becomes especially serious in narrow columns where the lines are very short. Because the text varies from one line to the next and word breaks at the ends of lines often create problems, there is an unevenness in the spacing that affects the visual rhythm of each line and disturbs one's reading: it makes the eye stumble. It makes reading tiring and more like work.	In order to set justi-← fied copy, you have to spread out the spaces be-tween the words and, sometimes, even be-← tween the characters in order to have those lines come out to the same length. This prob-← lem becomes especially serious in narrow columns where the lines are very short. Because the text← varies from one line to the next and word breaks at the ends of lines often create problems, there is an unevenness in the ← spacing that affects the visual rhythm of each line	In order to set justified copy, you often have to spread out the spaces between the words and, sometimes, even between the characters in order to have those lines come out to the same length. This problem becomes especially serious in narrow columns where the lines are very short. Because the text varies from one line to the next and word breaks at the ends of lines often create problems, there is an unevenness in the spacing that affects the

   Ragged right overcomes this artificial spacing by simply doing away with it. The type is set the way it should be—naturally spaced. An added advantage of natural spacing is the evenness of the type's color: by avoiding that extra spacing, there are no loose areas to contrast with tighter ones in the text. Tight ones appear dark, loose ones appear pale.

   Specifying ragged right setting can be a little more complicated than saying "10/11 Times Roman flush left rag right max x 15 pi," which tells the typesetter that you want the column set in 10-point Times Roman with one point of space between the lines, ragged right, with no line to exceed 15 picas in length. There are various degrees or raggedness you need to know about in order to be able to ask the typesetter to supply it.

The most ragged and feather edged (and also the messiest looking)—is **rough rag.** That is called for when you ask for *no word breaks*. It means that your line will be set as the copy comes, and if there is not enough space to accommodate the last word in full, it will become the first word of the next line. Rough rag can create some deep holes if that last word happens to be a long one. You can reduce the danger of extra-large holes by asking for "no hyphenations, except to avoid indents deeper than two picas," or whatever is appropriate to the type size and line length that you are using. That allows some word breaks, yet retains that rough feather edge. Some typographers call that **tight rag.**

You can have a much neater edge by calling for a setting that is the equivalent of justified (i.e., **hyphenation allowed**), but that skips the final step in the setting: pressing the button that opens up space between the words and characters in order to justify the line measure.

If the typesetting machinery can produce it, you can also ask for **kerning** (usually expressed in terms of minus units) by which the spacing between the characters is reduced. That way, you can produce a very tight and organized feeling to your typography that makes the ragged edge even more dramatic than it otherwise would be.

Identical copy set three ways:

ragged right max x 9 picas no word breaks	ragged right max x 12 picas hyphenation OK to avoid rag deeper than 2 picas	ragged right max 12 picas hyphenation OK
Rough rag.	*Tight rag.*	
In order to set justified copy, you often have to spread out the spaces between the words and, sometimes, even between the characters in order to have those lines come out to the same length. This problem becomes especially serious in narrow columns where the lines are very short. Because the text varies from one line to the next and word breaks at the ends of lines often create	In order to set justified copy, you have to spread out the spaces between words and, sometimes, even between the characters in order to have those lines come the same length. This problem becomes especially serious in narrow columns where the lines are very short. Because the text varies from one line to the next and word breaks at the ends of lines often create problems, there is an unevenness in the spacing that affects the visual rhythm of each line and disturbs one's reading: it makes the eye stumble. It makes reading tiring and more	In order to set justified copy, you often have to spread out the spaces between words and, sometimes, even between the characters in order to have those lines come out to the same length. The problem becomes especially serious in narrow columns where the lines are very short. Because the text varies from one line to the next and word breaks at the ends of lines often create problems, there is an unevenness in the spacing that affects the visual rhythm of each line and disturbs one's reading: it makes the eye stumble. It makes reading tiring and more

Warning: setting ragged right takes a little more space, though exactly how much more depends on the kind of setting that you are using. It also depends on your column width: if you have longer lines (nine words or so) then the raggedness tends to be much less pronounced that if you have short ones (six or seven words). Clearly there are fewer line ends in copy set wider than there are in the same copy set narrower because the copy is set in fewer lines if they are longer. So you have to add a safety factor to accommodate this unknown to your copycasting calculation.

There is yet another complication: the individual typesetter's interpretation of the setting. One operator may produce galleys that are much **tighter** (taking less space) than another whose setting is **looser** (using more space). These are variables that can only be settled through experience over time.

You have one option that will give you more control over the setting: you can decide where the lines should break and then type the manuscript accordingly. You then specify the setting to be 9/10 Helvetica, for instance, flush left, ragged right, set **line for line as typed**. The setter will do as asked, but watch out! What may look quite neat in the right-hand margin of your typewriter, or even on the screen of your word processor, is likely to come out very ragged indeed in type. That's because typeset characters vary in width, whereas each character is equally wide on your typewriter. It is also an awful nuisance to have to retype your copy (probably several times over to get it right), so this option is seldom used except for very special material such as decks, quotes in large type, and picture captions.

Display type

Headline or display type can be anything you want it to be. It can be picked to contrast with the body-copy typeface (if you use serif faces for the text, then you can use a bold sans serif for the headline), or it can be picked to complement it. In terms of the overall product's look and character, the greater the affinity of the two types—the text and the display—to each other, the stronger the effect of the product will be, since it will exhibit a consistency of typography throughout. There are some publications that use a variety of headline typography throughout the issue and a different face for every story. It certainly creates visual interest and lots of opportunities for cleverness, and it is especially useful when there are few pictures to enliven the product. But it can also create visual chaos. All of this adds up to an unhelpful observation that has been made several times in this chapter: there are no rules. You go according to instinct, preference, and experience.

To get enough characters into the headline, you have two options: you can pick a condensed face that crowds more into the same space, or a size smaller with your normal typeface. If you go a size smaller, you can make up for the loss of punchiness by increasing the weight or blackness, say from semi-bold to bold, or from bold to extra-bold. That way you have your cake and eat it too.

Headline set three ways to show that you can squeeze more words into the same space by using a more condensed face, or going a size smaller, while at the same time increasing the boldness.

This is a headline set in Helvetica

This is a headline set in Helvetica

This is a headline set in Helvetica

Headlines

Display type is intended to attract attention and performs two functions simultaneously.

1. It pulls the reader into a specific story—because of the way it is written, because of the promise of interest it holds, as well as its visual characteristics.

2. It affects the reader's awareness of the publication as a whole, as the progression from page to page coalesces into an overall impression of its character.

You need to be aware of these two factors in order to handle your options intelligently and respond to the specific needs of your particular publication.

Too often the editor is so involved with the story that the overall product's interests are shelved or forgotten, resulting in a conglomeration of effects that do not work actively together and lead to a weak, ineffective impression for the issue as a whole. Any one segment may be excellent, but the product lacks unity, let alone consistency, from one issue to the next.

Such consistency has an invaluable by-product: recognition of the product by the reader and the advertiser as a trusted, valued friend. The product probably gains more from such recognition of quality than it would from attempts to create "variety" through inconsistency, constant change of pace, and typographic fancy-dress fripperies. Also, the reader sees the product for a short time only, and so is not nearly as bored with it as the editor may be, whose life revolves around it. Thus, the "liveliness," "differentness," or "change of pace" that the editor seems unable to resist trying to create by artificial means is not only unnecessary, but probably even harmful. It is much wiser to stick to a simple, restrained, **recognizable format** than to start reinventing the wheel on every page, or every story.

That is why it is also advisable to use one typeface for both body copy and display type, although many people will dispute this—experts, as well as those who profess to know nothing about art, but who know what they like. Using one typeface creates a **unity of character** that cannot be improved. If that is going too far, then the next best thing is to pick one basic face for the display and use it exclusively in the many different versions in which it is available: regular, bold, extra-bold, italics, all caps, outline, drop-shadow, or whatever other variables there may be.

Whatever the choice may be, you can be certain of one thing: it will be outdated in a few years. Fashion is most strongly manifested in the display areas of publications, and what seems the proper and more "with-it" way to do things today will surely look outdated tomorrow or at least the day after tomorrow.

Even if you avoid trendiness and exaggeration by sticking with responsibly composed and expressive typography, whatever you are doing today will be old-fashioned one day. To attempt to work for eternity is foolish. Instead, handle the display as logically as possible, allow it to signal its story and content as clearly as possible, and style it as consistently as possible throughout the issue.

How big should headlines be?

The size of headline type is often predicated on newspaper tradition, which decrees that the more important a story is, the louder the trumpeting should be—the bigger the type ought to be. Furthermore, newspaper makeup also decrees that the higher up the story is on the page, the bigger the headline type should be because important stories go at the top of the page, which is the important area. Fine. You may choose to accept this or make your own decision.

What you must do in any event is make the headlines visible, big enough and bold enough to make for ample contrast against the body copy. If they are too small, they look insignificant. If they are too big, they overwhelm and become out of scale. If they hurt the eye with their size, make them smaller or shoot them through a screen so that the blackness is turned to a gray tint. In any case, follow your instinct.

The common practice is to have headlines set anywhere between 18 and 36 points. Bigger than that is fine for just a few words; smaller than that is advisable for minor elements. It is impossible to make laws about such subjective, interpretive, unique decisions. Just remember that headlines must work together as a group throughout the issue and must not appear to be individual impressions atop each separate story. Some restraint on your imaginativeness will make a better overall product.

What is the best place on the page to put your headline?

Since we read from left to right down the page, it is sensible to place the headline above the text so that the eye can travel comfortably downward as the stages of the story are revealed. That doesn't mean that you may not put the headline anywhere else that makes sense in a specific situation. It only means that you are giving up a natural advantage in order to achieve a special effect. Is that effect worth it? You have to be the judge. Will it come off? Only if you do whatever you intend to do strongly, deliberately, visibly, and courageously.

The top left-hand corner of the spread is where the eye goes first. Put your major headline up there and you will catch most of the readers.

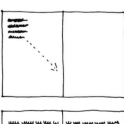

Jumping the gutter (crossing from one page to the other) with a headline tends to be dangerous unless the typography of that headline is so enormous and overwhelming that the gap between the pages is bridged by it. It is wiser to lay out the page in such a way that the headline remains on one page, even though it may refer to a story that covers the whole spread. If you must jump the gutter, avoid having the gutter fall within a word. You can also get a better result by writing a so-called **bimodal** headline, which consists of two sets of thoughts or phrases separated by a colon, a dash, or an ellipsis (. . .). The left-hand page holds the first half of the headline, and the right-hand page displays the second half of the headline.

A few technical terms about headlines

Since journalists are justifiably some of the proudest professionals and most verbally oriented people there are, a specialized newspaper jargon has evolved over the years. Here are a few terms you ought to be able to recognize.

Times roman bold set tight and without extra leading

FLUSH LEFT, RAGGED RIGHT

Times roman bold set tight and without extra leading

STAGGERED

Times roman bold set tight and without extra leading

CENTERED

Times roman bold set kerned minus-one unit in one line is strong in visual impact

WALL-TO-WALL
(filling out the space available)

The issue
Times roman bold

EYEBROW
(free-standing, centered, self-contained label over a large headline)

The editorial:
Times roman bold set tight and strong

KICKER
(positioned flush left or indented, or over an indented head, self-contained but tied into the head by meaning, often with a colon or ellipsis at the end)

The importance of the relationship of all editorial spaces in the issue

HAMMER
(kicker larger than its headline beneath)

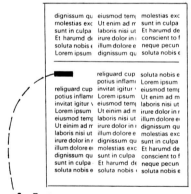

tight *from page 00*

This boldface *continued*

TOMBSTONING
(a depressing name for a depressing problem in page makeup. When two or more headlines align across the page so they read into each other by mistake, the problem is avoided by juggling the elements around in different configurations)

JUMP HEAD
(identifies the continuation of the story on another page usually by means of a key word or phrase from the opening headline)

RUNNING HEAD
(a small label in the top left-hand corner of the page identifying the subject matter being continued from the previous page)

Legibility of headlines: all cap, up-and-down style, or downstyle

recognition

RECOGNITION

We Type Heads This Way

But it makes more sense
to set them this way...

Than to Set Them This
Way Which Looks Funny
but We Are Used to It

typography
typography

We recognize words in character groups rather than letter by letter. The outline of such a group is a crucial factor in the process. Recognizing the word "recognition," for instance, is aided by the fact that the "g" pokes down below the type, the "t" pokes up above it, and the two "i's" have dots floating in the space above as well. But set the same word all cap, RECOGNITION, and you have a neat horizontal alignment across the bottom and top of the letters, which forms a nice neat box that holds no visual clues whatsoever to help identify the word. That is why all caps are harder to read than lowercase.

Yet a few words set all cap are no problem. Labels, department headings, logos, etc., are fine that way, as are special words picked out in headlines for their particular significance or meaning. There are also some demographic segments of readership, such as architects and engineers, who tend to letter their drawings all cap and who have no problem reading caps. Yet, even for them, setting long blocks of copy all cap is inadvisable. For the population at large, use all cap with discrimination for special effect.

The **Up-And-Down Style** of typesetting, to this writer's thinking at least, seems illogical and a hangover from the past that is accepted somewhat unthinkingly. It was invented as a makeshift solution to overcome shortages of capital letters when newspaper headlines were set all cap. Such shortages are no longer with us, and headlines are set large and bold to distinguish them from the body copy anyway. So such extra added differentiation as capitalizing the first letter of every important word (which is what this style entails) becomes excessive. Not only does it lead to arguments as to which words are important and deserve such treatment, but it also decreases the words' legibility because it is an unnatural way of presenting them. Furthermore, it decreases the distinguishing features of proper names in headlines by making everything look like proper names with initial capitalization. Why is it still done? Because of habit; because most newspapers still do it to make their publications look "newsy," and, above all, *because our typewriters do it.* On a typewriter, the convention is indeed useful in distinguishing heads from body copy. However, the translation of typewriting convention into typography makes little sense. If you want your product to read smoothly, look contemporary, and be logically made, start your headlines with a capital letter and continue in lowercase— **downstyle** —just as a normal sentence would, only set large and bold.

To ensure legibility, specify **tight setting**. It is easier to read words when the characters are close together than when they are spaced far apart, especially in sizes of type such as those used in headlines. The new typesetting machinery allows us to kern the characters, and this capacity ought to be made use of in any type size larger than 14 point. Unkerned typesetting creates unnecessary gaps between the letters. Closing those gaps up helps us to distinguish the word as a word more quickly. Incidentally, never open up between words or letters in a headline in order to fill out a predetermined width. Set the head flush left and ragged right.

Decks and blurbs

Often headlines are accompanied by a **deck**: several lines of display type that expand the meaning of the headline, explain its significance to the reader, or in some other way helps to persuade the reader to read the text. If the basic idea of the story is stated in the headline, if the deck points out its significance and the first paragraph of the text immediately tells the news and its usefulness, you have a sequence of reading matter that is practically irresistible. Since one thought flows from the previous one, it is logical to place the elements in a like manner. Headline at the top, deck beneath it, text below that.

Often decks are misused as a précis or repetition of either the headline or the first paragraph. Readers resent reading the same content twice because it wastes their time, and it decreases the deck's importance on stories where it is being used functionally.

If the deck is placed above the headline and is written in such a way that the headline flows out of it naturally (with or without ellipses or leaders), it is called a **precede**. Decks and precedes are also often called **blurbs**.

Decks should be distinguished in function as well as in form from summaries or synopses. Decks are active steps in a series of information-giving statements. Summaries are self-contained précis of the article. Usually in scientific journals they are used for information retrieval purposes or as fast overviews that allow the potential reader to decide whether or not to invest time and effort in reading the text.

Captions, legends, cutlines

Everyone brings his or her own background, experience and individual interests with them when they look at a picture. As editors, you must be aware of this natural human characteristic and react to it, if you want to get your interpretation of a picture across to the reader and avoid having it misinterpreted by the reader's own way of seeing it. How? By means of words that accompany the picture to explain its significance the way you, the editors, see it. The trouble is that pictures tell too much!

There are a few situations in which **captions** (in magazines), **legends** (in books), and **cutlines** (in newspapers) are unnecessary. When they are mood shots used as openers to a story, for instance, the headline that is seen near them takes the place of the caption and does the work of focusing the interpretation of the picture in its own words.

Captions should, whenever possible, do more than just describe what the picture shows or give the name of the person in it, because readers look at illustrations first, before they start to read the page. Their interest is aroused by images, which ought, therefore, to be utilized as hooks to pull the readers into the story. And a juicy gobbet of information in the caption is the best possible material with which to bait those hooks.

The caption should be closely attached to the picture so they are perceived together as Siamese twins are. Alignment and closeness are the two obvious techniques to make them appear that way. A precise measurement of appropriate closeness depends on the scale and context, of course, but perhaps a pica ought to be about maximum. As for alignment they should be flush with the edge and should align on the corner. The diagram shows the various alternatives.

Readers look for captions below pictures because that is where they expect to find them, so it is wise to put them there, all other things being equal. It is also wisest to keep them neatly aligned with the picture rather than indented because the crispness of effect thus created outweighs any advantage you may have from spots of empty space alongside such indents, which aren't big enough to be dramatic, but are sizable enough to appear messy.

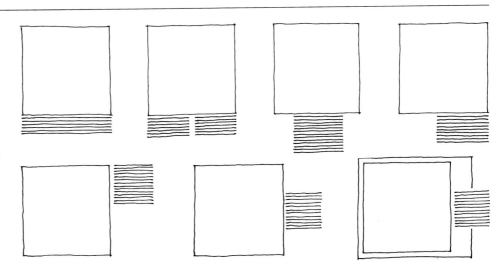

The purpose of this type is to study the effect that novarese italic might have when set in narrow columns, flush left and ragged right. The purpose is to use this format for picture captions (often called "legends" in books and "cutlines" in newspaper parlance).

It is often most attractive to set captions ragged right if the rest of the page is set in rigid, justified columns. The contrast of texture and informality adds flavor to the product. The flush edge of the type is the edge to which the picture should be aligned or made parallel, so the type lines appear to grow out of the photo, like whiskers. And you can get away with setting flush right and ragged on the left if your captions are not too long (a dozen lines perhaps) or too wide (more than 35 characters on average).

To help the captions belong to the picture, use any two of these three principles in conjunction: (1) Align flush-left captions with the left-hand edge of the picture and flush-right captions with the right-hand edge of the picture. (2) Align captions with the top or the bottom of the picture. (3) Set the inner edge of the caption (the one alongside the picture's edge) flush, letting the outside edge be ragged.

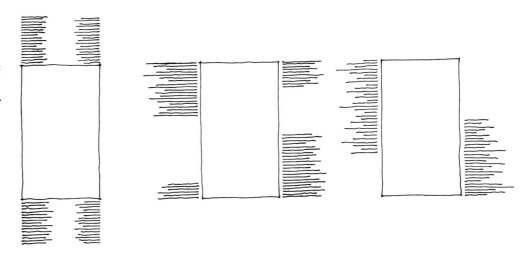

Setting captions very wide—the full width of the picture no matter how wide it may be—is perfectly all right if there is only one line to read. If you start adding lines you jeopardize legibility by going too wide. Your risk is fairly small up to about four lines, but any more than that will reduce the readership to just those people who are fascinated by the information and will, therefore, bother to plow through all that material. Better break it into two **legs of type** (columns). How wide is too wide? It depends on the face, the leading, and so on. But if you must have a rule of thumb, assume that going wider than 60 characters per line is dangerous.

Should captions be bigger than the surrounding body copy or smaller? Should captions appear darker or paler? Should they be set in italics? Who knows? Newspapers seem to prefer the darker/bigger direction, whereas visually sophisticated magazines seem to use the lighter/smaller type, often set in italics of the body-copy typeface. There are no rules, nor is there any logical argument that should sway the individual editor one way or the other from personal preference: "I like it that way."

Catch lines or boldface lead-ins

There are essential technicalities you should know about because they increase the communication value of both the picture and the caption it accompanies. Used correctly, they are editorial tools for speedy communication, which is what you want. If you think of a caption as the self-contained little story that it should be (if you are using the picture as a springboard for information, that is), then it is perfectly logical to write it so your main point is articulated in a little headline that starts the text. Such a miniheadline is precisely what the catch line or boldface lead-in ought to be. The **catch lines** are usually written as labels—self-contained and free-standing—and that is probably the easiest way to handle them. If the labels are interesting, they work. **Boldface lead-ins** whose visibility relies on typographic contrast with the first words of the first sentence of the caption (usually set bolder, or all caps, or larger, or in a contrasting face to the rest of the caption) are, alas, too often misused. Those words set in bold ought to be worthy of such emphasis in terms of their own significance. You should avoid blunting your precious weapons of emphasis, such as boldfacing, by giving something the *appearance* of importance without giving it the substance or meaning. The simplest test to determine such worthiness: do the boldfaced words make sense if you read them alone? If they do, then they indeed say something intelligent. If they cannot stand on their own, then you know that you must rewrite your sentence. Here is a diagram of caption variations.

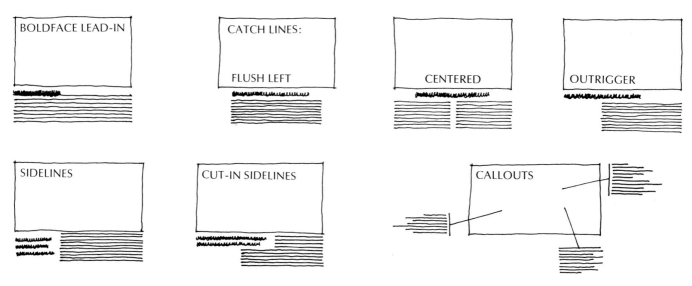

BOLDFACE LEAD-IN

CATCH LINES:

FLUSH LEFT   CENTERED   OUTRIGGER

SIDELINES   CUT-IN SIDELINES   CALLOUTS

Bylines

Two major questions need to be asked that will give clues to handling your bylines:

    1. Are there a lot of them in the issue? If so, it is certainly worthwhile to establish a definite format and placement for them so they add to the overall personality of the product.

    2. Are the names in those bylines important to the status of the publication? If so, you must give them the importance they deserve through placement, size, and visibility. If not, you can play them down. Here are a few of the typical placements to choose from.

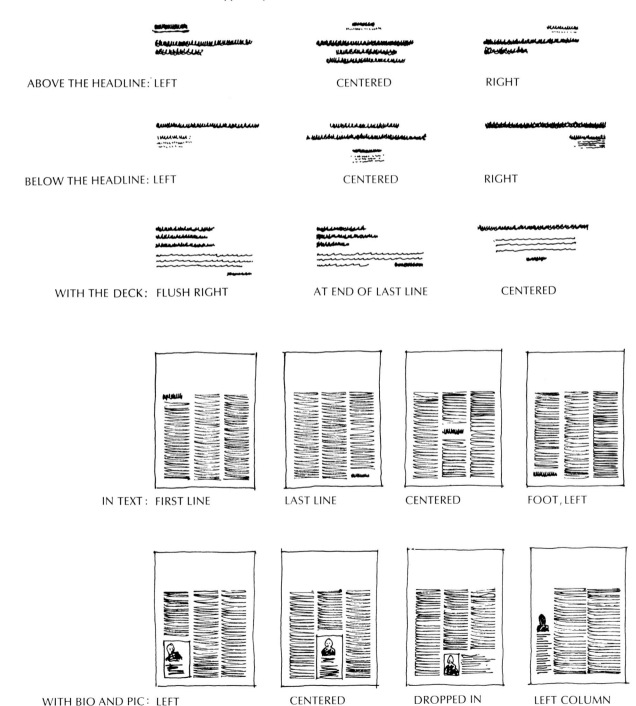

ABOVE THE HEADLINE: LEFT   CENTERED   RIGHT

BELOW THE HEADLINE: LEFT   CENTERED   RIGHT

WITH THE DECK: FLUSH RIGHT   AT END OF LAST LINE   CENTERED

IN TEXT: FIRST LINE   LAST LINE   CENTERED   FOOT, LEFT

WITH BIO AND PIC: LEFT   CENTERED   DROPPED IN   LEFT COLUMN

5

Tips to help you take better photos for your publication

Move in as close as you can

That way you help define what you are trying to capture on film. You are deliberately getting rid of the confusing surroundings and homing in on the area that matters. The closer you move in to your subject, the more positive, striking, and detailed the quality will be. The bigger the image, the more powerful its journalistic and design impact. (Incidentally, you can retrofit images that encompass too much by cropping. See page 98)

Use lenses that will move in close for you

If you cannot get nearer, but still want to capture close-up detail, technology can come to your aid: Getting the right lens just costs money.

Having everything in focus is dull

All but the simplest cameras allow you to choose your **depth of field**. That allows you to make the important part of the picture crisp and sharp, whereas the part in front of and beyond it can be made to look fuzzy. This is just another technique of "editing": drawing attention to that which is important.

You control depth of field by changing the aperture of the lens. The smaller the aperture (the higher the f-number, like f-16, for instance) the greater the depth of field; the more you open up the lens (to an f-stop of 2.8, for instance) the tighter the depth of field becomes. If you use a long lens, your desired effect is automatically produced: You focus on the subject and fuzz out the foreground and background, which are still there as a recognizable context but do not compete for the viewer's attention.

Put the center of interest elsewhere than plumb in the middle

In the middle is where you expect to find it, which is precisely why it makes a boring photo. If you imagine a pattern breaking the viewfinder into ninths, like this diagram, placing the center of interest at one of the four intersections will give it a dominating position. Also, use one of the two horizontal lines inside the diagram as an edge for the horizon. That way, either the upper two-thirds or the lower two-thirds become dominant.

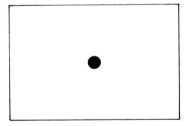 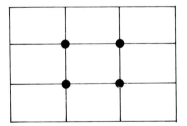

Make something dominant in every picture

The very fact that you do so implies an editorial statement of some kind: It shows a point of view. By selecting one element, you show that you have something specific to say, which in turn makes it more interesting *to listen to*—which is precisely the same thing as finding something interesting to *look at*. Reading/hearing/seeing are all related aspects of communicating.

Compose your shots with an awareness of the lines of force

Horizontal lines, flatness, lots of left-to-right elements, give the resultant image a placid quality. Lots of verticals can be interpreted as strong and tough. Diagonals or angles convey a feeling of action and motion. By itself, such knowledge may not be all that useful, but knowing these effects can help you give the photo the requisite mood if you use such lines of force as contrasting background to the foreground element that you are expressing. Concentric or converging lines can help draw the viewer's attention to your focal point.

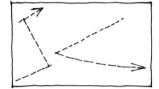

Allow moving objects plenty of space

The composition of the frame can underscore or even imply activity that may not actually be visible, such as the direction in which people are looking or pointing. What you want to do is to take the motion's direction into account and allow ample space in the frame for the action to grow into. Keep moving elements away from the edge of the photo, unless you want to be very tricky. A useful action-exaggeration manipulation of existing images is shown on page 115.

Use the rectangle format to best advantage

Most cameras produce rectangular images. Look at the subject to decide whether it is a broad and flat shape (in which case you shoot it as a horizontal) or a tall, skinny shape (in which case the vertical would fit it better). Shoot verticals as often as the subject matter is suited for that, or as often as it seems to make sense. So look for arrangements that fit naturally into a vertical shape. They will give you variety and a change of pace on the page. Maybe you can even get them on the front cover.

Enliven your picture with foreground interest

Looking through something at the subject beyond gives a feeling of "being there" to the onlooker. Photographs are illusions of reality. One of their purposes is to foster that feeling of participation in their viewers. That's what gets people involved in the story.

Pick a background that explains the character of the personality

Allow the context within which the subject is to be seen to help the reader understand at first glance what you deem significant about the subject. By substituting job backgrounds for sterile studio set-ups, you can make even the most ordinary people pictures become documents of people in true-to-life settings instead of catalog mug shots. Their offices, workplaces, and surroundings can be highly revealing of the subjects' characters.

Don't let the background become a nasty surprise

Be aware of everything seen in the frame. The camera isn't selective. It cannot judge. The photographer must do that. That's why *you* have to notice the Eiffel Tower growing out of the woman's head—and move the woman and/or the camera. It might be wise to leave the tower where it is.

Perhaps it is best to shoot people against plain backgrounds: It is safer that way—but is it more interesting?

Watch out for booby traps

We see differently than the camera does: We see selectively—filtering or editing out what is unimportant or misleading; the camera, alas, has no brain, so it is up to the photographer to do the noticing and **visual editing**. The contrast of dark objects against light backgrounds, or vice versa, can ruin the image. We take no notice of telephone poles or wires when walking down the street. But take a photo of the same view, and the black cage we live in slashes across the skyline. We ignore and look beyond the dirty dishes on the table when the after-dinner speaker rises to pontificate, but take a photo of the scene, and all you see is dirty crockery white against the dark dinner jackets.

Check the edges of the picture in your viewfinder before you shoot

That may help to prevent chopping off the tops of people's heads, cutting off their feet, and other such generally unsatisfactory mayhem. Tilting the camera or moving it a few inches this way or that could allow you to concentrate on the focal elements without having the surroundings just appearing by happenstance or accident.

Shoot people as the individuals they are

This is often a problem when you have a number of people to show: anniversaries, honorees, officers, new employees, and so on. Since everyone is different, their pictures should reflect those differences in character, personality, and attitude. Then having to arrange them in groups of equal-sized pictures will not create such a boring result. The faces will make themselves interesting.

Bunch people into tight groups

That way, you can come in closer and get them bigger. It is in the details that the interest lies. The normal space that people prefer to have around them to make themselves feel safe and secure looks like very large gaps when frozen into photographs.

Figure out fresh angles for cliché situations

The typical (and worst) problems are the "grip-and-grin" or "grin-and-shake" congratulation or welcoming pictures. If the story cannot be told another way, neatly avoiding the use of the standard set piece, try to cover the handshaking event as spontaneously and freshly as the circumstances will allow: shoot over the presenter's shoulder; crawl on your belly and shoot upward at the symbolic hands; use a periscope; drill a hole in the ceiling from the room upstairs and shoot downward—*anything* to get a bit of variety. But remember that people are interested in people, and that what you, as communicator, deem to be deadly may well be fascinating to your readers. And, most certainly, it is crucial to the people who are appearing in the picture.

Sunlight is great, except that it makes strong shadows

Shadows are dangerous, especially if they are under the noses and in the eye sockets, turning living people into cadavers. The brighter the sun, the more hard-edged the shadows and the greater the need to squint. Better to shepherd the people into the shade and then shoot in indirect light.

Flashbulbs create shadow monsters on walls

Move the subjects at least six feet away from the wall to prevent casting shadows as well as throwing the wall itself out of sharpness (which may be all to the good if you are shooting against motel-lobby wallpaper or its patterned equivalent).

Don't blind your subjects by shooting flash too close

It is better to stay about ten feet away from the subject to prevent flash hot spots, and it is much better to separate the flash from the camera and hold it to one side. It is even better to bounce the flash off the ceiling, if the ceiling is not higher than about ten feet. If circumstances dictate getting in closer with the flash, cut its progressive starkness with a piece of gauze laid over the flashbulb. Incidentally, a flash probably doesn't work at all beyond 20 feet. Ten feet is optimum. But new, fast lenses coupled with new, fast film can avoid the use of flash altogether, which makes it possible to take far more lifelike pictures in existing light.

If you want animated reactions from people, be funny

You want to have people appear alive in the pictures, but that is *not* the effect that saying "Cheese!" engenders. Forced smiles create waxworks. If you are going to start shooting people who are supposed to smile, give them something to smile about.

6

People pictures don't have to be boring

People are interested in people.* That is why people pictures (**mug shots** in police and editorial jargon) have become such an essential ingredient of publications. Yet editors all decry their fate, because they persist in seeing these pictures as dull and boring. The boredom may well be in the editors' rather than the readers' minds. It isn't just the people whose pictures appear in print who are pleased to see them (although those people seem to react as though it were more important than it really is). The readers, too, care to see them because they don't just want to *read* a story about personalities; they want to *see* personalities too. Whether this is instinctive human curiosity or whether it is a need we have acquired from television and other visual media is not important. What is important is that readers want to see the person because they are looking for personality clues. They don't really care what someone looks like, unless that someone's claim to fame happens to be his or her looks. They care very much about character—as expressed in the look of the eyes, the body language of the stance, the revealing glimpse caught and frozen for inspection by the sensitive photographer. That is why the first duty for the editor is to search out those pictures that show such insight. Naturally, these shots are "dangerous" to use: the subjects may well be less than happy to have their innermost selves revealed to the public this way. Yet it is precisely that revelation that becomes the essence of lively publication making. So you have to weigh the politics of the situation: You have to calculate the cost/benefit ratio. It may cost you your job to run a certain not-very-flattering picture of the chief executive officer—but the benefit to the publication will be the recognition of its pioneering spirit! (Perhaps such a risk/reward ratio is stacked against you: too much risk for the wrong sort of reward?) Well, J. P. Morgan, talking about the risks of investing, said, "You eat better at 10 percent, but you sleep better at 2 percent." You have to judge the pros and cons of going out on a limb for yourself. Good luck!

Let's be a bit more realistic, then, and accept the fact that the safe shot is what you are likely to be stuck with. That is, indeed, boring. But there are two basic kinds of situations: (1) a story where you have one or just a few mug shots to handle, where the pictures are incidental to the story; and (2) a story or section where you must accommodate a large number of people pictures in some kind of catalog format. In the first case you can (and should) play with the material to make it as graphically varied and interesting as possible. In the second case, you are stuck with the images—it is not worth the investment or time to manipulate them—and you must make the *group* or *pattern* appear interesting.

*Has it ever occurred to you that there are never any people in pictures of *rooms* in magazines? When you want the surroundings to be noticed, don't put people in the picture, because if you do the readers will study the people and forget the room settings.

The individual mug shot and how to make it more interesting

Clean up the background

If it is distracting, if it is part of a snapshot with other people in it, if it is an ugly wallpaper pattern, if it has nothing to do with the focus of your story, if it is too pale to give good definition to the edge of the halftone—darken it, lighten it, make it fuzzy, do something with it that makes the personage "pop out" and get attention, so that the background becomes secondary.

How? By **retouching** the photograph—having a professional retoucher spray gray paint over the bad area, or by "ghosting" the background (see page 108). Or . . .

Get rid of the background altogether

This results in much more interesting shapes because it is a change from the everlasting rectangular halftone. Furthermore, it creates the illusion of the personage sitting right there on the white paper.

This is an easy trick, especially if the person is facing the camera—you avoid the problem of chopping off a piece of nose or mouth. (A bit of ear or top of the head doesn't matter nearly so much.) And, if you do create unintended baldness, you can always counter the criticism by maintaining that there are only a few perfect heads, the rest have to be hidden under hair, and you are just helping out.

To make a silhouetted picture you can either do it yourself or instruct the printer to do it for you. As far as doing it yourself is concerned: it is extremely unwise to cut up pictures. It ruins them for future use, and it may be very unpopular with the owners. But you *can*, of course, take your trusty scissors and cut out a paper-doll personage, stick it on a piece of white cardboard, and instruct the printer to "**silhouette** as cut out." It is much

safer—and the results are better if you give the printer a transparent overlay marked where the edge of the silhouette is to appear. By far the best procedure is to prepare a **mask** on acetate; that way, you are in total control of the final results.

Here are diagrams to help you visualize the process.

Original picture attached to white cardboard backing, with register marks in position.

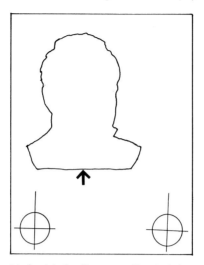

Method 1: keyline or outline in ink (black or red) drawn on tracing paper.

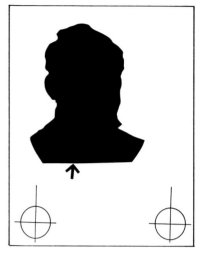

Method 2: mask cut from cut-and-peel overlay film (amber or red).

Insert the silhouetted personage in a box

The contrast between the head-and-shoulders halftone and the white paper background is enhanced by deliberately framing a piece of that background. The person is then placed in an individual bubble of space and, if the box is smaller than the head, can appear to emerge from it in dramatic fashion. Here are four typical variants.

The linework can be done by the printer, but it is best done by you on an overlay the same way that any line art is added to halftones.

Add quotes and identification in the box

The combination of a disembodied photo inside a defined area is an ideal starting point for unusual treatment of the usual name, title, and function, and an opportunity for a more-or-less-provocative statement. Be as courageous as you want to on this, because here is a chance to turn something rather ordinary into something quite extraordinary.

Crop courageously

The usual shape is not prescribed by law, just by habit and laziness of thought and, possibly, lack of courage. It is perfectly acceptable to chop off the top of the head and bottom of the chin. There is ample precedent even for cutting off an ear or two (Van Gogh did it in real life!). Here is President Lincoln, taller than ever because of the extra-narrow cropping; George Washington is peeking through a slit; Ulysses S. Grant is right up close to you.

Keep the hands in, if there are any

They may well be more expressive than the face itself. And they invariably add some activity to the image.

Utilize screens other than the expected halftone

Mezzotints, steel etch, line screen, line conversions, and the like (see page 130) are ideal for use on people pictures, but they must be used boldly, to make it quite obvious that the treatment is deliberate and not a mistake or the result of bad printing.

Bring individuals into groups

If your story deals with several people who are connected in the sense of the story, perhaps a grouping might be more expressive than a presentation of the individuals as ducks in a row. But the photographers didn't catch them together, and several of the pictures are of individuals who submitted their studio portraits after the fact. What do you do then? You cheat: You take the prints you have and have copies made—sized in such a way that the heads measure more or less the same. The easiest way to do that is to decide on a standard dimension to cover the distance from the top of the head to the bottom of the chin and ask the photo lab to blow up or reduce new prints to that dimension, given a reasonable tolerance. It won't be precise, but variation within reason is perfectly acceptable since nobody's head is the same size as anybody else's anyway.

When you get the duplicate prints, you then take your trusty scissors and carefully cut out each mug shot. Then you compose them in such a way that the shoulders overlap in ways that appear natural, with some people apparently standing behind others, nice and tight. Any kind of arrangement of people talking to each other or people talking as a group will appear believable and realistic, if the eye level remains constant and in alignment. You then glue the group down, using rubber cement or hot wax from a wax dispenser, burnish the whole thing down carefully, and your art is ready for the camera. The more precise your paper-doll-cutting craftsmanship, the better and more realistic the final result will be. To prevent the edges of the photo paper from appearing as white lines in the printed piece, darken them (only in the dark areas of the photo) by running the edge of a black felt-tip marker on the edge of the paper itself, being sure not to mark up the face of the photo. Then, when the edges are dry, start the assembling process. Darkening the edges once they're in place is impossible if you want to avoid damaging the picture beneath the one you're doctoring.

Other patterns than the **collage of silhouettes** described here are possible, of course—and your imagination, common sense, and editorial restraint are the guiding factors as to what to do and how far to go with it.

Five commonsense principles for using people pictures

People ought to face inward into the spread

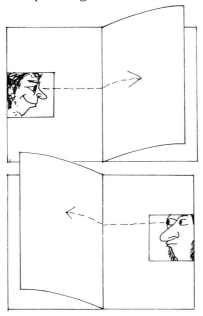

The direction of people's gazes ought to be exploited

The curiosity aroused by such a trick may well impel the reader to turn the page. Remember how everyone looks up at the sky when they see one person doing it? Curiosity is a powerful motivating force and the direction in which people are looking—whether in real life or merely in pictures—should be utilized. It works.

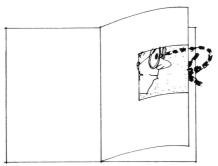

Relationships between people should leap to the eye

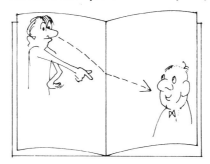

Size is interpreted as a measure of importance

This raises political problems, unless you are aware of it. The highest ranking personage gets the biggest size, the next rank down must be a little smaller, and so on. Of course, you could decide to make them all the same size. Rarely does it become possible to have fun with sizes for purely decorative or superficial purposes of design and, unfortunately, what you may perceive as playfulness is likely to be misinterpreted by the reader and surely by the subjects themselves.

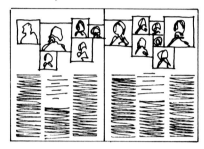

Editing down to the most telling image pays off

That is, unless those extra photos help to show a variety of characteristics or emotions, or unless it is a photo essay, of course. Where the story (such as an interview) flows on for several pages, an effective and enlivening trick is to put different mug shots of the same person in the same position on each successive page. It ties the pages together and creates a sequence of images whose deliberateness comes across more strongly for its regularity of placement.

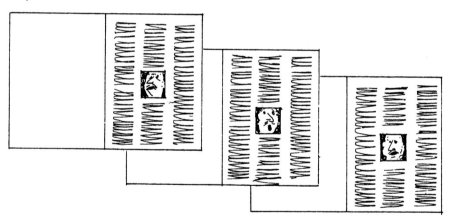

Make the best of those unavoidable catalog arrangements

Groups of people whose existence must be acknowledged or recorded for some reason—new employees, 25-year veterans, honorees, graduates, and so forth ad infinitum—have to be accommodated and handled as neatly and as cleverly as possible. They are, admittedly, not very fascinating raw material, yet the publication has a responsibility to show them. So you show them: you don't make a feature of them, you give them as little space as is commensurate with the dignity of the subject matter. You make the pictures as unassuming as seems right, and you get it done as fast and expeditiously as possible, so there is more time to spend on areas of the publication that deserve more creative attention.

You must think in terms of pattern making when facing a number of mug shots and biographies. The effectiveness of the handling must be sought in the *group* rather than in the individual images themselves. Such grouping arrangements can vary from the simplest rectangle to all sorts of arbitrary patterns such as pyramids or other geometric shapes that are seen in depressing variety in high-school yearbooks.

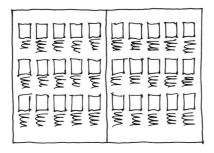

Adding rules (drawn lines) can help break the arrangement into smaller units for more sensible variety. It creates contrapuntal patterning with two elements: the rules, which define a geometric structure for the page, and the mug shots themselves, which create a smaller-scale pictorial spotting. If you also separate the biographies from the pictures (leaving the identifying names, of course), you have a third element to work against the other two.

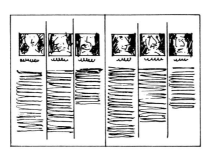

Here the mug shots create a horizontal emphasis strong enough to camouflage the irregularity of the words beneath. The vertical rules organize the space most visibly and thus deliberately by extending into the space above the mug shots.

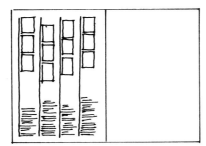

Postage-stamp-sized mug shots appear more interesting when their placement is staggered slightly. The vertical rules make it possible to demarcate the four vertical slivers of space, implying that each sliver is independent of its neighbors. The spacing between the mug shots in each sliver is constant—making makeup very simple. The success of this trick is to have enough space separating the pictures from the description at the foot of each column. It is that luxurious **empty space** that lends drama to the arrangement.

Here are three slivers of space, three columns' worth. Each is divided vertically into two, allowing two mug shots to be placed next to each other. The horizontal placement of the mug shots is the same in all of them—there are none off kilter or out of alignment as in the example above. What makes the arrangement lively is the arbitrary omission of one or two mug shots in the right-hand sliver within each column. The left-hand sliver must remain full so as to create an obvious "belonging" to the vertical rule, but the right-hand pictures are expendable. Further, to emphasize the illusion of

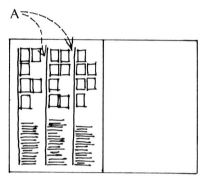

flags fluttering from a vertical mast at left, it is important to leave a little more space at "A" than there would be had the area been subdivided arbitrarily into equal parts. As in the examples above, the words act as a foil to the decorative pictures. Cross-reference between them by numbering, lettering, or running the last name of the person both beneath the picture and in the text below.

Cluster individual shots into close groupings

Here is where the greatest fun can be had with people pictures. Clearly, this is also a highly specialized situation, where a greater degree of importance is intended than in plain catalog-type presentations. It is far more likely to be used for combining two or three personages than for a crowd.

Frieze run across the top. By placing names in the empty space "behind" the heads, or aligned neatly beneath them, you have a good opportunity to contrast the clean, neat horizontal alignment of the mug shots with the raggedness of the columns at the foot of the page, which are deliberately unaligned.

The same frieze run across the foot of the page. This is a much more dramatic arrangement because the white space "behind" the people's heads seems to flow up into the text above them and, by so doing, makes the text belong more intimately to the people below. This illustration would not exist were the columns of type all the same length, rather than **scalloped** as sketched here. Names would have to go below the pictures to avoid disrupting that valuable illusion of white background flowing up into the text.

Vary the sizes of the faces arbitrarily. Assemble the original photos the way they were received—at all sorts of different scales—to create a grouping where some people appear close up in the foreground and others far away in the distance. That's the effect of varying sizes creating an illusion of depth in perspective. Also essential to this effect is the clearly defined edge of the text above the mug shots. It emphasizes the variations in the pictures by its own horizontal precision.

Vertical overlapping is perfectly possible in multipage stories, if it creates a very startling effect. In this case, identification of individuals other than by numbers is much more difficult. Also, it is somehow implied that the persons shown this way are going to be referred to in the text on the same page on which their photos appear. For some peculiar reason, the informality of the horizontal arrangements shown in earlier examples does not carry that same implication. Is it perhaps because the horizontal arrangement looks like a party, whereas the vertical arrangement is more closely akin to catalog-type presentation?

7

Tips to make more effective use of pictures

Let's face it: Most of the photographs you are likely to be faced with are not very exciting. They are the expected view of an ordinary event, scene, or person frozen on film in a documentary fashion—the way it was. You are lucky if the shot is crisp and in focus and reasonably well lit, and the composition sits in its frame comfortably. As far as having much reportorial value or point of view is concerned, that's rare indeed. Yet that's the raw material you have to work with. You have only two options.

Option 1: throw the ugly ones out

But how can you publish printed matter without pictures in it? Pictures do so much to attract curiosity in readers, open them up to accepting information, enliven the product, and make it "interesting." (Yes, even deplorably dull pictures have that effect, because readers respond to visual information so much more readily than to verbal information. It is much less work than reading!)

To throw them out is too drastic a step. Besides, if you have no pictures to enliven your pages, your typography will have to bear the full brunt of pulling readers in and retaining their attention—a task that is perhaps even more daunting than facing . . .

Option 2: make the best of what you've got

A crummy picture will always remain a crummy picture, no matter how you doctor it. Don't think of it in terms of improving the image, because that's a problem you cannot do much about. Do think of it, rather, in terms of editorial value: finding what is worth publishing in the picture, and then focusing the reader's attention on that point. That inner significance makes the original's visual shortcomings unimportant. It justifies the picture's use on a higher level—not just as decoration for the page, not just to break up the type, not just as filler for empty spaces—but as a functional segment of the communication package.

Under such conditions, it is perfectly legitimate for you to consider the photo as malleable material, yours to do with as you—the editor—deem appropriate. It may make the photographer unhappy, but your prime consideration is to publish a story, a message, significant content, and anything that helps that process along is likely to be permissible. It is the story that matters, not the photographer's feelings. Again: If you do have *fine* photography, then leave it alone. Let it stand on its own. But if you have ordinary material to start with, then summon up the courage to tamper with the unprecious image for the sake of that valuable story. A whole list of such tampering trickery for the sake of editorial meaning starts on page 105. But before you delve into that, it is necessary to understand some fundamentals about pictures in publications. These are the normal approaches that good pictures demand.

The pretty picture: beguiling, but off the point

Often you are faced with the problem of what to do with a lovely image— here, available, ready to use; yet paradoxically you know that it is a side issue and doesn't really advance the cause of the story. In fact, it may well lead the reader to incorrect conclusions. What to do? Rejecting a beautiful image out of hand may well rob the product of an opportunity for uplift, but it is worse folly to pretend that it adds communication value to the story. (It is cheating even worse to twist the story in order to tie the picture in somehow.) Such pretense backfires in loss of credibility. Instead, be honest: Use the picture as an object worthy in and of itself, and present it to the reader as a treat to savor and enjoy.

Quarantine it in a box away from the story itself; build it into the story where it will do the most visible good to the product as a whole, rather than the story itself; run it as a **precede** to set a mood; or add it as a **shirttail** at the end of the story. Or use it as a **frontispiece** opposite the table of contents, or refer to it and run it in a strategic location elsewhere, like opposite the inside back cover. In short, the aim is to give it the requisite product-enriching visibility without at the same time confusing the reader.

The awful picture: depressing, but informative and essential

You'll be faced with this situation considerably more often than with the opposite problem described above. Here you have a bunch of images— embarrassingly bad they are, too, yet inescapably important to the story— and you cannot improve on them because there is not time and, besides, the subject has disappeared. The only sensible thing is to use them—but not splashily. Blowing up a second-rate picture doesn't improve it; all that does is bloat it and flaunt its inadequacy. Instead, run such pictures small and near the foot of the page, and don't attempt to catch attention with them. Instead, use a big headline or some other technique. But remember, photomechanical variations on originals may well be useful trickery (see page 130).

Have the courage needed to use that unexpected image

Obviousness is probably dull. The easiest way to spice up the story (or the entire product) is to accompany it with unanticipated imagery. The more startling the effect, the more likely it is that a dangerous, courageous decision has been made. But there is no question that there are numerous options at the editor's disposal that ought never be rejected out of hand: unusual viewpoints; peculiar lighting; surprising juxtaposition of elements; surrealistic transpositions of function, scale, relationship. They don't necessarily make the subject funny or foolish; they do, however, add attention-getting sparkle to a page.

How bleeds create an illusion of size

First, to **bleed** a picture is to print it right out to the edge of the page. A picture thus "bled" is called a "bleed."

↙bleed

Let's assume that we have a photo of a landscape. When it is printed on the page, it is a miniature reproduction of that original view. If it is framed by the margins of the page, it is contained—held in—imprisoned by that page. But if the picture is expanded to cover those margins, the image appears to burst out of the confines of the page, creating an illusion of continuation into spaces beyond the page. The page itself becomes merely the physical focal point of a much wider scene in our imagination. It is an exciting illusion if you have the right subject. What you have to do is look at your picture with great care and decide whether the illusion of continuation is appropriate to the subject matter. Are the significant elements in the picture bleeding off the page? In this landscape, is the sky or the foreground or the river at the left flowing off the page? The blank wall that is a neutral background to a vase of flowers would not be a sensible subject for bleeding off the page because it is not material to the vase of flowers, which is what the picture is about. Clearly, editorial judgment has to come into play here.

Interrupt the margin by bleeding pictures

Every printed page has a **live-matter area** that is surrounded by a frame or margin. It might be appropriate to name those margins here, remembering that nomenclature varies, but these are fairly standard.

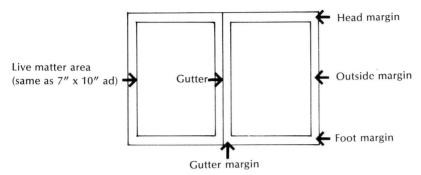

Standard-sized magazines are based on the 8½″ x 11″ dimension. But as paper costs have risen, the page has been chopped down, until it now measures about 8⅛″ x 10¾″, which are irreducible minimums. Why? Because ads are sized to a standard 7″ x 10″ proportion, and publishers must provide a page large enough to display them—or else. The reason for going into this rather technical side issue is simply this: The wider the margin, the more noticeable any interruption becomes. By reducing margins to the minimum, magazines have robbed themselves of the capacity to surprise by bleeding, because the difference between bleed and nonbleed is so insignificant that it is hardly worth talking about. So you aren't likely to be impressed by the capacity of bleed to interrupt the flow of margins and thus gain attention for your picture in a normal magazine any more.

Narrow margins, small photos

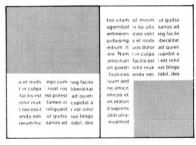

Wide margins, large photos

None of the above alters the principle: Anything that interrupts a pattern attracts attention. Bleeding does exactly that if the margins are wide enough to be discernible, and if the picture that is made to bleed is big enough to make it worthwhile pulling such a special stunt. Warning: To accomplish the trick of bleeding, you will have to print on a sheet of paper slightly larger than the finished page size. After the printing, then, the sheet is trimmed back to the correct page size, lopping off slivers of the bleeding picture.

Most pages are printed on slightly larger sheets anyway, with at least ⅛″ on all outside edges of pages, except the gutter, where the pages are folded and not trimmed. Clearly, you must size the picture to be ⅛″ bigger on any edges where it will bleed. That is reasonable and logical. What is infuriating is that one edge of the sheet of paper is needed by the press machinery for picking up and passing the sheet along to the next step in the printing process. That narrow edge is called the **gripper edge** because—you guessed it—that's where the gripper picks it up. Unfortunately, it is technically impossible to have two things touching the paper simultaneously. You cannot, therefore, have a picture bleeding in the place where that accursed gripper will be doing its gripping. Under Murphy's Law, where everything that could go wrong inevitably will, your bleeds will fall right there You must therefore check with the printer and ask for the **imposition**; the printer will provide you with a diagram showing how the pages fall on the sheet of paper and where the gripper will be. You can then shift your bleeds from this page to that, or make the printer turn the sheet around to accommodate your bleeds. In any case, though, check with the printer about any premium charge for bleeding pictures, for it is better to be prepared for surprises.

Typical imposition diagrams. The various standard paper sizes offer various page combinations. The printer can outline the available options in diagrams like these, which are essential planning tools for both bleeding and utilization of color.

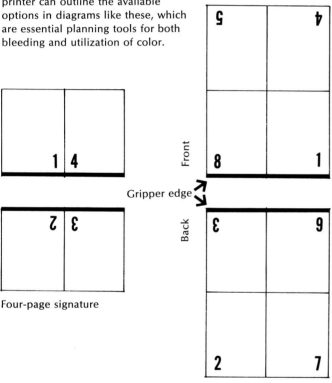

Four-page signature

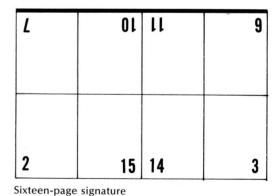

Eight-page signature

Sixteen-page signature

Gripper edge

Front

Back

How the reader interprets meaning through size

The bigger something is, the more important we think it to be. That is so obvious that we take it for granted. But once we realize its potential, we can use the principle to guide our decision making about pictures. It affects two distinct areas of that process.

First, are we just using the picture to fill up an empty space, and if so, is it worth it? Will the extra size given to an unworthy picture mislead the reader? Or worse, will it devalue our technique of creating emphasis by size next time, when we do have an image we want to bring to the reader's

Here's a picture we want to use to go with a story about *"When in doubt, ask a policeman." Don't think of it as being a filling for a predetermined space (though, of course, it will be exactly that when it is printed!). Instead, see the original as being an image that ought to be given a size that is commensurate to its importance in the context of the story — a value judgment that is purely editorial, affecting the "design" of the page, of course, but based on the intrinsic value of the original — NOT the final "beauty" of the page. So: give it the size it deserves. Do not fit it into an arbitrary, preconceived hole.*

Lorem ipsum dolor sit amet, consectetur adipscing elit, sed diam nonnumy eiusmod tempor incidunt ut labore

When in doubt, ask a policeman

et dolore

dignissum qui blandit est pra molestias excepteur sint occa sunt in culpa qui officia deser Et harumd dereud facilis est soluta nobis eligent optio est c Lorem ipsum dolor sit amet, co eiusmod tempor incidunt ut la Ut enim ad minim veniam, qu laboris nisi ut aliquip ex ea co irure dolor in reprehenderit in v illum dolore eu fugiat nulla par dignissum qui blandit praeser molestias excepteur sint occa sunt in culpa qui officia deser Et harumd dereud facilis est e conscient to factor tum poen l neque pecun modut est nequ soluta nobis eligent optio con religuard cupiditat, quas nulla potius inflammad ut coercend invitat igitur vera ratio bene s Lorem ipsum dolor sit amet, co eiusmod tempor incidunt ut la

eiusmod tempor incidunt ut la Ut enim ad minim veniam, qu laboris nisi ut aliquip ex ea co irure dolor in reprehenderit in v illum dolore eu fugiat nulla par dignissum qui blandit est prae molestias excepteur sint occa sunt in culpa qui officia deser Et harumd dereud facilis est e soluta nobis eligend optio co soluta nobis eligent optio est c Lorem ipsum dolor sit amet, co eiusmod tempor incidunt ut la Ut enim ad minim veniam, qu laboris nisi ut aliquip ex ea co irure dolor in reprehenderit in v illum dolore eu fugiat nulla par dignissum qui blandit praesen molestias excepteur sint occa sunt in culpa qui officia deser Et harumd dereud facilis est e

1-column: a subsidiary image, hardly worth being there for all the good it does (so minuscule).

When in doubt, ask a policeman

dignissum qui blandit est prae molestias excepteur sint occa sunt in culpa qui officia deser Et harumd dereud facilis est soluta nobis eligent optio est c Lorem ipsum dolor sit amet, co eiusmod tempor incidunt ut la Ut enim ad minim veniam, qui laboris nisi ut aliquip ex ea cor irure dolor in reprehenderit in v illum dolore eu fugiat nulla par dignissum qui blandit praeser molestias excepteur sint occa sunt in culpa qui officia deser Et harumd dereud facilis est e conscient to factor tum poen l neque pecun modut est nequ soluta nobis eligent optio con religuard cupiditat, quas nulla potius inflammad ut coercend invitat igitur vera ratio bene s Lorem ipsum dolor sit amet, co eiusmod tempor incidunt ut la Ut enim ad minim veniam, qu laboris nisi ut aliquip ex ea co

irure dolor in reprehenderit in v illum dolore eu fugiat nulla pari dignissum qui blandit est prae molestias excepteur sint occa sunt in culpa qui officia deser Et harumd dereud facilis est soluta nobis eligend optio co Lorem ipsum dolor sit amet, co eiusmod tempor incidunt ut la Ut enim ad minim veniam, qui laboris nisi ut aliquip ex ea co irure dolor in reprehenderit in v illum dolore eu fugiat nulla pari dignissum qui blandit praesen molestias excepteur sint occa sunt in culpa qui officia deser Et harumd dereud facilis est e conscient to factor tum poen l neque pecun modut est nequ soluta nobis eligent optio con religuard cupiditat, quas nulla potius inflammad ut coercend invitat igitur vera ratio bene s Lorem ipsum dolor sit amet, co

dignissum qui blandit est prae molestias excepteur sint occa sunt in culpa qui officia deser Et harumd dereud facilis est soluta nobis eligent optio est c Lorem ipsum dolor sit amet, co eiusmod tempor incidunt ut la Ut enim ad minim veniam, qui laboris nisi ut aliquip ex ea co irure dolor in reprehenderit in v illum dolore eu fugiat nulla pari dignissum qui blandit est prae molestias excepteur sint occa sunt in culpa qui officia deser Et harumd dereud facilis est soluta nobis eligend optio co Lorem ipsum dolor sit amet, co eiusmod tempor incidunt ut la Ut enim ad minim veniam, qui laboris nisi ut aliquip ex ea co irure dolor in reprehenderit in v

2-columns: a neutral image. OK. So what?

When in doubt, ask a policeman

conscient to factor tum poen l neque pecun modut est neque soluta nobis eligent optio con religuard cupiditat, quas nulla potius inflammad ut coercend invitat igitur vera ratio bene sa Lorem ipsum dolor sit amet, co eiusmod tempor incidunt ut la Ut enim ad minim veniam, qui laboris nisi ut aliquip ex ea cor irure dolor in reprehenderit in v illum dolore eu fugiat nulla pari dignissum qui officia deseru soluta nobis eligent optio est c

conscient to factor tum poen l neque pecun modut est neque soluta nobis eligent optio cong religuard cupiditat, quas nulla potius inflammad ut coercend invitat igitur vera ratio bene sa Lorem ipsum dolor sit amet, co eiusmod tempor incidunt ut lal Ut enim ad minim veniam, qui laboris nisi ut aliquip ex ea con irure dolor in reprehenderit in v illum dolore eu fugiat nulla pari dignissum qui blandit est prae sunt in culpa qui officia deseru soluta nobis eligent optio est c

conscient to factor tum poen l neque pecun modut est neque soluta nobis eligent optio cong religuard cupiditat, quas nulla potius inflammad ut coercend invitat igitur vera ratio bene sa Lorem ipsum dolor sit amet, co eiusmod tempor incidunt ut lal Ut enim ad minim veniam, qui laboris nisi ut aliquip ex ea con irure dolor in reprehenderit in v illum dolore eu fugiat nulla pari dignissum qui blandit est prae sunt in culpa qui officia deseru soluta nobis eligent optio est c

3-columns: a dominant image. Eye-catching and thought provoking. The story flows out of it.

attention? Making an unworthy picture bigger than it deserves to be just bloats it.

Second, how does the picture relate to the words? How do they balance, complement, enhance each other? This area of analysis affects mostly the **opener picture** and the headline of a story, since there is a standard pattern: The photo is intended to catch the reader's attention; the headline, which relates to it as precisely as a caption, then focuses the reader's attention on the idea you want to feature. The size of that opening picture should grow out of the excellence of the image—excellence in terms of its *meaning for the story*—and only incidentally out of its beauty or cleverness. If the picture is beside the point, don't play it big. If it is pertinent, play it as big as you can. Avoid allowing space to dictate the size. Instead, start with a value judgment and then find the space to display it properly.

The **first impression** of your pages is communicated by the sizes of pictures and by the page arrangement. If the reader learns that size is not arbitrary, but that big images are meaningful in terms of the story, every big picture will then be a strong signal for attention, leading to effective, fast, intimate communication and thus a better product. Don't expect readers to realize *why* this is happening. All they will think is that yours is an interesting publication. That is music enough to an editor's ears.

Why it is wise to crop the picture until it hurts

This is the retrofitting you have to go through if the photographer didn't get close enough to the subject. What you have to do is to search out in the original print what is significant about it, to determine which part of the image is important enough to publish. All the rest then becomes expendable. Expendable, however, is too weak a word—it is *essential* to remove unnecessary material, for it may well distract the reader's attention from what you as editor want to be noticed.

Furthermore, changing the **cropping** of a photo can alter its meaning—

Original

Dynamic

Static

not just by simplifying or homing in on which is important, but by other visual implications. Obviously, every picture is a case by itself, and there are no rules. The only rule is to become aware of the possibilities and then follow up on your insight. An extra added attraction: By chopping the

original down to its irreducible minimum, you can use what is left at a much larger size and with much stronger impact; or you can gain valuable space on the page by running it smaller than it otherwise would have been.

Crop to make pictures work together better

A picture is never just a gray rectangle on a page. See it as a piece of communication that has its own natural sense of scale, proportion, feeling of distance, special mood, and individual statement, and it is much more than something printed on the surface of a piece of paper. It is the *illusion of a view* beyond the surface of that paper. As such, it is perfectly logical to perceive the photograph as though it were a view through a window and that window is in fact a hole cut through the wall our printing paper represents.

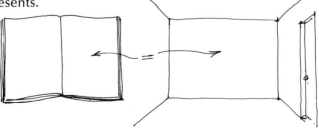

This concept of a picture being a view through a window is especially important when you have more than one picture to accommodate. How often does it happen that there are two images that have to run next to each other on the page, yet how seldom do they relate to each other visually! They may make sense together in meaning or as illustrations of related events happening to the subject; but do they look it? Think about it for a moment: Imagine that a carpenter has come to cut two holes in that far wall. Let's call them "windows":

99

The view from those windows has a unity—a logical connection that we expect.

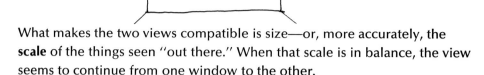

What makes the two views compatible is size—or, more accurately, the **scale** of the things seen "out there." When that scale is in balance, the view seems to continue from one window to the other.

That's why this macro/micro cow is unrealistic. The unnatural juxtaposition of disparate sizes feels wrong and disturbing.

The illusion of a continued view applies whenever we have two or more images of similar size placed in close proximity on the page.

Readers look at our page twice, the first time in glancing fashion, to decide whether to give it more time and attention, to find out whether it promises to be interesting. The second time, when they have been hooked by what they saw, they actually pay closer attention—reading, studying, and absorbing.

What succeeded in bringing the readers in? Most probably it was the pictures, if the headlines managed to explain their significance. And even if those pictures were relatively small, they could have seemed important acting as a huge image *as a group*, if they were made to blend together in

scale. Only at second viewing does each individual image gain its point—
at first viewing they all worked together to create this synergetic result
where $1 + 1 = 3$.

Unrelated scale: These two photos
don't "work" with each other,
because the people in them vary in
size so much that the pictures seem
related to each other only in content
and overall shape and size.

Equalized scale: By cropping and
enlarging the photo at far right, the
two images have been brought into
balance. They now appear to be two
views of the same event.

Crop for continuity of the horizon in neighboring pictures

Continuity of scale is the first fundamental relationship between neighboring
pictures, if you see them as views from windows. The second and intimately
related one is the horizontal relationship between adjacent images. This basic
relationship is so seldom regarded that it might be an interesting exercise to
look through any publication for two adjoining landscape views. Draw a line
through the horizon of the left-hand picture, then draw a line through the

horizon of the right-hand picture. One hundred to one they don't align! Do they? Why not? Because nobody thought much about it, because they were busy sizing and cropping the pictures to fit arbitrary spaces that happened to be contiguous without thinking of the relationship between the pictures. So the nonrelationship you get looks like this:

That's the result of tunnel vision, seeing each image as a separate entity. By widening that tunnel to include more than one image at a time, you can expand the *effect* of the pictures. It is much like coming out of a constricted vertical canyon onto the broad plains of the moon (which is where these NASA pictures happen to have been taken).

By cropping to make the horizon flow from one image into the neighboring one, a more expansive overall view is created.

Edit pictures so one image becomes dominant

There are very few situations where you have several pictures, each of which has equal value to the story, the reader, or the publication. When it becomes quite clear in your mind precisely what the underlying message of the story really is—its reason for being published—then it will likely become obvious to you which image supports or embodies that idea most clearly and effectively. *That* is the picture to use big. The bigger, the better. Even if it isn't all that marvelous in terms of photography, it is probably marvelous in terms of meaning. Remember that we are in the business of publishing *stories* and not photography as art!

That important picture then will carry the major burden of intriguing the reader into the story. To help it do that job, it is highly effective to support it with small images if you have them. Why? For two reasons. First, if you want to make something big look remarkably big to the reader, you have to contrast it to something tiny—that way, it suddenly becomes overwhelming. Second, the big picture arouses the potential reader's curiosity. That curiosity can be at least partially resolved by more visual images. They work faster than long-winded verbal explanations, and they themselves can start fresh directions of curiosity that force the reader to delve ever more deeply into the hard work of reading the text. This is especially true if the captions have given additional useful information—though not all! We must always keep the reader hungry for more. If that sounds a little bit manipulative, so be it. We are fighting for attention, and the end justifies the means.

Help pictorial scenes by cunning page arrangements

A sequence of ideas or thoughts can be placed on the page in such a way that it becomes a maze for the reader to puzzle through. Or, it can be made simple and forthright by alignment, overlapping, growth in scale, and numbering. **Sequences**, of course, are the most elementary examples of thematic subject flowing through pictures. Other perhaps less obvious but no less valid relationships ought to be made equally evident in all stories that consist of more than just a hunk of text with a couple of shots thrown in to break up the type.

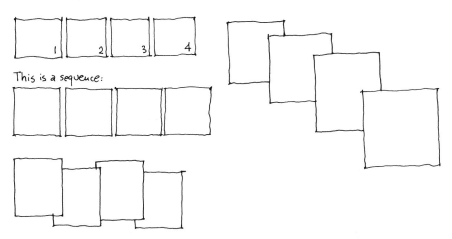

This is a sequence:

Cluster small, spotty pictures to give them greater visibility

Peppering pages with insignificant odds and ends is less impressive and much less attention-getting than pulling them together into groups—if such groups make editorial sense, that is.

How? Dozens of techniques: Place them on a unifying background of a simple shade of gray, texture, or better still, a symbolic image that unifies them by sense as well. Or install them in a box container of some sort. Or butt them close together. Or deploy them within an encompassing grid. Or fix them in a graphic net. Or give them repetitive shapes that make them links in a connecting chain. Or best of all, juxtapose them so that one image's meaning flows out of one into the other. Or—what else? There must be as many solutions as there are problems. Devising the ideal one depends on the specifics of the situation, and that is what makes this profession so rewarding and so interesting.

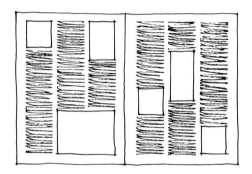 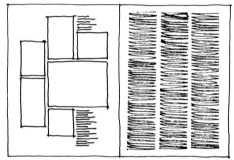

Link images to create a cumulative impact

Often a story cannot be told in merely one image—however excellent that image might be. Two or more are needed to do the job. This applies to sequences over time, relationships in space, development of ideas, contrasting of subjects, and so on. If you have them, use them, but be sure you know why you are using them. Be certain of the editorial points you want to make and then handle the pictures in such a way that those points are indubitably made. And be sure you aren't using more than the minimum simply because it is easier to use all of the pictures than it is to go through the mental gymnastics of deciding which one to throw out. In other words, the task of editing, which applies just as much to pictures as it does to words and everything else we print, is to *edit*—to be courageous in using the blue pencil and the wastebasket, in order to leave only those sparkling nuggets in the pan (to mix a few metaphors for the fun of it). The principle is simple: You don't improve the reader's understanding of a person's character by showing more than one dumb picture of that person. If, however, you have several views that can add another dimension to our understanding of that person, then the situation is changed. Then you have to ask yourself: Which one picture embodies those characteristics that need to be brought out, or are they all important, or do we hone it down a bit by showing only three of the six available, two extremes and one neutral one in the middle? Such analytical thinking applies to any group of pictures you may have, obviously not only to people pictures.

How to expose the sense of the story in pictures

It is often possible to turn an uninspired or uninspiring picture into a sharp tool for communication if you have two prerequisites: clear understanding of what it is you are trying to say, coupled with the courage to allow nothing to stand in the way of your saying it. As mentioned on page 93, and strongly repeated here: This is not the treatment of choice when one has good photos to work with. It is the treatment of desperation, when one is faced with the difficulty of illustrating or expressing a message that demands visual aid, yet the raw material available cannot stand on its own because of lack of excellence. In other words, it represents 85% of the typical editor's normal predicament. This is not to sound cynical. It is a simple statement of fact observed over years in the business. Only some 15% of the material included in a publication is potentially "exciting." The rest is pedestrian, workaday, and uninspiring, and, if you've been at it for any length of time, it tends to be depressing. It follows that to do some alchemy and turn your lead into editorial gold, you have to use a lot of imagination, see clearly, decide forcefully, and carry through deliberately. What follows is a list of gimmicks (to use a pejorative term) that are not gimmicks when used correctly—where the end justifies the means. There, they turn into *techniques*—a much more palatable term. Let us think of them that way.

Clearly, the editorial interpretations of any of them depends on the specifics of the situation, the particular subject matter, the context in which it will be seen, and so forth. So use these techniques with care and circumspection, and don't use them too much or too often; do use them when the idea or the product would be poorer without them.

Publish pictures of pictures

Normally, the image in the photograph is what gets reproduced on the page. What is forgotten is the simple fact that the original photo was an object in and of itself: a piece of paper, a thing to hold in the hand and tear, spindle, and mutilate. Why not reproduce it as that object? That way, you get two for the price of one: You reproduce the image (the picture) *and* you give it a special flavor of being seen as something more than just that image. How? By one or more of the following tricks.

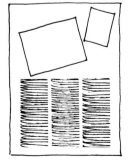

Tilt it at an angle on the page. That way it immediately ceases to belong to the column pattern. You indicate this to the printer by drawing a rectangle on the page where the picture is intended to go.

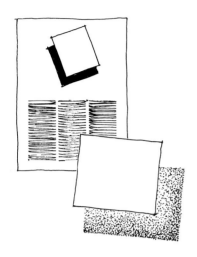

Emphasize nonbelongingness by making it appear to "float" above the surface of the paper by casting a shadow. There are several ways to accomplish this. The easiest is to make an overlay: Take a piece of tracing paper and draw the shadow line in black ink. For more details on how to make overlays, see page 84. If you prefer, you can manufacture those lines out of any of the many rub-off or stick-on tapelike products available at any art supply shop. They come in a variety of widths, and all you do is chop off a piece and make it adhere to the overlay paper. A little trickier, although much more interesting to look at, is to make the shadow a bit fuzzy and transparent—not pitch black. That is much more realistic. You accomplish this with a soft pencil on an overlay. The technique takes practice, and the end product also has to be reproduced as a halftone and stripped to the picture itself.

Frame the image. Most pictures have a sliver of white edge framing the actual image. It is hard to reproduce that sliver of whiteness, for nobody would notice it printed on white paper. Instead, one creates the illusion of that sliver by printing a thin line or rule around what would be that frame, and the reader perceives our intentions. The printer can scribe this line on the negative for you, or you can do it for yourself on the mechanical, or on an overlay on that mechanical.

Mutilate the paper of which the photo is made. Turn a corner over, curl it in some way, tear off an edge. How? Again, by combining the photo with hand-drawn art that describes your idea. It is best drawn in black ink—and perhaps in this kind of venture it is wiser to get the help of a professional pen pusher, because the illusion is dependent on good draftsmanship. But first you have to explain the idea of what you want done to your draftsperson. If these diagrams are not detailed enough, see *Graphic Idea Notebook*, also by this author.

Combine several pictures by an informal arrangement of overlaps to make them appear as though they had fallen onto the page. This obviously requires a carefully crafted mechanical that both instructs the printer as to which picture goes where and to what size, and also gives the requisite line art (outline of the "frames" and "shadows") that is an essential ingredient of the illusion.

Add naturalistic symbols to the pictures that might help in getting your desired illusion to work more colorfully or strikingly. Paper clips, photo corners, a piece of an envelope out of which the pictures have fallen, the stub of a pencil—you name it. They can all be incorporated into the setup, either as individual elements to be stripped in or as integral elements of the overlays. Get the printer's advice on technique, but don't allow yourself to be discouraged or talked out of the idea. (By and large, printers tend to be conservative. Sad experience has made them that way.)

Run the pictures with the photographic paraphernalia surrounding them—film sprocket holes, sheet film frames, notches, 35mm slide sleeves, and so forth. How do you manufacture that? There are so many variables that professional advice should be sought here.

Bring attention to the important part of the image

This goes beyond merely cropping (that's like losing excess weight around the edges). Here we are talking of major surgery: carving away what isn't wanted—going as far as one can—in fact, silhouetting. That simply means you print only that part of the photo you deem useful and do not show the rest. How? There are two basic methods, neither of which is difficult.

In the first method you instruct the printer as to what you want done by drawing a **keyline** or **outline** on an overlay over the photo. All the halftone dots on the inside of the line are to print. All those on the outside of the line are to be removed. How the printer accomplishes this is something you need not concern yourself with. All you need to worry about is the accuracy of your line, which must be drawn in a clean, thin, ink line and must be accurately keyed to the photo. Furthermore, you must also worry about not marring the surface of the original photograph with ruts left by pencils tracing over the surface. The emulsion of a photograph is very soft material and marks easily, and any such marks can appear in the reproduction as highlights or shadows.

The second method is to make a **mask**. This does part of the work for the printer. You have to use a piece of material that will protect the area you want to print and allow the unprotected area to be burned away (overexposed) by the printer's halftone-making camera. The material is regularly available in sheets or rolls—yes, it is expensive—at art supply shops. You ask for amber or red **cut-and-peel film**. (The amber color is easier to see through.) You place it over the original and carefully draw the outline of your desired image with a cutting blade. You then peel away the amber film from the area you do *not* want, and that's all there is to it. As always, key the overlay to the original with **targets** or **X-marks**.

What has just been described is known as a **silhouette** halftone—silo or silho for short. Obviously, it is more expensive than the plain halftone. Anything that isn't a plain halftone is inevitably more expensive. But—used right—the effect is cheap at the price.

There is a third method you should *never* use. You never cut out the original picture with a pair of scissors. The only time you ever do that is when you are combining pictures, such as a group of mug shots in which you overlap shoulders. But even then you would get duplicate prints to do that, if you are at all circumspect! For normal silhouettes, work on overlays and let the printer accomplish your results for you.

Another technique for drawing attention to a specific feature in an image is to make the important area appear crisper, lighter, darker, or somehow more clearly defined than its surroundings. If you are describing a cog in a machine, you have to show both the cog (which is what the story is about) and the machine (which is the context of the cog). But it is hard to find a cog in a machine. Therefore, you have to create some sort of contrast in order to draw attention to your important cog.

Make the surroundings paler or darker. This can be achieved in several ways, the easiest of which are:

☐   To give the original to a **photo retoucher** who sprays the background with lighter or darker paint, leaving the cog as is. This is obviously a fairly expensive proposition, but essential if that cog is a complicated object or if the background is tricky to handle.

☐   To make an outline or a mask on an overlay, just as in the preparation for silhouetting. Then, you instruct the printer to **ghost** or lighten up by overexposing, or conversely, **darken** the area you want to disappear a bit. You can control the degree of ghosting or darkening by expressing it in percentages. One hundred percent is deemed to be "as is" in the original. Ninety percent of original is 10% ghosted, or made paler by a factor of 10%, and so on.

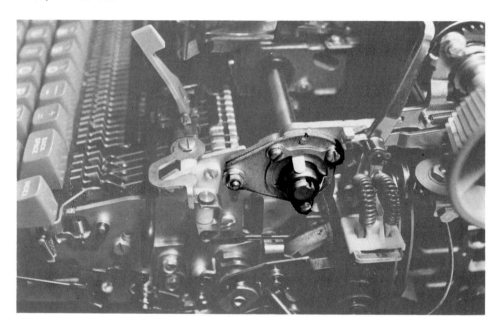

Use different kinds of screens for the cog and the surrounding machinery. The finer the halftone screen, the better the detail. On very good paper you can print comfortably using a 150-line screen (that means there are 150 dots to every inch in both directions). On newsprint stock, you usually use a much coarser screen: 65 lines per inch, or even 55. By using the 150-line screen for the cog and the 55-line screen for the machine, you can contrast textures.

Use color. Run one of the elements in color, the other in contrasting black and white. Or add an overprinting tint over the surroundings and let the cog appear crisp black and white, or any number of other such combinations. Clearly, this is more complicated to think through, but it is no more difficult to accomplish technically than any of the others. All you need is that simple guideline to instruct the printer's platemaker as to which part of the picture is to be treated which way.

Add line art to the picture that emphasizes the cog in question—arrows 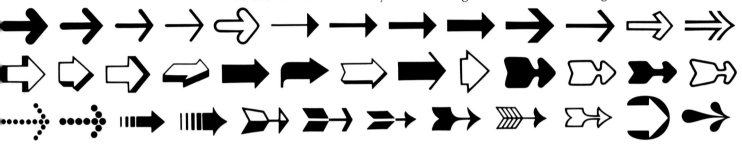 pointing to it, circles encircling it, asterisks referring to it, fists ☞ highlighting it, and so forth. All of these can be done as drawings or bought in a store, be they rub-off, stick-on, or clip art that has to be glued on an overlay and keyed to the original photo. The lines are then **dropped out** from the halftone, if you want them to appear white against the picture, or **surprinted** or **stripped in** if you want them to appear in black against the picture. You must determine which you prefer by studying the darkness of the picture area in which the line work will be seen. If the background is very pale, obviously dropping out in white will make the line work invisible; therefore, you must surprint it. If the area is very dark, obviously you must drop out the line work in white. If the backdrop is medium, you flip a coin and hope for the best. In any case, whenever it is medium gray, it is wise to make your line work bolder, using thicker lines or larger symbols, so that whatever you do use will be more likely to be seen against that neutral background.

Do things with the edges of the pictures

Fuzz them out so that they are vignetted—so there are no definite edges at all. Fade the picture away into the white paper as though it were disappearing into a fog. This has to be done by a retoucher using sprayed-on paint.

Make rounded or other unusually shaped corners. The printer can do this for you if you specify the radius. (A quarter-inch is about right. Anything smaller tends to be insignificant, and going much bigger tends to make it look horsey.)

Surround the picture with a ruled line. This is a favorite mannerism of some magazines to make them look different. It is, however, particularly useful in publications printed on newsprint stock where the edges of photographs tend to disappear, especially when they show light areas such as the sky. Defining the edge with a line makes the product appear much crisper.

Frame the picture with an outline of the object through which the view is seen, such as a keyhole, porthole, window, mirror, or the like. The surrounding symbolism of the shape will probably have to be stripped in as line art. The shape itself must, of course, be indicated on an overlay.

Shape the picture into geometric shapes, such as circles, triangles, rhomboids, trapezoids, or anything else. Indicate it on an overlay.

Manipulate the image for symbolic purposes

Analyze what the thrust of the story is and how you can turn the ordinary illustration into more of an expression of concept. For instance:

Show vibration or up-and-down motion, as in this example. Don't try to be literal about it. A picture of a pothole is not very inspiring, nor is a picture of a road with a tiny invisible spot on it (labeled "pothole"). Instead, illustrate what the potholes do to the driver: Bump-a-da-bump! Take a duplicate of the photo (never destroy the original, you'll be sure to need it some other time!) and cut it up in slivers, then repaste them out of alignment. Result—bumps that you feel in the pit of your stomach.

Show danger, shattering explosion, as here. See the standard skyline picture as a fragile object made of glass, and then appear to shatter it. How? The simplest possible ruse: Paint the outline of shards in ink on an overlay and then reverse them or drop them out in white from the background picture.

Show threat, fear, or menace by running the photo as a **negative**. Reversing the light and the dark throws our perception out of kilter. It is spooky, upsetting, and startling, and it can be a very strong statement. Just inform the printer that you want this image run as a negative and that, yes, you know what you are doing.

To show the What as well as the How when all you have is a picture of the What, add line drawings growing out of the image. Such **extension drawings** can expand the original image into a broader understanding of the context of the picture. The photo is the focal point of a larger image encompassing the entire subject matter. The drawing is done on an overlay the same size as the photograph, and the two are keyed to each other so that the two separate pieces of film (halftone and line) are then stripped together accurately without a gap between them to spoil the illusion.

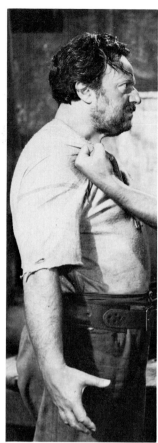

This is eight point garamond light one point of space between lines, flush left and ragged right

This is eight point garamond light with one point of space between lines, set flush left and ragged right, to a maximum measure that varies

This is eight point garamond light with one point of space between lines, set flush left and ragged right, to a maximum measure that varies

To show the makeup of a complex object, split the image into its component parts and describe each of those parts in a separate caption. This merely represents a more complex cropping and sizing problem and calls for accurate instructions to the printer.

To create an illusion of motion, tilt the horizon, even when there isn't any movement in the picture at all, or when you need to emphasize speed. This is the sort of situation where a photocopy sized to the printed size is essential: You can actually chop it up the way you want to see the final halftone. A dry run for such trickery is usually a good safety measure.

Use partial silhouetting to emphasize action

When you look outside your window, you feel protected from the view by the wall that is between you and the outside. It may be storming out there, but you are comfycozy in here.

Now imagine that you are looking out at a horrid seven-headed dragon. It is not terrifying, because it is so far away that it appears tiny.

But when that seven-headed hydra waddles closer, it is a little more unpleasant: It is getting bigger. Yet we have that protective wall between us and it.

As it comes closer, the flimsiness of our protecting wall becomes a major factor in our feeling of safety and involvement. Will it hold?

Will the dragon break the glass and shove one of its slobbering heads in to bite us?

The wall is the publication's page; the window is the photo. Photos are illusions of windows in walls, but so long as that window has a rectangular outline, the view appears "out there" and we are uninvolved spectators "in here" (and we can take the dragon or leave it, as we wish). But when that distinction between "out there" and "in here" is blurred by the breaking of that rectangular outline—by the insertion of an element of the object "out there" into the inner space "in here"—we are immediately forced to pay attention; we are no longer in control, the dragon is. Partially silhouetting a

picture, having an active element poke out of it, is a compelling trick to gain the reader's attention. How do you do it? In precisely the same way you prepare a complete silhouette: by drawing an overlay that shows the edges of the picture that you want to appear as the rectangular halftone and includes the parts that poke out beyond that rectangle. Of course, you can also cut it out of the masking overlay material. It must be done the size of the original photo, and the printer then reduces it to the required size for printing.

Combine words with pictures so 1 + 1 = 3

Place the name of various elements needing identification around the outside of the picture, instead of putting them in a long caption that nobody wants to read and that is invariably hard to decipher. Then lead **arrows** from the words to the actual element in the picture. This turns a photo of a probably uninteresting object into a visual diagram—in itself much more fascinating to study.

As far as those words themselves are concerned, they must be physically attached to an overlay on the original so that you can coordinate them with the arrows. That requires you to attach the original photograph to a piece of illustration board large enough to accommodate the space that will be needed for the words. If the original is an 8″ x 10″ print, then that board is likely to be a monster. (But don't worry, you can buy it 20″ x 30″ as a standard size, and 30″ x 40″ is also available, although that is perhaps a little excessive.) The words themselves can be typeset, cut out and glued on, or handwritten.

Whichever you choose, remember that the reduction from the original will have to be taken into account. So if your original comes down to half the original size (focus 50.0), your lettering will need to be twice the size of what you want it to be. Most likely, you will want a type size of about 9 point for legibility. That then means you must have your words set at 18 point so that they will reduce to 9 point in the final version. The equivalent proportions must be used for handwriting.

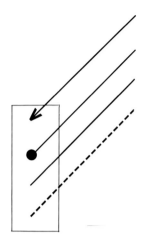

As far as the arrow lines are concerned, those are drawn or attached to the overlay also. They should not be too thin, or they will disappear in the halftone—which defeats the purpose of the exercise. If they appear printed on white paper surrounding the halftone, obviously they will need to be black. But if the arrows appear on the picture itself, you will have to instruct the platemaker as to whether you want the lines to drop out in white or surprint in black. That decision depends on the darkness of the areas in the picture through which the lines pass. There is no reason that some should not be white while others are black. It is money well spent if you get a result that communicates clearly. If you have another color available, then you can start having more fun—but remember to specify that the rules must all be dropped out from the black in order to make a clean white background for the color to print on. Otherwise your precious color may not be visible over the black ink of the picture.

Should the arrows have arrowheads or dots at the end, or should they be plain lines? Your personal aesthetics and common sense come into play here. Dots look technical. Arrows add an active, dynamic atmosphere. Plain lines are simple and elegant.

It is perfectly possible to make up the photo with just the arrow lines inserted by stripping in from an overlay on the original, and to have the descriptive words appear in type on the page itself. That way you avoid having to get all that outside typesetting and a huge overlay. But errors are easier to make on a small scale. However, if there is lots of wording to be accommodated, perhaps this is the wisest way to handle the problem.

Another technique is to place the words in relation to the object inside

BY JOVE!
How did it get here?

the picture, rather than in relation to the outside rectangle of the picture. The geometry of the page is usually made up of rectangular elements working with each other by alignment, stacking, centering, and so on. To get extra mileage from pictures where it makes sense, why not break away from this norm and knit the words with the picture more intimately? Drop them out of the picture, surprint them, lead them from the pictured object out into the surrounding spaces. Anything is acceptable if it grows out of the sense and meaning of the photo and the editorial idea, and if it is graphically handled so that all the words are truly legible.

To be sure the idea is workable, it is advisable to obtain a photocopy of the picture in the intended size, have the words set in type, adhere them to an overlay in the desired position, and give instructions to the printer as to stripping in in black or dropping out in white.

You need just a modicum of *courage and humor* to make clichés sparkle

n'est ce pas?

8

Inescapable technicalities about pictures

Must all originals be black-and-white prints?

Can you use **color prints**? Or 35mm **transparencies**? Or bigger **chromes** (color transparencies)? What about Polaroid™ shots?

It is perfectly possible to reproduce any of these in black and white, although quality and cost may affect your decision. The best results and the cheapest processing, however, are to be expected from plain black-and-white prints (normally 8″ x 10″ or 5″ x 7″). The glossy finish of the emulsion allows reproduction of the subject matter with the greatest precision and crispness. Other finishes, such as matte, silk, sepia tone, and the like are available, and you may be forced to use them when Important Personages supply you with studio portraits to use as mug shots. They are less likely to give you as good a result as the plain old black-and-white glossy.

Contact sheets

The roll of 35mm black-and-white film is developed and then usually cut into strips of six or seven exposures and assembled for printing same size onto an 8″ x 10″ sheet of paper. This gives the photographer and editor the entire "shoot," allowing them to choose which shots should be blown up for possible use. Enlargements are usually made to 8″ x 10″ or 5″ x 7″. The contact sheet is an extra cost, of course, but it is useful as a catalog of what is on the negative for future use. It is also much cheaper than enlarging the entire batch.

To discern details in such tiny images, it is necessary to study the pictures through a magnifying glass or loupe, available in various degrees of quality at camera or art supply stores. 8X magnification is most common. Mark the pictures you want with a grease pencil or felt-tip marker on the contact sheet, and send it together with the negatives back to the lab for processing. You can indicate cropping by outlining the area of each picture that you want enlarged and printed. In your instructions to the photo lab, refer to each picture by number, for example, "Contact Sheet No. X, Frame Y," since each contact sheet and picture is numbered.

Prints in color

They are as good to reproduce from as black-and-white prints, as long as they have a smooth, glossy finish. The cameraman shooting them for halftones may opt to use filters, and the new platemaking machines are also equipped with processing variations that accept color originals. But if those originals are printed on textured paper, fuzziness in the reproduction is practically unavoidable.

It is possible to print black-and-white prints from color negatives if the correct paper is used. Check with your photo lab. Incidentally, it is wiser to work with a professional photo lab than the cheaper mass-production or drugstore-type photo services. The labs give individual attention, can improve the quality of the prints by handwork, and—most importantly—will help you with practical advice.

When reproduced, instant photos in color seem to lead to mushy results, unless the originals have been very skillfully shot.

Transparencies

Transparencies of whatever size must first be converted to black-and-white prints; the prints then become the "art" that is reproduced. The most faithful reproduction of color to black and white requires making an **internegative** from which the black-and-white print is then taken. Naturally, internegs cost money, and however well they may be made, they remove the final product a step further away from the original; quality, crispness, and detail cannot help but suffer. Such second-step black-and-white prints are, however, better to reproduce from than *color* prints made from color transparencies (unless you pay for custom printing, which is horrendously expensive).

All the above applies only to reproducing photos in black and white. For full-color ("process color") or two-color ("matched color") reproduction, you need good, crisp transparencies of whatever size, or you can use **reflection copy** (such as a painting) as originals.

Pictures already printed elsewhere

Often you may only have an existing halftone as original copy. The safest way to handle this is to reuse it at exactly the same focus (same size—unless you choose to chop off an edge here or there, of course). That way you are reproducing the original as though it were line art, dot for dot. It is bound to get a bit cruder, but that will seldom be noticeable; the dark areas will probably turn muddy and highlights become less sparkling, but you can live with that. If you find that it is unavoidable to reduce the original, it is wise to ask the printer or platemaker whether it is possible to have the item **rescreened** (that's some magic with angled screens and what-not that you don't need to know the technicalities of). It ought to give surprisingly good results. A disaster is liable to happen only if you have to enlarge the original, because when you do that the dots grow, and the results look as coarse as newspaper photos. This may well be an interesting trick when you are looking for trickery, but as a good reproduction of a photo it leaves much to be desired.

How can you tell that the picture is the right way 'round?

Transparencies can easily be printed flopped left to right by mistake. Furthermore, when you have the transparency itself, it is often hard to tell which is front and which is back. Here are a few pointers—which are not 100% infallible!

By common sense

Does lettering on street signs or book spines read backward in the picture? If so, flop left to right—unless the signs happen to be in Arabic.

Is the man's jacket breast pocket on his right? Then it's wrong. If he's only wearing a T-shirt, then you are in trouble. Check the part in his hair. Most men part their hair on the left. Buttons help: Men button clothes left over right; women do it right over left, for some peculiar reason. You have to put yourself in the subject's place to figure that one out.

Steering wheels on cars are on the left (except in Great Britain), and they are mostly driven on the right-hand side of the road (except in scenes of accidents).

There must be other obvious signs, but let's get technical.

By emulsion

The negative gives you two clues. First, the shiny side should be toward you, the dull, emulsion side should be toward the paper, away from you. Second, if you are seeing the film the right way, you'll be able to read the trademark and the numbers in the margins of the film material itself. Your contact sheet will also show these markings legibly, assuming you have a contact sheet available to check your prints against. The same principle applies for **color prints** as for black and white.

If you're working with **color slides**, the shiny side of the slide should be toward you, the dull side with the emulsion on it away from you. Dullness is often hard to identify, but if you turn the transparency at a slight angle to the light, you can clearly see contourlike ridges on the edges of the color areas. They are caused by the different combinations of layers of emulsion. The side with the contours should face away from you.

By notches in sheet film

The first thing to check for is whether there is any kind of wording on the edge. If you can read it, then you are looking at it the right way around. The second thing to check for are the notches. **Sheet film** (anything 4″ x 5″ and up) has actual notches cut from the top left-hand corner. They are there for practical reasons: to help the photographer insert the film into the camera correctly, to help the lab technician print it correctly in the dark, and to distinguish one type of film from another by the patterning of the notches themselves. It doesn't matter whether the piece of film has been used as a vertical or a horizontal. You must turn it around until the notches appear at the top on the left-hand side. If you cannot achieve that goal, flop the picture, and it will work. Alas, you cannot depend on this 100%, because duplicate transparencies are often made emulsion side to emulsion side to

achieve optimal quality—and so the notches end up on the wrong side of the dupe. How can you tell? You can only guess and hope. You have a 50/50 chance of being right, which is pretty good odds, especially if you say the magic words ("To hell with it").

A vital point to remember about flopped pictures comes at the stage of production when the printer submits proofs of the pages prior to printing. These are called **blues** when they are printed in blue or **vandykes** when they are printed in brown (there is a color called vandyke brown after the Dutch painter Van Dyck) or **brownlines**, or by various other locally used names. It is very easy for the page assembler (the **stripper** or **compositor**) to flop the negative by accident and strip it in flopped left to right. Then, if a man's pocket turns out to be on the right side, which is wrong, mark the **cut** (old-fashioned term for "picture") with this sign ⟲ , which means *flop left to right*. (It also means *turn upside down*, but never mind, you will also write "Flop left to right" in words alongside, and it will be understood.)

Why and how do you crop pictures?

Cropping means working out how to alter the existing proportions of an original so that it will fit into a space of a different proportion on the printed page, probably smaller than the original. (How to get it to the right *size* is a question of "scaling," which we will cover shortly.) So, for instance, if your original is rectangular and you have a square hole to fill, you will have to determine which part or parts of the original rectangle you will sacrifice in order to produce the requisite square shape. In principle, that's all there is to it. In practice, however, how do you do it? Well, you do *not* physically cut up the original—ever. You mark on the edges where you wish it to be cropped,

using a blue **grease pencil** (made of wax, but everybody calls it a grease pencil). It rubs off easily by wiping with a tissue dipped in rubber-cement thinner. If a hunk of the grease pencil falls off and gets stuck to the face of the picture it will probably not show in the reproduction if the pencil is blue. If it is red, it will certainly be visible, because red, under the kind of light used for making halftone reproductions, turns black. Ordinary pencil doesn't write on the shiny emulsion of the print. A ball-point pen makes indentations, and the ink cannot be removed. Other inks tend to smudge—permanently, in the wrong places. Avoid writing on the back of the photographs. If you do, you run the danger of embossing the writing into the emulsion from behind.

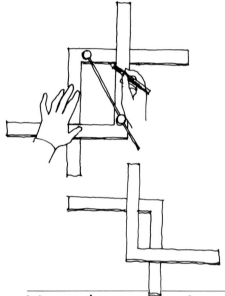

If the photo has no white border on which to make the marks, glue it to a piece of blank paper with double-faced sticky tape and make the marks on the paper. A few more technicalities on this minor aspect of how to inform the platemaker are discussed on page 127.

To help you determine how and where to crop, you can buy a device that is very impressive looking. It has two **L**-shaped templates attached to a bar on which they slide so that they can be fastened in the position you find correct. The device is particularly useful for reproportioning a group of pictures all to the same shape. You can also make your own device by cutting the two templates out of illustration board. By placing these **L**s on top of each other, you can move them in any direction and to any size, as far as the length of the arms will allow. Then you can determine which part of the photograph you wish to have reproduced and make your marks—only in the margin of the photograph—according to where the **L** has been placed.

How do you scale pictures to the size you want them to be?

Scaling is sometimes also called **sizing** —for obvious reasons. It is simply figuring out the dimensions of an original print to make it fit into a usually smaller space on the page. Normally, only one dimension of that space is known (the width, because we tend to conform pictures to the width of type columns). So the question is: If you know that a picture needs to be 3″ wide, how high will it be, assuming you use the original the way it is without cropping any of it? There are six techniques that can be used.

By arithmetic

Let's assume you have an 8″ x 10″ print that you must fit into an area 3″ wide. How do you find the height? The formula is simple:

$$\frac{\text{original width}}{\text{original height}} = \frac{\text{desired width}}{\text{desired height}}$$

$$\frac{8''}{10''} = \frac{3''}{X}$$

cross multiply: $8'' \times X = 3'' \times 10''$

$$\text{therefore } X = \frac{30''}{8''}$$

$$= 3.75''$$

This is slow, cumbersome, and daunting to the nonmathematically inclined.

Yes, the same thing can be done on a calculator, but the necessity to turn fractions of inches into decimals for the calculation and then back into fractions again makes it even more difficult. In the future, when we do all our measuring metrically, the struggle will be less difficult. But for now, there is another way out: We can do all our measurements and calculations in picas, as typography is measured. Unfortunately, here we come up against one of those anomalies in the publishing business: The typesetters work with picas, whereas the photo people (processors, platemakers) work in inches and dislike picas. Yet the page assemblers (the film strippers) have to marry the two units of measurement together, in spite of the fact that inches do not coordinate with picas very cleanly. No doubt this will all be resolved when everything is done on the computerized grids on cathode ray tubes, and when all our old-fashioned picas, points, inches, and even centimeters will be turned into units or bytes or what-not. Although these systems are being introduced in large operations, it will be some time before they trickle down to our humble level of endeavor.

By geometry

If you take your original and trace its rectangular shape on a sheet of paper, you can then work out how it will enlarge or diminish by a very simple process of draftsmanship. First, you need to draw a diagonal from one corner of the rectangle to the other, and extend it out into the space beyond.

You then have to extend one of the width lines of the original diagram, like this:

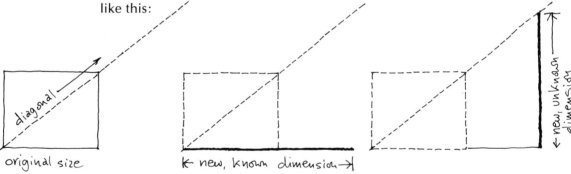

You then measure the desired dimension that you know (probably one that corresponds to your column width). Once you have defined that point, you can draw a line at right angles from it, to meet the diagonal. That will give you the vertical dimension of your new rectangle.

This is fairly time consuming; you have to be an accurate draftsperson, and it isn't really useful when you have a great many pictures to handle. It is a useful trick to remember, however, when you have to manipulate an image or two in some way.

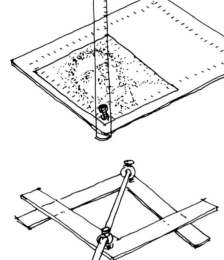

By a proportioning grid

This is a useful tool purchasable at art supply dealers. You position the corner of the photograph under the riveted corner of the machine; rotate the movable arm to the corner diagonally opposite—and the reduction or enlargement of that proportion can be read off anywhere the diagonal arm intersects the vertical and horizontal. These instructions sound dauntingly complicated, but are in fact child's play.

By a proportioning device

This is also an instrument available at art supply shops. It consists of two **L**-shaped transparent plastic angles attached to each other by a free-floating diagonal rod; one end is a pivoting device, the other has a sliding and fastening gimmick. The purpose of this device is to determine cropping as well as scaling simultaneously. It is easy, once you read the instructions that accompany the machine. The great advantage of its complicated looks is that it is a very impressive object lying on the desk. It is also fast and easy to use, however.

By a proportioning wheel

Often called an **engraver's scale**, it comes in two shapes: the straight version, reminiscent of an engineer's slide rule, or the same thing bent around into a circle. The slide-rule-shaped gadgets are somewhat archaic. The circular ones are the cheapest as well as the most widely used and most easily obtainable, because they are flat, light, compact, cheap, and efficient. The larger the diameter, the easier it is to read off the various scales, and the more accurate the result will be.

The two circles are marked off in inches. The inner one represents the original sizes; the outer one, the desired future sizes. You turn the inner circle

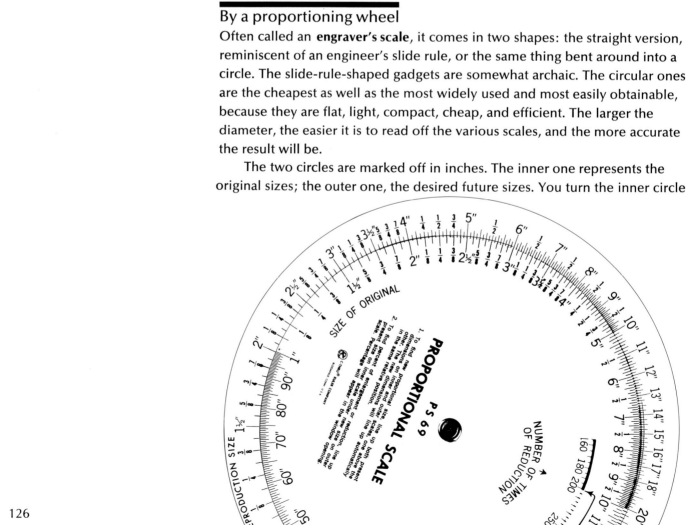

around until the original dimension aligns with the desired dimension. Then all other dimensions will be shown in proportion so that you can read off whatever you need. Again, in words it sounds complicated; in reality, given three minutes of practice, it is easy. The great advantage of the circular proportional scale is that it also has a window cut into it where you can read the enlargement or reduction percentage. So it automatically gives you the "focus" with no extra action. Example: If you place the 1" mark on the inner circle opposite the 1" mark on the outer wheel, the percentage will show 100. But if you put the 1" mark on the inner scale against the 2" mark on the outer scale, the percentage will show 200 (which is correct—after all you are blowing it up to twice the original size). That's all there is to it.

By using a calculator

If you can follow formulas with trigonometric functions and press magic buttons, you can somehow succeed in eliciting the needed answers. If you know how to do *that*, however, you are a National Asset and ought to be helping to balance the budget, or at the very least forecasting when the next comet is going to collide with Earth.

How do you inform the cameraman about what you want?

It is interesting for *you* to know the shape, size, and configuration of the picture on the upcoming page, but it does you no good unless you can instruct the cameraman who will be making the halftone film. And those instructions had better be clear, concise, and legible, or it will cost money and time for remakes. The **cameraman** or **platemaker** (working at the printer or in some cases as subcontractor to the printer) expects you to give those instructions in one of three different methods.

1. By attaching a tag to the picture giving a **focus** value. These focuses are expressed as a percentage that the cameraman transfers onto the machine that exposes the film. Those percentages correspond to the percent enlargement or reduction of the original that you desire: 100% is the same size, labeled as "SS" on the original; 50% equals half the size of the original; 200% is twice the size of the original or "twice up"; 75% is—what? Correct: three-quarters of the original. If you want to appear knowledgeable, talk "focus." If no cropping is to be done, all the cameraman needs is the desired focus and your result will be shrunk or swollen to the right percentage. But if you want to crop, then you have to show the cameraman where to do so.

2. By marking the required dimensions on the margins of the photo using blue grease pencil. (For more on this, see page 124.) One further caveat should be added to what you find there. Never draw instructions on overlays over the photo using pencil or ball-point pen. The emulsion will be furrowed by such hard instruments, and the ridges will show up in the reproduction as thin shadow lines or highlights.

3. By giving the cameraman a photocopy of the original made to the desired size and cropped to the desired shape. Such images are then

duplicated in film by the platemaker. This is the most expensive method, but it is ideal because it enables you to work out the result you want precisely. And you can be reasonably sure that the cameraman will follow instructions.

What will the picture look like when it is reduced?

It is hard to know, without having had some experience, whether the image will disappear and become illegible when it is made smaller, or whether it will hold its own. There are several methods of finding out.

Look at it through a reducing glass. This is obviously not a very accurate method, but it works in a rough kind of way, and a reducing glass costs about what a good magnifying glass does.

Project it in a projector. A variety of machines are available, all of varying design and capacities that affect the size of original art a machine's **copyboard** can accommodate and the degree or reduction or enlargement possible on it. Of course, if you would use such a projector only seldom, the investment in a **lucy** (as it is generally called) may not be amortized.

Have a reduction made on a photocopier. Many machines can reduce originals down to a set of standard focuses: 98%, 74%, and 65% on some machines; 95%, 75%, 62%, 50%, and 45% on others. You can combine focuses, ordering a reduction of a reduction, and come pretty close to what you imagine the final ought to look like. Naturally, electrostatic copiers don't give you very good reproductions of your pictures, so details may be lost—which defeats the purpose of the exercise.

Have a photostatic copy made. **Photostat** is the name for a negative/positive process using inexpensive materials, and the result is called a "stat" for short. New materials and processes have been invented that are slowly replacing stats, but the name lingers on. Depending on the kind of paper used, the photostat can be shot as a halftone or as a continuous tone, to your desired size. You then crop it according to your wishes. One shot (usually priced according to the paper size used) will set you back several dollars; if you have several originals that can be shot to the same focus, **gang them up** to fit in one larger shot. That way you get more for your money. The only problem: If some originals are very dark and others are very pale, the operator won't be able to adjust the exposure to improve on the originals but will need to shoot at an average.

Unless you supply Veloxes (defined on page 130) with the mechanicals, the printer will need to make a halftone anyway, so you could gamble and ask him to shoot them ahead of time and send you proofs (**salt proofs**—cheap prints that tend to disappear in time, or **warren** prints, which are similar) for your assessment and possible remake to a different size. Chances are you'll not need to reorder.

What is a halftone?

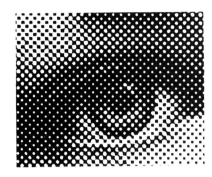

A photographic print shows a gradation of tones ranging from white to black in a continuous blending. This, alas, cannot be reproduced in printed media the same way. It must be turned into a printing plate whose results appear similar, but whose technology takes the limitations of the printing process into account. The limitation? That you can only print straight, solid black ink, and any "graying down" of that ink must be achieved by trickery.

By rephotographing the original photo through a mesh or screen, the original **continuous tones** of the image are broken into a pattern of tiny dots. The dots appear in a regular pattern, but within that regularity, one irregularity is possible: variation in the *size* of the dots. Where the dots are tiny, less ink is transferred to the paper, more paper shines through between the dots, and the result appears as a pale or light gray. Where there are no dots, it appears white—or as white as the paper will allow. Where the dots are big, the result looks dark gray. Where the dots touch each other, the result is, of course, black. That's practically all there is to it.

If you are using newsprint to print on, the surface of the paper is absorbent. If you use heavy, shiny, "coated" stock, the surface is hard, reflective, and nonabsorbent. The kind of paper you are using (as well as the printing technology itself) affects the choice of screen that is appropriate. Absorbent paper makes each dot a little bit fuzzy, so the dots need to be more widely spaced. Coated stock resists absorption of ink into its fibers, so each dot remains precise and clearly defined; even if they are smaller the dots will retain their precision. **Screens** are specified in number of lines per inch: 65 is coarsest, 150 is probably the finest you are likely to use. Newspapers use about an 85-line screen. Normal magazines usually use 120- or 133-line screens. The finer the screen, obviously, the closer to the original the result looks. The printer will tell you which screen should be used for your particular combination of stock, printing processes, ink type, pressrun, and so forth. That decision is out of your hands, but you ought to know about it.

You should also know that the shorthand for "halftone" in all communications in the trade is "HT." You can also write it as "½ T."

Who makes halftones?

The printer's cameraman or the reproduction service—or you, if you are a do-it-yourselfer.

The printer almost always has a **platemaker** on staff to make the printing plates. In offset, the actual plate that does the printing is made from a negative. That negative of a halftone is made by the platemaker to the size and cropping specified by the editor or designer. That negative is then **stripped in** on the page, along with negatives that have been made of type and all other elements supplied by the editor on the mechanical. Many editors, however, prefer making up the pages as paper paste-ups so they can control the entire process. In such cases, what you need instead of the negative film is a halftone positive print. Where does that print come from?

The printer can make a contact print from the negative, or you can bypass the printer altogether and order a **Velox** from a reproduction house. Velox is the name of the Kodak paper used. It is more expensive than the next option, but the results are brighter and more contrasting. As always, you get what you pay for.

You can also order a **PMT** (photomechanical transfer) instead of a Velox. This, too, is a Kodak product that is faster and considerably cheaper, although somewhat flatter in appearance. Obviously, all halftone prints must be made to the size you require for printing. You can save money by **ganging up** several shots and having them made into PMTs together—if they are all to the same focus, of course, and if they are more or less similar in their tonal values. The operator of the PMT machine can vary exposure a little to create darker or lighter results, but that won't do you any good if your ganged material varies all over the lot, because it can only be shot on an average setting.

Usually, the Velox or PMT is shot to the correct focus, but you receive it from the supplier uncropped. In other words, the entire original is reproduced, leaving the actual cropping up to the person who is going to be making the paste-up. This simply means that you will have to work extremely carefully to trim the excess parts of the picture accurately, cleanly, and straight. For that, you will need a steel-edged ruler, single-edged razor blade or cutting knife, and a good set-up to mark right angles accurately. There is a hidden problem with doing it yourself: It takes time.

You can make screened prints in your own darkroom by placing the halftone screen over the paper that you will be exposing. If you are confident enough of your own technique to have such a set-up, however, you certainly don't need generalized instructions here.

What are photomechanical variations?

The plain halftone reproduces the original photograph by turning it into an array of dots, which are usually circular, although some quality printing processes demand oval-shaped dots. It is not ordained that only dots be used, but they do yield the optimal reproduction of the original, so if you want detail, dots are what you need. If you are willing to give up detail for the sake of drama or startling special graphic effect, then any number of different screens exist that will yield spectacular results. Here are a few:

Clearly, these will cost more money—but if they are used spectacularly to get visibility, the investment will pay off in enlivening the product. Whatever you do, make the most of what you are doing by running it large enough to be discernible.

What is a linecut?

This is material that is black or white with no **middle tones**, like type or pen-and-ink drawings, none of which require halftone screens to reproduce them. The great advantage of line work on the page is that it has no hard outline like photographs do, so it lets in a little contrasting openness, informality, and air to the page.

Street scene in Seville drawn in dry brush and ink technique by Emil Weiss.

The Statue of Liberty through nine different screens: left to right: horizontal line, coarse mezzotint, steel engraving, linen, fine grain, coarse grain, fine mezzotint, circle line, steel etching. Courtesy of Carl Moreus.

What is a line conversion?

If you take a photograph (which has continuous tone in it) and reproduce it as though it were line art, terrible things happen to the picture: Everything that is darker gray than about 50% (black is said to be 100% and white is said to be 0%) congeals into solid black. Everything that is lighter than 50% disappears, drops out, turns white. Your details disappear. All sorts of blotches and textures appear, and the results can be tremendously startling and exciting.

Clearly, there are many variations on this technique, here described in its crudest, most elementary process. Discuss your idea with the supplier, be it reproduction house, photo lab, or printer, and ask to see samples. Then make your choice based on a show-and-tell example of the supplier's capabilities. Don't forget the capacity of your office copier to transform continuous tone into unexpected line art, especially if you make several generations of copies; in other words, if you copy a copy of a copy—even unto the fourth generation.

Normal halftone (133 line screen)   . . . line conversion   . . . electrostatic copier conversion

What are screens and shading tints?

They are patterns of dots or lines that can be added to line art, or the white paper of the page, to give it the appearance of gray tinting. The degree of darkness is defined in percentages, 100% being solid black and 0% being pure white. As in halftone screens, there is the equivalent designation of lines per inch, the coarser screens being suitable for reproduction on cheaper stock. The decorative quality of the dot structure may well be useful, however, to embellish artwork by tonalities, so a coarse screen need

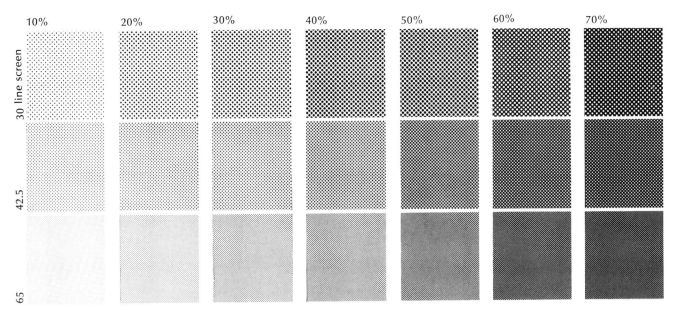

not be equated with a "cheap" result. It depends on how it is used. The screens can be added in two ways:

By the printer or compositor. The instructions are simple. On an overlay you draw the outline of the shape you wish to have appear tinted, using either black or red ink. This **keyline** in red ink will be understood by the printer as "not to be printed." If you use black ink, you had better mark the keyline clearly as "Guideline only. Do not print" or you will find your gray area neatly outlined with a black border. In either case you must specify what kind of screen is to be stripped into the area thus outlined (for example, "Strip in 20% screen, 110-line").

Many people still call these things **Bendays** after the inventor of an equivalent process used in letterpress printing, now nearly obsolescent.

By the do-it-yourself editor or designer. Far greater latitude is possible here because all sorts of screen patterns are available at art supply stores as material to be attached to artwork or a paste-up. The material comes in adhesive sheet form, which needs cutting out and burnishing down onto the artwork, or it comes in rub-off form, which is transferred to the artwork by rubbing with a tool.

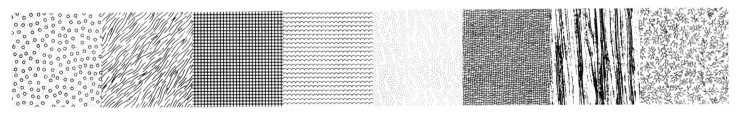

In printing, publishing, and editorial terminology,* anything that is not typographic is dubbed <u>art</u>, be it photograph, halftone, line art in pen and ink, technical illustrations, cartoons, and so on. Its merits as "art" may leave much to be desired, but "art" it remains. Even logos (such as department headings) that repeat from issue to issue or page to page are called **standing art**.

*See Patricia Barnes Mintz, *Dictionary of Graphic Arts Terms* (New York: Van Nostrand Reinhold, 1981).

9

Illustrations and their substitutes:

where to find them, how to use them

One of those conventional wisdoms that are accepted without question is that there is something inherently wrong with a page of plain type. Such thinking assumes the product will be dull and remain unread if it isn't gussied up and broken up with pictures, headlines, interruptions of various kinds, and flamboyant excesses of all sorts.

Well, that isn't necessarily so. It depends on the subject matter and the writing of the text. If the text is important and well expressed, flowing smoothly with points following in logical sequence, then visual enrichments are counterproductive because they call attention to themselves at the expense of the story. Furthermore, it is likely that your specialized, in-house, intimate-circulation publication has an audience to whom the subject matter doesn't need to be sold with exaggerated effects. They already care and need to know; they are already interested, and therefore they don't need to be "caught." They do need to be kept interested so they'll look forward to the next issue—but that is slightly different from beguiling them the first time around. Here the crucial factors of usefulness and accessibility of the information come into play. Once you've established that, you've created loyal readership.

On the other hand, it is undoubtedly true that the greater the variety of material on the page, the more hooks there are to pull casual or uninterested readers into paying attention. Each small item is another opportunity to persuade them to stop skimming and start reading. Such potential readers peck at the pages, apparently at random, looking for juicy gobbets here and there. Some tabloid presentations are specifically tailored to such an approach, breaking up stories into tiny subcomponents, each with its separate headline, picture, caption, box, sidebar, arrows, angled overlaps, shadows, and every possible unexpected combination of visual/verbal material intended to amaze, titillate, and intrigue—and they do it with enviable success. You can find racks full near any supermarket checkout counter.

At which extreme does the ideal lie: the dignified sophisticated publication that melds subtle visual effects with restrained typography, or the brash, spotty, but indisputably exciting one that entertains between short attention spans? The ideal, alas, doesn't exist. It all depends on the subject, audience, and purpose of the publication, and ultimately on the hunch of the editor. There is also no such thing as "good" or "best," there is only *effective*. Does the publication succeed? Does it come off? Even that is something one can seldom be sure about, but it is fun to keep trying to experiment with it and, maybe, help it along.

The material in this chapter is assembled with that purpose in mind. It lists and explains the basic options at the editor's disposal. The question of their appropriateness is left completely unanswered except for these three comments:

1. If the visual ingredients are poor, the temptation is to save the situation with fancy typography and so-called **design**. Resist that temptation. A worthy story can stand on its own and cosmetics will only cheapen it.

2. Elegance, dignity, and perceived value grow from the clever editorial judgment that uses the right **embellishment** in the appropriate place and nowhere else. If such embellishment grows organically out of the stories' own subject matter, the likelihood is that it will make editorial sense.

3. The purpose of publications is to disseminate information, and anything interposed between the message and the reader that disturbs the clarity and **speed of communication** should be questioned, no matter how amusing, original, or clever it may be. Your decision may well be to keep it in—fine!—but you must know what you are doing and, more importantly, why you are doing it. Only then can you weigh the cost/benefit ratio and come to a cogent decision.

Custom-made art vs. existing art

Budget. That's the operative word. If only you had the money and could afford to have photographs taken by some of those famous photographers whose evocative work gives so much depth and meaning to material in national magazines, or those artists whose skills meld thoughts and images into an irresistible transmission of ideas, or those imaginative illustrators who can take complex technical facts and transmogrify them into accessible, expository artwork, or those sagacious cartoonists who penetrate to the heart of the matter and expose its essence in a few deft, symbolic strokes, or those skilled typographic designers who turn a row of dry statistics into compelling charts, graphs, or easy-to-use tables—but you don't. Very few of us do. Most of us have to rely on existing artwork, easily applied graphic embellishments, and our own imagination. That is why there is just this short paragraph on the subject of **commissioned artwork** in this book.

If you have the good fortune of using such custom-made material, be sure that you use it with flair to get the most mileage out of it. Be doubly sure, however, that you aren't bamboozled by its visual excellence. You, as editor/designer, are the final arbiter of the sense and the content of the publication, and however good the art may be, if it is off the point, it is bad art. You must either change the art and force it to conform to the editorial point, or you must amend the editorial point to have it correspond to the art. Only when they work in tandem can you derive the best possible communication value from them.

Sources for photography: expensive, cheap, free

Anything you could possibly want a picture of has been photographed somewhere, sometime—but where is it to be found? There are huge collections of **stock photographs** and illustrations, both general and specialized. Many of them are listed in *Magazine Industry Market Place* under "Stock Photo Agencies." Many more, including international and government sources, can be found listed in the new *World Photography Sources*, both distributed by R. R. Bowker Company. The many agencies and departments of the United States government have extensive collections of material available at nominal expense (although not for implied endorsement of product or service). Check *Pictorial Resources in the Washington, D.C., Area* by Shirley R. Green, available from the Library of Congress. The library's own prints and photographs division has an enormous collection.

Individual photographers make their stock available as well. They are listed in the books mentioned above. In addition, an invaluable clearinghouse of information is Rohn Engh's computerized listing of professionals and semi-professionals working in the unlikeliest of places, itself in Osceola, WI 54020; telephone (715) 248-3800.

Then there are the various associations whose promotion departments exist to provide material. And don't forget the public relations departments of the big companies and the public information offices of service establishments. The list is awesome.

The real problem in finding pictures isn't their availability, it is your time. When you need a picture, you need it now. No, not now, yesterday. By then, it's a bit late to do the research, call for a batch of pictures on approval, and get angry at the mails for not delivering any faster. The secret is not at the picture end of things, but rather at the editing end: do not wait until the copy is finished, retyped, edited, and okayed by the CEO before starting on the chore of figuring out how to illustrate it all. Think pictures while you are writing the first draft, do your research, and call your sources right then and there.

Old engravings in the public domain

Before photography and halftone reproduction became available, all illustrations had to be engraved by hand: cut from wood or scratched or etched from metal. The pictures were made to appear as natural as possible through shading that was created by cross-hatching—yet they were all **linecuts**, in spite of the variety of techniques used. That is a most fortunate advantage for us because we can easily reproduce those illustrations as line work, and we can even reduce or enlarge them without spoiling them. It is unwise to attempt that with pictures that are halftones because the dots either become too tiny and disappear, or worse, combine into large blocks that make the image look muddy. Or, if you enlarge them, the dots become gross and overscaled.

To reproduce from existing material, you either cut up the original

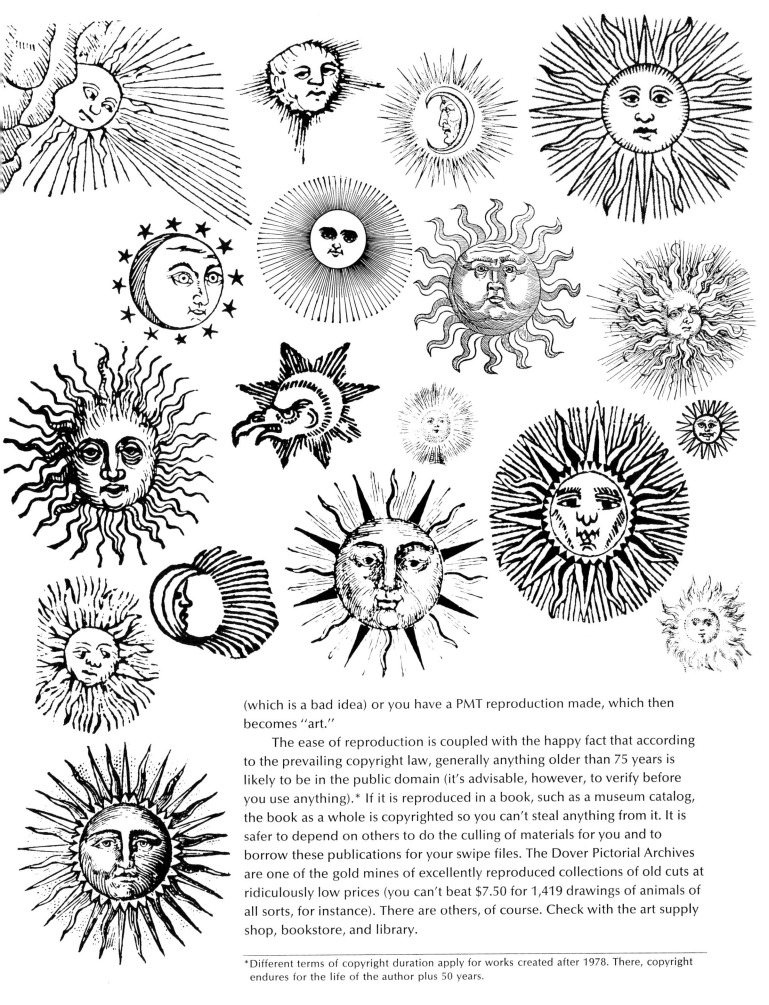

(which is a bad idea) or you have a PMT reproduction made, which then becomes "art."

The ease of reproduction is coupled with the happy fact that according to the prevailing copyright law, generally anything older than 75 years is likely to be in the public domain (it's advisable, however, to verify before you use anything).* If it is reproduced in a book, such as a museum catalog, the book as a whole is copyrighted so you can't steal anything from it. It is safer to depend on others to do the culling of materials for you and to borrow these publications for your swipe files. The Dover Pictorial Archives are one of the gold mines of excellently reproduced collections of old cuts at ridiculously low prices (you can't beat $7.50 for 1,419 drawings of animals of all sorts, for instance). There are others, of course. Check with the art supply shop, bookstore, and library.

---

*Different terms of copyright duration apply for works created after 1978. There, copyright endures for the life of the author plus 50 years.

Clip art: its uses and dangers

If old-fashioned woodcuts and steel engravings are stylistically inappropriate, an equivalent mass of more contemporary artwork is available from clip book services. There are many that offer ready-made illustrations in any style imaginable, organized by subject and category, that probably include anything you can possibly need or think of. They are available at art supply stores as well as by mail. Fresh material is constantly being added, and they all supply you with catalogs for the asking. Three leaders in this field are: Volk Art, Box 72L, Pleasantville, NJ 08232; Dynamic Graphics, Box 1901, Peoria, IL 61656; Graphic Products, 3601 Edison Place, Rolling Meadows, IL 60008.

One potential problem is the likelihood that you will see the art you are using being used somewhere else (and if you are the sort of person who would be embarrassed rather than amused by seeing someone else wear the same dress as you have on at a party, then you are in trouble). What to do? Don't run the art exactly the way you cut it out of the book, but disguise it in some way. Combine parts of one drawing with another. That's easy to do, and all you need are scissors and some glue. Or add tints or background to camouflage the original. It is not at all difficult, and it is fun to try.

Transfer art and the easy way to become an "illustrator"

The manufacturers of acetate lettering also produce a vast array of graphic symbols of all sorts, many of which are pictorial. Especially useful for **graph symbols** and **pictograms**, they can also be combined easily into custom-tailored solutions for your particular needs. With the most limited skill, you can produce remarkable results, if the ideas underlying the graphics make good editorial sense. And that's the key, isn't it? Well, interestingly enough, ideas often grow out of the graphics in front of you, even if you believe yourself to be thoroughly unimaginative in this area and find it difficult to dream up graphic ideas from scratch—and who doesn't? You can start your creative juices flowing by playing around with such readily available materials, and who knows what brilliance may be lurking just under that quiet surface? The investment is modest and the payoff can be impressive. It makes sense at least to give it a try.

Handwritten notes: art at the end of your arm

Hey! That's a great idea!

What an unexpected effect to see handwritten annotations in the margin—and what an attention getter! Especially if they are run in blue ink and in a handwriting that isn't too formal in character so that it appears genuine. The whole trick is to make the reader believe that they are privy to someone else's private commentaries.

The art is prepared as a simple overlay after the type has been put down on the mechanical; then it is stripped into the plate or left alone to run in a second color.

You don't have to restrict this trick to verbal annotations. Just as body language is a tongue distinct from regular speech, so there are all sorts of scribbled symbolisms that communicate: underscores or overscores; emphasis lines alongside the text; brackets; arrows leading from one element to another; formulas in the margins; exclamation points or question marks; arrows leading into the text; check marks; deletion marks; even blots. And a deliberate fingerprint or two may raise some eyebrows.

Rubber stamps and the danger of being funny

Here is a graphic material whose texture and informality give it a special effect of immediacy. You can have anything made into a rubber stamp, be it verbal or pictorial, or you can buy ready-made stamps at stationery stores. You can also find pictorial ones in those gift shops that smell of incense. Those that are not sickeningly sentimental are meant to be funny or outrageous, as are those you can send away for to such sources as the Visual Lunacy Society, Box 308, Great Falls, VA 22066.

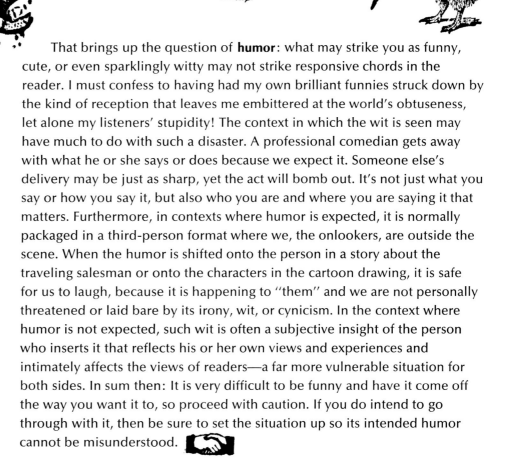

That brings up the question of **humor**: what may strike you as funny, cute, or even sparklingly witty may not strike responsive chords in the reader. I must confess to having had my own brilliant funnies struck down by the kind of reception that leaves me embittered at the world's obtuseness, let alone my listeners' stupidity! The context in which the wit is seen may have much to do with such a disaster. A professional comedian gets away with what he or she says or does because we expect it. Someone else's delivery may be just as sharp, yet the act will bomb out. It's not just what you say or how you say it, but also who you are and where you are saying it that matters. Furthermore, in contexts where humor is expected, it is normally packaged in a third-person format where we, the onlookers, are outside the scene. When the humor is shifted onto the person in a story about the traveling salesman or onto the characters in the cartoon drawing, it is safe for us to laugh, because it is happening to "them" and we are not personally threatened or laid bare by its irony, wit, or cynicism. In the context where humor is not expected, such wit is often a subjective insight of the person who inserts it that reflects his or her own views and experiences and intimately affects the views of readers—a far more vulnerable situation for both sides. In sum then: It is very difficult to be funny and have it come off the way you want it to, so proceed with caution. If you do intend to go through with it, then be sure to set the situation up so its intended humor cannot be misunderstood.

Rules and how to use them to advantage

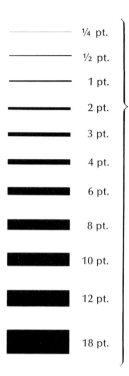

¼ pt.
½ pt.
1 pt.
2 pt.
3 pt.
4 pt.
6 pt.
8 pt.
10 pt.
12 pt.
18 pt.

Any typesetter or printer using any kind of machinery has the capacity to provide lines as part of the typesetting process. Those lines can be vertical or horizontal (although horizontally set rules are easier to accomplish on most equipment), and they can be virtually of any width. These "weights" are the most commonly available.

They can be set to any width up to the maximum the equipment allows (usually 43 picas). They are also available as tapes and on acetate sheets, either in rub-off or cut-out-and-adhere form. They can be known as **border slides**, although the most common term for them is rules. Plain ones are called plain rules, reasonably enough.

Double-lined ones are parallel rules

multiple ones, multiple rules

gray ones, shaded or tone rules

dashed ones, coupon rules

fancy ones, fancy rules

double lines, one fatter than the other, oxford rules

Dotted rules can be made by setting periods as though they were type, in which case they are called **leader** rules

Many rules come with ready-made box-corners rounded or embellished in some way

Tapered rules are these things

Due to their availability and cheapness, rules are a potential aid in making up pages for a number of reasons.

1. Rules are marvelously useful in organizing the geometry of your **space** by defining areas within that space. They define the edges of things, contain things, enclose things.

2. Rules separate disparate components of the page from each other, and good fences make good neighbors.

3. Rules can give emphasis or individuality to whatever it is that they isolate from its surroundings.

4. Rules have the invaluable capacity to add **color** by contrast. Imagine a page of gray type with a fat black rule on it, or a delicate hairline rule next to bold black type. The combinations are limitless, and they give life and sparkle.

5. Rules can be used to underscore or overscore individual words or phrases to give them emphasis.

6. Rules are decorative elements if used in conjunction with white space. Often, a hunk of empty space deliberately edged with a rule can be as interesting looking a counterpoint to the text as a picture, which might well pull the reader's attention away from the text.

7. Rules can be used as a patterning element for the page or series of pages, or even an entire issue, which in turn creates a subliminal character for the product that stays in the background, yet gives the whole package a flavor of its own. Think how ordinary *Time* magazine would appear without its geometrical patterning of the hairline rules on the pages, or *The New Yorker*'s wiggly lines used as rules alongside the text.

The use of rules—or better said, the overuse of rules— can be blamed on the vagaries of fashion. At times the use of rules is anathema, and then tastes swing to the opposite extreme and you can't see the type for the "furniture." But the functional capacity of rules to help both editor and reader is unaffected by fashion. That's why they can and should be used when they can be helpful, despite current trends in taste.

Boxes: what's in them for you?

A great deal, if you don't limit your thinking to the usual scrawny outline surrounding the block of text in the unimaginative way that they are usually handled. Too often, the people who are antibox on principle are right: boxes can, indeed, be just a crutch. Too often they are superficial, nonfunctional cliches; but they can be extremely useful if you understand why they are being used.

1. To separate one part of a story from the rest, to quarantine it away.

2. To make a part of the story less important by playing it down at the foot of the page, setting the type smaller, and deliberately bypassing it.

3. To make a part of the story more important by placing it near the top of the page, setting the type bigger, using active or exciting language, and adding attention-getting graphic embellishment.

4. To make the overall page look less gray by breaking it up into smaller units.

5. To make the story look less daunting and faster to read by breaking it up into smaller-looking, **self-contained components**.

6. To break out statistical or other self-contained **sidebar** matter that would be a stumbling block in the smooth reading of the main body of the story.

7. To increase the readership of a story by giving the editor the opportunity for yet another headline with which to intrigue readers (often

readers read the short sidebar first, because it is short) and entice them into tackling the main body of the article.

How can boxes be used more effectively? It is worth thinking that question through. How do we separate things from each other in the real, nonprinted, three-dimensional world?

1. You imprison the object inside a fenced area

If you are flying in an airplane looking down, what does that fence look like? A thin line; yet we know the line must have height, or else it wouldn't keep the cow penned up. In print, a box made of a single line of whatever thickness is the equivalent of a fence or wall seen from the air

Fence seen from above ----→ COW

2. You make the object hard to reach

Putting it on a level higher or lower than its surroundings separates it, as well as implies a change of emphasis. An illusion of a change can be created on the surface of the page by creating a false second plane with shadows. Even without legs, this table top appears to be "floating" above the floor because of the shadow it casts

From that airplane (with good binoculars) it would look like this | CAKE

3. You make the object impossible to reach by hiding it in a container.

Here is a shoebox in real life

This is what the shoebox looks like from the airplane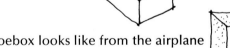

This is a shape that lends itself to two further illusions: by leaving out the walls that define the "inside," you create the illusion of a low pedestal on which an object has been placed  ----→ Outside walls shown

By leaving out the outside walls and showing only the inner ones, you seem to have carved a niche in the surrounding surface of the wall (the page) into which you insert the object  ----Inside walls shown

4. You make the object special by a symbolic setting. A jewel seems so much more valuable when laid gently in the middle of a velvet cushion than if tossed on the kitchen countertop

Translate that velvet cushion into flat printed terms, and what do you have? A tint block of some sort: in color, in a screen of black so it looks like gray, textured or smooth

5. You make it extra special by framing it and hanging it on the wall for everyone to admire.

    Each of these yields a different sort of box. Next time you are faced with breaking out some material and putting it in a box, remember these differences, for they may well be a clue as to how you should handle it graphically. Any such logical, functional, graphic symbolism will not only enhance the page and your product (by making it more interesting to look at), but it will improve the communication value of that product by utilizing symbolism to help to explain the thrust of the material.*

    They are very easy to make. At any good art supply store you can buy all sorts of ready-made sheets of different box frames printed on acetate. All you do is cut them out, trim them to size, and attach them to your layout. Here's a trick to help make the corners accurate: use graph paper printed in light

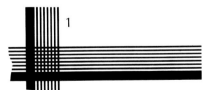

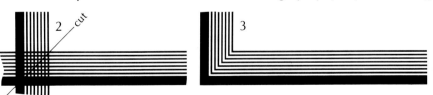

nonreproducing blue ink to ensure accuracy. Overlap the acetate rules at the corners of the box. With a razor blade or sharp X-Acto knife and a 45° triangle, cut through both layers simultaneously, and remove the excess. You'll be left with clean, precisely aligned corners. Take great care in your burnishing not to displace any of your butting joints. Are there any tips to make curved corners easier to accomplish? I wish there were!

---

*For much more on boxes, see *Graphic Idea Notebook*, by Jan V. White, p. 103 and following.

Here is a group of boxes just to start your imagination working.

Geometric

Sinuous

Pictorial

Naturalistic

Multiple rules

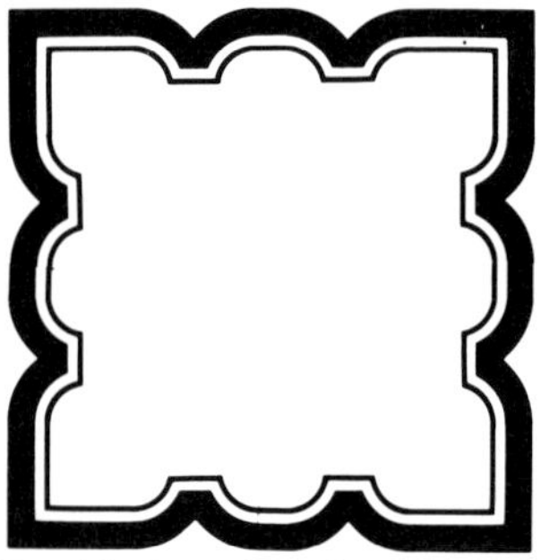

Double (scotch) rules

Fancy corners

Turned inward

Shadowed Frame

Encircling Frame

Identification in corner

Title as part of frame

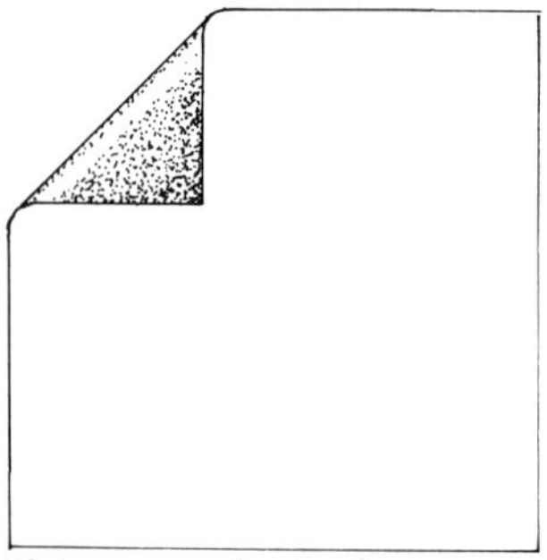

Flatness emphasized

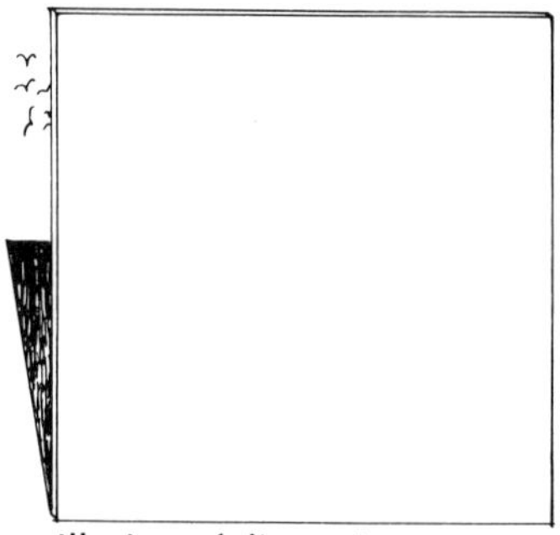

Illusion of dimension

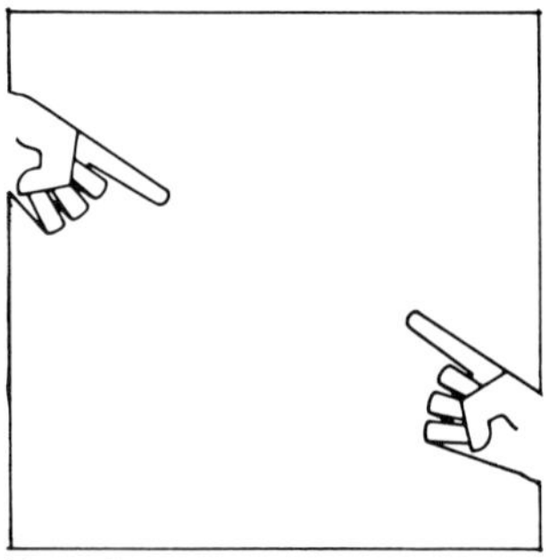

Negative space

Part of something else

Nonpictorial odds and ends as illustrations

Visual accents made of typographic elements add sparkle and color to the page. Large **initials**, available on acetate sheets of type, can be inserted if the text has been set to allow room for them. Measure the letter's width on the acetate sheet and specify the intended indention so that you can accommodate it on the mechanical. **Breakouts** or **callouts**—those provocative quotations set off in larger type, embellished in some way, and dropped into the text—interrupt the makeup of the page and act as verbal illustrations. Anything that interrupts a pattern attracts attention to itself.

Color variation in type, whether you actually have part of the text printed in red ink and the rest in black, or whether you use darker type for one area of the text and lighter type for another, can give life to a presentation, especially if the color differentiation reflects differences in meaning, such as questions and answers. The difference in color of type can be visualized as the different voices speaking to each other.

Headlines and subheads can be placed in unexpected relationships to the text and to each other so that they become expressive of their inner meaning or create an unusual pattern. Both will do some of the work that a traditional pictorial image might be expected to do, but they will do it in a more roundabout fashion.

You can set **text in shapes** whose outline is pictorial, or you can use a typeface whose character is such that it immediately communicates the mood or context that you wish to create.

Specific words that embody a thought can become the focal element on a page and can be set much larger than their surroundings to become the functional accent you need—at little cost other than the courage to do it.

■

You can make your own artwork by using symbolic materials evocative of the subject matter in hand, such as money: make rubbings of coins through a piece of tracing paper, or use photostatic reproductions, other than life size, of bits of printed currency. Small objects of any kind that you can make **xerographic prints** of—such as keys and pencils, flowers, you name it—are a-dime-apiece images that are easily reproducible in the publication. They can be reduced in size, of course, but their dramatic surprise value lies in their full size, if you have the space for them.

It is quite impossible to list all the means at the artful editor's and designer's disposal. It is far wiser for you to establish a **good ideas swipe file** in which to secrete tear sheets of astute devices that you come across. That file is an essential catalog for finding details, because we tend to remember ideas in a vague sort of way, yet when we actually need them, we can't quite remember what it was that made that idea so marvelously effective. If you know where to find them, you can overcome such infuriating frustrations.

Besides, the very act of establishing such a file and adding to it as you come across material worthy of remembering is a self-education process by which your awareness of visual/verbal technique grows and improves— so much so that your own creativity and confidence encourage you to begin inventing your own solutions without needing to depend on those seen elsewhere. At that point, you'll only need that file when your own muse is away on vacation.*

*For much more on this subject, see *Editing by Design,* by Jan V. White (New York: R. R. Bowker, 1982), p. 167 and following.

10

Making mechanicals:

a crash course for the uninitiated and disinclined

There are two basic approaches to preparing editorial material for printing. Which of them is to be followed depends on the size and complexity of your publication, the sophistication of the available equipment, and the printing processes to be used.

If yours is a complicated product printed in color in large quantities, a sequence of steps is followed that will allow you to respond to the need for speed, efficiency, and cost, using the capability of the technology at hand. The assembly of the various elements that go into making up pages is part of the printer's service (in the **stripping** department). Nowadays, there is a tremendous variety of ways to supply that material to the printer: All sorts of marvelous new devices are being invented, debugged, and coming on-line, up to and including computer-assisted full-page makeup with full-color capabilities, concentrated in individual terminals at each editor's desk. Such marvels of the electronic era are already with us and will, inevitably, grow in use. They will displace our current working arrangement, replacing it with better, faster, more productive techniques. But for now, if you are involved in this large-scale end of publication-making, the way you are likely to communicate with the printer or page maker is by means of **dummies.**

Dummies can vary in appearance and finish from detailed paste-ups showing every line of type in place and all the pictures as correctly sized and cropped photostatic reproductions pasted in position, all the way to **keyline** diagrams that merely indicate rectangular outlines of each element, coded to the material to be inserted. The choice depends on the preference of both editors and printers, as well as on what the contract calls for. There are, however, two characteristics that all dummies must have in common.

The first is accuracy: The stripping department ought not to have to make up your mind for you, nor ought it to be put in the position of having to interpret poorly worded instructions. Chances are that such interpretations will be wrong, and fixing them later will cost time and money.

The second is all-inclusiveness: There is no excuse for not supplying the printer with everything needed to make up a page in its entirety. Forgetting is amateurish, and submitting pages with holes in them marked "TK"* may make you feel delightfully "hold-the-presses" journalistic, but is probably self-indulgent.

---

*TK is short for TO KUM, deliberately misspelled so that printer knows not to print those words by mistake, and indicates that fresh material is to come at a later date.

If yours is a more modest product, basically one color, with comfortable lead time for production and a reasonable number of pages, then a far simpler procedure is followed. That procedure is the subject of this chapter.

Taking the fear out of mechanicals and where to get advice

Mechanicals are assemblies of the type and all the other visual elements to appear on the page, and they are presented to the printer to work from. They consist of **spreads**—facing pages—assembled to look precisely as you intend them to appear in the printed piece. You glue all the **line work** such as type, page numbers, ruled lines, line drawings, charts, tabular matter, and so on, onto sheets of stiff paper. (Yes, you must have a good idea of the layout before you start the gluing process!) Wherever pictures occur, you either glue in a **Velox** (see page 130) or, if the printer will be making the halftones for you, indicate where they are to go and how big they should be. The platemaker will photograph your mechanical as line art, and your pictures as halftones, and will then strip them together as negatives. The printing plates will then be made from those negatives.

When the mechanical is perfect and all-inclusive, it is said to be **camera-ready**. Mechanicals or **boards** are also sometimes called **keylines**— from the term used to describe the outlines of halftones to be stripped in.

Mechanicals also contain written instructions to the printer in the margin or on an overlay, and should be complete and perfect in every detail so that all the printer need do is what he is supposed to do: the printing.

Your most important source of information, advice, and help, as well as your ally, is the printer. A relationship of cooperation and trust is essential for comfortable production as well as finding the most cost-effective solutions to your particular set of problems. So it is wise to bring the printer in at the earliest possible stage, for he will be able to answer important questions that will affect your own working techniques. Basic things need to be asked: How does the printer prefer camera-ready copy to be presented? Should halftones be keyed to areas defined by outlines on the layout, or should you paste in black areas into which the halftones will be stripped? How does he prefer to schedule the work flow, on an **as ready** or **when can** basis (piecemeal as you can get it to him) or as a complete job? How should mechanicals and artwork be marked for efficient and convenient handling? When does he prefer to have the material delivered and what are the optimal schedules (and how much flexibility is built into them) to make the job as economical as possible? There's a lot more like that to determine. But you only know what to discuss with him after you have rooted through this chapter's worth of technicalities. So suspend the detailed worries about the printer for the time being, remembering only the principle that the printer is your friend, someone you will want to involve in the final decisions.

The tools and materials you cannot work without

If you must do it yourself, you must prepare yourself for the physical aspects of the work: the mental (planning, coordinating, scheduling, designing) part of the job is complicated enough without your having to struggle with the mechanics as well. So invest the necessary treasure in the tools you will need. They will help. No, that is an understatement: They won't just help—without them, you cannot do the work.

First and foremost, you must have quiet space to work in, and an uncluttered surface to work on. Assembling bits of paper from all over, keeping it all organized and clear, being able to see what you are doing (not just the page you are working on, but the other pages of the same issue), and keeping track of the glue and the pencils and the triangles can't be done on top of a mound of accumulated stuff. It needs S P A C E. Clear, uncluttered, broad, empty space. Ideally, you should have a full-sized table, at least 2'6" x 6', with a tackboard on the wall behind it to the same width, and ample, comfortable light. Whether that table is of sitting or stand-up height is a matter of personal preference. Standing allows you to walk around more easily, fostering a broader, looser field of action that, in turn, encourages freer layout. Sitting in one position tends to concentrate your vision on the details at the expense of the broader picture. An easel-type desk, specifically made for artists to sit at, is not ideal because you need to accommodate three separate functions with your table top: storage as well as drawing and pasting. An angled top allows only two, the drawing and pasting. Anything that isn't tacked down slides off, which is irritating. The ideal arrangement is to have a drafting board placed at an angle atop a flat desk. You need a separate side table on which to do the gluing and keep your coffee cup and ashtray. (If anything can spill on the mechanicals, it will.) And lastly, you must have easy access to a sink to wash your hands in. Nothing—*nothing*—is as important as cleanliness in making mechanicals. Every little spot, smudge, particle of soot, broken pencil tip, and foul fingerprint will pick up in the reproduction process. You strive for perfection—and dirt is even more shameful on mechanicals than it is in the laundry, in spite of what detergent commercials may want you to believe!

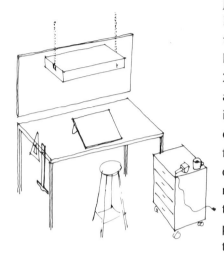

A list of essential tools

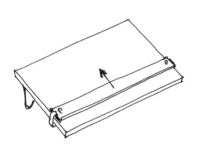

☐ Drawing board, big enough but not bigger than necessary to accommodate your paper size.

☐ T-square; the most essential tool to ensure that your product will be square and true. You can buy it separately or as a sliding bar attached to the drawing board. It is easier to use if it is attached, and just by being there it reminds you of the need to use it.

☐ 30°/60° triangle with the vertical side tall enough to span the height of your page.

☐ Steel ruler 24" long, marked in inches and picas.

☐ Scissors with blades at least 8" long, called editor's shears.

☐ X-acto knife with lots of #11 blades. Always use sharp blades, replacing ones that are blunt or whose tips have broken off. If you prefer, you can use single-edged razor blades.

☐ Cutting base. This is a sheet of gray or green plastic about ⅛" thick with grid lines imprinted on it. Made of a new material that makes cutting small pieces of paper a joy, it also protects your desk top.

□ Mechanical pens (tubular points) of two or three widths, with the appropriate india ink dispenser to fill them with.

□ Hard pencil (2H or harder), or a lead holder into which leads are inserted.

□ Nonrepro-blue pencil or fine ball-point pen.

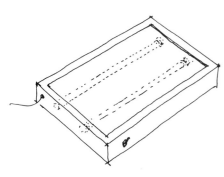

□ Rubber cement for gluing, a dispenser with a brush for applying it, a can of thinner or solvent to thin it with, and a pick-up to remove it with. But you might prefer a larger initial investment that will make for cheaper, easier, and more flexible use later: a waxer. Large table-top waxers are available, but you need only invest in a hand-held model. It has a heating element that melts specially formulated paraffin wax and allows it to be rolled smoothly and evenly onto the paper. The advantage of the wax is that it is cleaner and easier to work with in that it allows for moving the pieces of paper around until you are finally satisfied with their placement and burnish them down permanently.

□ A type gauge divided into a series of point size measurements—commonly showing 6-point, 7-point, 8-point, 9-point, 10-point, 11-point, and 12-point measurements.

□ Burnisher for burnishing down waxed type, rub-off lettering, etc.

□ Enlarging wheel or other device for scaling pictures.

A list of essential materials

□ Paper on which to make mechanicals. Any smooth white stock is acceptable, although it is wise to use a fairly heavy stock for ease of handling. If the final mechanical will require lines to be drawn on it, then the surface must be hard and smooth to allow that to be done without danger of lines spreading or picking up surface fuzz. Lightweight **illustration board** with a smooth or **hot-pressed** surface is specifically made for this purpose.

If your publication will have the same column format from issue to issue, have the printer run off a stack of **dummy sheets** showing the outlines of columns and the trim edges of the pages in nonreproducing blue ink. That will facilitate your work by giving you accurate positioning guidelines for type and photos without your having to measure and draw the lines every time. Nonrepro blue is a color that is not picked up in the photographic process when the mechanicals are turned into film.

An alternate technique at your disposal is based on using a **light table**. The paper you paste down on must be translucent; then you take a sheet of acetate on which your grid has been drawn and place the paper over it. The light from the light table shines through from below and gives you the requisite guidelines. Obviously, you don't use the drawing board in this case, but you have to solve the problem of accurate squaring up without a T-square by using the acetate grid.

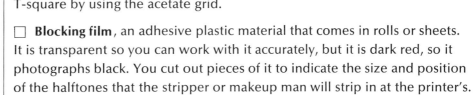

□ **Blocking film**, an adhesive plastic material that comes in rolls or sheets. It is transparent so you can work with it accurately, but it is dark red, so it photographs black. You cut out pieces of it to indicate the size and position of the halftones that the stripper or makeup man will strip in at the printer's.

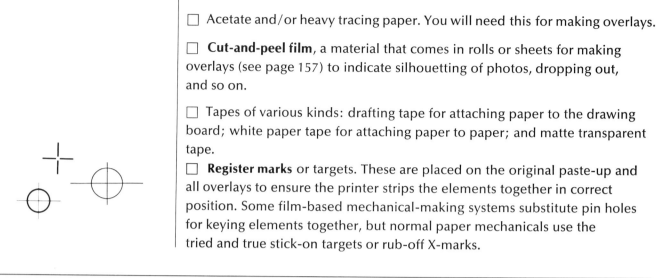

☐ Acetate and/or heavy tracing paper. You will need this for making overlays.

☐ **Cut-and-peel film**, a material that comes in rolls or sheets for making overlays (see page 157) to indicate silhouetting of photos, dropping out, and so on.

☐ Tapes of various kinds: drafting tape for attaching paper to the drawing board; white paper tape for attaching paper to paper; and matte transparent tape.

☐ **Register marks** or targets. These are placed on the original paste-up and all overlays to ensure the printer strips the elements together in correct position. Some film-based mechanical-making systems substitute pin holes for keying elements together, but normal paper mechanicals use the tried and true stick-on targets or rub-off X-marks.

The need to keep clean

Cleanliness has already been mentioned as far as your hands are concerned. It cannot be stressed too strongly that your tools must also be kept immaculate. The glue you use cannot help but transfer onto the triangle and T-square, so wash them regularly. Be very careful with ink lines, especially when they are made with a soft-tip pen. That ink leaves residue on the edge of the triangle and will smudge on your paper. The second major source of dirt disasters is the type itself. If your type has been set by photocomposition and your proofs are photographic printouts, then you have no problem. But with all other systems, watch out: Type proofed on a proofing press will have ink that must dry thoroughly before it is safe to touch (which sounds simple, but who ever has time for anything in real life?). Strike-on or cold-type proofs, including those made by typewriters using carbon ribbon, are nearly as dangerous to touch. You must either handle them with great care or protect them from smudging by spraying them with a light coat of clear acrylic (matte finish) spray. When it has hardened, you can relax a bit.

Working in miniature

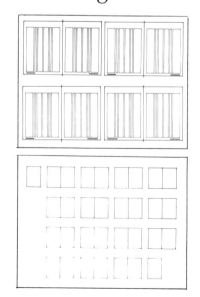

Before cutting galleries and starting the rough dummy, sketch out on paper what you intend to do. You probably have a pretty good idea of which story should go where as far as the pages are concerned (important ones on top, fillers down below; pictorial ones sandwiched between textual ones, etc.). You also probably use a **planning sheet** to sketch out each issue anyway if your product has more than eight pages.*

Now comes the time to crystallize those scribbles and vague ideas into some more precise form. For that purpose, you should have your dummy sheet reduced to miniature size and run off in a stack of several hundred copies, so you can waste them if necessary; a good workable size is eight pages (four spreads) on an 8½" x 11" piece of paper turned sideways.

*A planning sheet is an 8½" x 11" piece of paper with rectangles representing each of the 32 pages that are to be printed. Each rectangle is just large enough for you to be able to scribble the name of the story in it.

That is small enough to prevent you from getting lost in detail, yet large enough to force you to think in realistic proportions.

When you have sketched out your space allocations in miniature, you can then start to take the next step.

Making a rough dummy

Before you do a final mechanical, it is advisable to do a rough to make sure that everything will fit the way you intend it to. The camera-ready material you will be using to make your final mechanicals ought not to be handled too often in order to keep it in pristine condition. So you experiment with photocopies. At this stage, you must determine several elements.

Proper spacing. The paste-up stage is not the time to be deciding what looks best. You should know beforehand what your standard spacing between the elements is supposed to be. The dummy allows you to check whether it is going to work according to Hoyle.

Position of rules. Ink lines should be drawn first, before anything else is glued onto the page, because ink doesn't take on the slick surface over rubber cement or wax. Unless great care is taken in the gluing and all excess is carefully removed, you should put down your ink rules on a perfectly clear, clean surface. The rough dummy allows you to plan the placement of all the major elements on the page, including rules, so you can then copy them onto the mechanical.

Handling pictures and captions. Make up your mind about how big they will be, where they will be placed, how much space there is to be left between them and their surroundings, and so on.

Handling the space in the display areas. The space within which the headline is placed should be standardized. There is a comfortable, optimal proportion that should be worked out and, once determined, carefully repeated. Unfortunately, this doesn't always happen because we all tend to take the easy way out: We place the text on the page and allow the space around the headline to take up the slack—be it a bit too tight, or much too loose. That is letting the tail wag the dog: The catchy headline in the display area (those words you spent so much effort in writing) is what ought to take pride of place. The text is what you should doctor to fit by cutting or adding a few lines. Compromising on proper spacing around the headline destroys the overall look of the product—and the rough dummy allows you to find out what needs to be done before you start the final.

Practical tips on making mechanicals

It isn't all that difficult. You have to work cleanly, cut accurately, draw carefully, measure precisely, place elements on the page consistently—but you know all that already. What you may not recognize, though, is the need to give yourself enough time to do it properly.

This is absolutely crucial to your success. You cannot hurry a hand-crafted process and cut corners and squeeze it in as a last-minute rush and hope to

151

have it come out perfect, the way you want it to be. Especially if you are not yet skilled at doing it! Unfortunately, since the mechanical is the last major stage in the production of the printed piece before printing, its schedule gets squeezed between the immovable publication date and the inevitable delays in work that have preceded the final assembly. So you rush it through, work until midnight, exhausted, when your minor motor skills suffer. You accept the compromises ("nobody will notice"), spill coffee in your nervous haste— no wonder you dread the mechanical stage. Self-discipline, adhering to the schedule before you get to this segment of the job, is the secret to bringing the monster under control.

In the list of tips that follows, the assumption has been made that the mechanicals you are preparing are for use in offset lithography, which is the most commonly used method of printing short-run publications. Clearly, preparation of material for in-house reproduction processes must be done according to the requirements of the reproduction machinery available there.

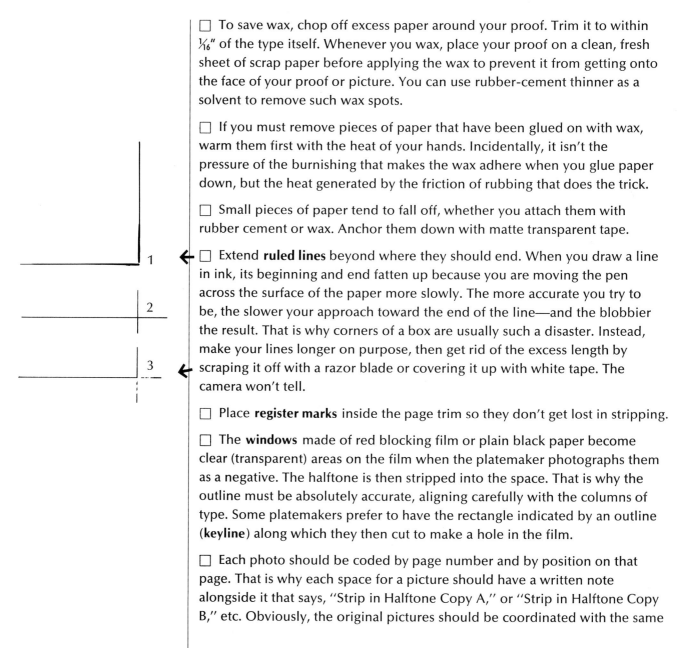

☐ To save wax, chop off excess paper around your proof. Trim it to within ¹⁄₁₆" of the type itself. Whenever you wax, place your proof on a clean, fresh sheet of scrap paper before applying the wax to prevent it from getting onto the face of your proof or picture. You can use rubber-cement thinner as a solvent to remove such wax spots.

☐ If you must remove pieces of paper that have been glued on with wax, warm them first with the heat of your hands. Incidentally, it isn't the pressure of the burnishing that makes the wax adhere when you glue paper down, but the heat generated by the friction of rubbing that does the trick.

☐ Small pieces of paper tend to fall off, whether you attach them with rubber cement or wax. Anchor them down with matte transparent tape.

☐ Extend **ruled lines** beyond where they should end. When you draw a line in ink, its beginning and end fatten up because you are moving the pen across the surface of the paper more slowly. The more accurate you try to be, the slower your approach toward the end of the line—and the blobbier the result. That is why corners of a box are usually such a disaster. Instead, make your lines longer on purpose, then get rid of the excess length by scraping it off with a razor blade or covering it up with white tape. The camera won't tell.

☐ Place **register marks** inside the page trim so they don't get lost in stripping.

☐ The **windows** made of red blocking film or plain black paper become clear (transparent) areas on the film when the platemaker photographs them as a negative. The halftone is then stripped into the space. That is why the outline must be absolutely accurate, aligning carefully with the columns of type. Some platemakers prefer to have the rectangle indicated by an outline (**keyline**) along which they then cut to make a hole in the film.

☐ Each photo should be coded by page number and by position on that page. That is why each space for a picture should have a written note alongside it that says, "Strip in Halftone Copy A," or "Strip in Halftone Copy B," etc. Obviously, the original pictures should be coordinated with the same

coding system and bear a notation (such as "Page 3, Copy A," or "Page 3, Copy B") on the tab that shows the focus.

☐ Check periodically the tightness of your T-square screws or the roller mechanism of the vertically sliding bar on your drawing board. They can loosen up and throw all your accurate construction askew.

☐ Copy the lines printed on your dummy sheet (delineating columns, page trim, position of page number, etc.) onto a sheet of clear acetate. You'll have to use specially prepared **wet media acetate** that will accept india ink lines. You can use it as an overlay on the mechanical to check your horizontal and vertical alignment for accuracy.

☐ The mechanical is for all intents and purposes the final copy. You may get a proof of some sort, but that ought not to be considered an opportunity for making changes. So read, proofread, double-check the mechanical and avoid making **changes in page**, i.e., after **page proofs** have arrived from the printer.

☐ Protect every mechanical against damage and dirt by putting on a **flap**. This is simply an overlay of translucent tracing paper on which you can write instructions to the printer. Its very existence helps to protect the mechanical from damage, dirt, stain, and rubbing off of small bits of paper stuck on it, and, worst of all, fingerprints. A hidden advantage of the flap: It is the *only* place the boss ought to be allowed to make notes. Incidentally, you should never write on the flap with a ball-point pen. It makes indentations in the soft surface of the mechanical beneath that can show up as shadows. Instead, use a soft pencil. Mechanicals produced by professional mechanical artists are always double-flapped: once with a transparent sheet, as described, and then with a second layer of brown kraft or equivalent strong stock that acts as a protective cover.

☐ Identify each mechanical by name, issue, page number, and date, and include boxes for the appropriate initials. The best place for such information is the lower right-hand corner. You can then **code** your halftones with the same numbering system and label each picture with an "A," "B," "C," etc., to identify its position on the page.

11

How to use color effectively

(and stay within budget)

Color can add richness, beauty, excitement, decorativeness, and personality to the product. It can add clarity to charts and diagrams. It can add believability to the images of objects (because the real world is in color rather than a black-and-white abstraction). But it costs more to produce a publication with color because of the technology, the extra steps, the original materials, and the printing techniques involved. Therefore, it must be used with great care in order to get the biggest effect from the investment.

Color, however, must never be seen as a trick to make a bad product better. All color can do is to make that bad product more colorful. It is, therefore, essential to avoid using it just in order to make the product look richer, or because there is money in the budget for it, or because the competition is doing it. Instead, it has to be used *right*.

The definition of *rightness* in this context is extraordinarily simple: color is used right if it helps to get the message across to the reader, if it clarifies the story, if it improves communication value, and, yes, if it enriches the product as an object (so long as that enrichment doesn't get in the way of the product's main purpose, which is *journalism*).

You can narrow down segments of that definition to reasons such as these.

☐ It is logical to use color as background tint to help organize small elements into big ones.

☐ It makes sense to use color as a decorative element to improve the look of the overall product in large areas, such as over a whole section or sequence of pages.

☐ It is obviously useful to utilize color to emphasize specific, small-size elements, to which you wish to attract attention.

☐ Color is legitimately used to separate one set of things from another on the same spread.

☐ Color can also be justifiably used to create continuity in a series of otherwise unlike units.

To follow up in much more detail about the editorial use of color in specific situations, please see *Editing by Design*, page 226 and following. For some thought on color in logos, see page 24 in this book; the subject of colored paper is discussed on page 165.

Does the purpose for which color is used affect the choice of color?

Indeed, it does. There are four fundamentally different functions that color performs in a publication, and each demands a different understanding and approach.

1. Color as **background** tint. If it is to be background, it must be subservient to the material printed on it. Therefore, you need to make the color quiet, pale, and restrained, so it doesn't demand more than the subliminal consciousness that the area is subtly different from its surroundings.

2. Color as **decoration**. Here, color is part of the foreground, and can therefore be more powerful, stronger, and more deliberately visible. However, it ought to be controlled sufficiently to keep it within the bounds of character appropriate to the publication.

3. Color as **articulator** of detail. By definition, details are small. It is therefore appropriate to pick a hue that is bright, cheerful, attractive.

4. Color as a tool for **emphasis**. This is where most care must be taken, for a rather unexpected reason: the lack of contrast between paper and the color printed on it. Black is the strongest contrast because black is *dark* and white paper is *light*. Red ink—however bright it may be—is much less dark and therefore its distinction against white paper is much weaker than that of black ink. If you want to achieve emphasis (i.e., strong visibility), you have to do one of two things: choose either colors that are both colorful and dark to give you that essential contrast, or enlarge the area to be seen in color so the amount of color used compensates for the decreased level of contrast.

What is the difference between process color and second colors?

Four-color process is the technique used to print pictures in full, natural colors. The original picture is photographically or electronically **separated** into four hues: yellow, red, blue, and black. Each of those colors is made into a halftone printing plate that, when superimposed one on top of the other, result in an illusion of the natural colors. Thus, printing presses must have four separate rollers, each bearing the requisite ink for printing those four colors. The four ink colors are standardized, and by themselves are not very beautiful hues. The red (magenta) is an aggressive pink; the yellow is rather crude; the blue (called cyan) is a greenish sky-blue; and the black isn't even a good black, but a pale, wan kind of black.

Second colors are much more interesting: they can be any color you want because they are **matched**. There are standard hues (often demanded by advertisers and called AAAA Colors, and they look bright and crude). And there is the broad range of printing ink recipes that can be specified to produce the colors in the PMS or Pantone Matching System color swatch books (a widely available and easily followed means of communication available at the art supply shop or from the printer). You can even get the printer to match the color of your eyes, though supplying a swatch might be somewhat painful!

Two-color presses are smaller, simpler, and therefore less expensive to run than process color presses, since they need merely two cylinders to carry the inks instead of four. But, as in all printing, the simple difference between process color and matched color isn't quite as simple as we have described it. If you are using a process color press, you cannot also use matched colors (unless that press has a **fifth cylinder** or **unit** on which such an extra ink can be run, obviously at added expense). So you face the problem of what to do if one signature or form of the publication is run on process equipment and the rest is run on two-color equipment, yet you simply have to have the same matched color throughout because all your charts have a special background color. It is possible to come pretty close to any "second" color by superimposing tints of the process colors one on top of the other. For instance, you can specify the exact process color equivalents for a large proportion of the PMS Second Color palette from a guidebook. The disadvantage is that screens of color tend to be rather expensive when you add the cost of the artwork, the making of the film, and the stripping charges. In a nutshell, then: four-color process can give you any color you want, if you are prepared to pay for it. Second color can do the same thing much more cheaply, but there is another difference too. Four-color process can give you any color you want anywhere you want it, even on the same page. Second color is restricted to that single color of ink. (The one possible variation is to use tints in a second color in combination with tints of black. There are always those two colors that you can mix together in the form of tints to give you exciting, subtle combinations.)

To save money, it is possible to use the four-color-process inks as though they were simple second colors—just by themselves rather than in superimposed proportions or screens. The red is a most unsatisfactory hue, whether used solid (100%) or screened down to a percentage. Pink it looks, and pink it will always remain—unless you superimpose it on a screen of black, in which case it turns to a darker pink. The yellow is a useful color used solid, but it becomes invisible when screened down. The blue is an excellent color that can also be enriched by a light screen of black. Unfortunately, used pure, these three hues are rather unattractive, and you don't get much praise for using them, because every publication uses them and so they are commonplace.

To get more for your money in second color, it may well be possible to **split the fountain**: the roller picks up ink from a trough along its entire length and transfers it to the four-, or eight-, or 16-page sheets of paper as they pass through the press. It is possible to put a dam in that trough so that you can have green ink on one side of the barrier and purple on the other. As a result, half the pages (those in the green rows) can have green; the other half, purple. The paper size, as well as **butting bleeds** in color, may be troublesome restrictions; but the printer may well know of a few other tricks available for your use. Solicit his help and be aware of the way the pages fall on the form, because you don't want to have a purple page opposite a green one—if you can avoid it.

What colors should you use?

Every color has three characteristics: hue, value, and chroma. **Hue** is the kind of color it is (its redness, blueness, greenness). **Value** is the degree of darkness or lightness that it has (its equivalent on a gray scale going from very light to black). **Chroma** is the degree of brightness or dullness that it has.

We tend to pick out a color because we like its hue, but you must remember that even more important than its hue is its value: if it is too dark, you will not be able to read the type that is surprinted on it. If it is too light, you will not be able to drop the type out in white and have it be legible. The midrange is ideal. To help you visualize colors, many ink manufacturers' sample swatch books show black surprint and white drop-out from each color. Others accompany the swatch book with an acetate overlay that has the black-and-white type imprinted on it, and you look at the color under the overlay in order to check the relationships.

How much color should you use?

Enough to make it noticeable, and thus worth the effort and expense. What you need to achieve visibility depends on the context, surroundings, and hue. If it is a brilliant color with strong chroma, and if it will be seen in a sea of white space, then a tiny dot is all that is necessary. If it is a dull brown, dark enough to be nearly black, then its colorfulness is hardly noticeable unless it is run in a large swath or as a tint over the whole page. The principle is simple, though: if it's worth doing, it's worth doing with gusto.

Flat color or spot color

Color can be used solid or as a screen or tint. It is usually run in combination with a black subject, such as a drawing or table. If so, then the black plate, probably carrying the information, is the **key plate**, and the color is prepared as an overlay related to it.

The overlay can be made of paper (tracing paper that can be seen through and drawn upon easily in ink to make keyline outlines) or cut-and-peel amber or red film (see page 150). The overlay must also carry the specifications for color and screen percentages, if any. The procedure for making mechanicals when you use colors superimposed on top of each other is identical, whether you will be using process colors or matched inks: you just make as many overlays as you have colors.

The difference between pictures with color tint and duotones

Covering a plain black-and-white halftone with a **tint of color** is a simple and cheap variant on the expected black-and-white photograph. Unfortunately, it dulls down the picture because the color fills in and darkens the photo's highlights, robbing them of the contrast that creates a sparkling image. If the color you use is light enough, then you can get away with it. If it is a dark color, however, it is wise to make it paler by screening it to a low percentage of the solid. Unfortunately, that tends to rob it of its colorfulness.

A **duotone** is made from a black-and-white original just like the tinted photo, but in the duotone, two halftone plates are made, one of which is run in black and the other surprinted over it in color. That way, the highlights don't fill in and a very interesting third color is achieved overall. By overexposing or underexposing one or the other of the plates, the proportions of the two colors can be manipulated so that the resulting image can be made to be more or less colorful: brighter or duller, browner or blacker (assuming you start out with a brown and black ink).

The duotone is considerably more expensive than the halftone with the tint on top, but much less expensive than full four-color process, and, of course, you don't need to have an original in color.

It is possible to make **triotones**—using the duotone principle in three colors—or to print a duotone in two colors atop a screen of a third color. Furthermore, it is also possible to take a black-and-white photograph and pretend it is a colorful subject and separate it as though it were full-color process, resulting in the richest printed effect. And there is such a thing as **double-dot printing**, where the duotone is made of two black plates (one perhaps a slightly tinted black that prints a little brownish, a little bluish, or a little grayish) that, when combined, give a velvety richness to the pictures. There is nothing esoteric about these techniques; all you need is money. (Warning: Avoid printing **halftones in color**; they look washed out unless you happen to be using a color that is appropriate to the subject matter, like brown that symbolizes age.)

Running type in color

You should do this only if the color is strong enough to be legible—in other words, if there is enough contrast between the whiteness of the paper and the darkness of the color. Furthermore, it is also wise to set the words in a type size and weight that will give ample area for ink: make it bigger and bolder. That is the same principle you need to remember when you drop out type in white from a background. By making it bigger and bolder you compensate for the reduced legibility of reversed type.

How color separations are made

Turning original art into plates for process color printing is a highly specialized technique. There are three common ways.

1. **Conventional** separations. The original artwork, photograph, or transparency is placed in a process color camera, which makes four separate exposures in the four subtractive primary colors: magenta (often called "process red"), cyan (often called "process blue"), yellow, and black. These negatives are continuous-tone (i.e., not screened) negatives and can be modified to some degree to correct or change the colors. When they are

ready, they are converted to screened negatives or positives from which the plates are made.

2. **Direct-screen** separations. This is a faster technique that skips the conversion step from continuous-tone negatives to screened negatives, thus making color correction more difficult. Other than that, the process is similar to the conventional separation process in that the four halftone negatives are used to make a proof, or are converted into positives from which proofs are made. When the film is corrected, it is used for exposing the actual printing plate.

3. **Color-scanner** separations. The scanner is an automated electronic machine in which the original transparency is placed on a drum and a light-sensing stylus travels over it; by means of a computer it activates another stylus that exposes the screened film separations. Since it is a very fast procedure, it is the least expensive. Its quality depends on the sophistication of the equipment, however (for instance, with or without laser?), as well as the skill of the machine's operator.

Proofs to check what you'll be getting

Three methods of proofing are commonly employed:

1. **Color keys**. This 3-M system is the most economical. It consists of sheets of acetate superimposed one upon the other; each has been chemically treated with a light-sensitized pigment (such as the four process colors) and is then exposed and developed like any photographic material, yielding a color image on translucent plastic. Placing one sheet atop the next gives you a good idea of what the printed effect is likely to be. When four sheets are superimposed, however, a grayish cast is created by the layers of the acetate itself and is bound to alter the accuracy of the color. Accuracy, therefore, cannot be expected from color keys, but they are a most useful guide, especially for checking stripping of tints in colors.

2. **Cromalins**. Made from positive film, the cromalin consists of a sheet of paper to which a thin sheet of photosensitive film has been applied whose image becomes visible when a powder of the appropriate color is spread on it. A second exposure is made for the second color, a third for the next and so on, until the full series has been built up. The sandwich is then topped off by a protective layer of plastic. It is an accurate preview of the final product. (Watch out for the jargon: you have a set of separations "cromed," i.e., made into cromalins. Don't confuse the verb "cromed" with the noun **chrome**, which describes a transparency larger than a 35mm slide.)

3. **Press proofs**. A press proof is an actual printed version of the plates, which have been printed in a small quantity on a small proofing press. Obviously it is expensive, and is not completely reliable since the press, the inks, and possibly even the paper on which it is printed may be different from those that will finally be used. Furthermore, greater care is taken on an individualized run than on the fast run. So the result may be misleading, and perhaps not worth the expense.

Progressive proofs

Process color printing is done in a standard sequence: first, yellow is placed on the sheet, followed by magenta, and then cyan, and the black prints last as the top layer. If the press has a fifth cylinder carrying a special matched color, it would probably go down last, although this aspect of the sequence could vary. Progressive proofs or **progs** are paper proofs printed as press proofs showing each individual color by itself, as well as all the various combinations in a sequence that matches the printing sequence. What you get is a stack of sheets that are stapled together and that look very impressive indeed, which you examine, nodding sagely and hoping for the best. The purpose of progs, of course, is to decide on the corrections that need to be made. The bottom sheet is yellow (since that is the first color to go down), the next one over it is red;   then yellow + red;   then blue; then yellow + blue; red + blue; yellow + red + blue; black; yellow + black;   red + black; blue +black; yellow + red + black; yellow + blue + black; red + blue + black; yellow + red + blue + black, i.e., the final image is on top.

You may often wistfully wonder what it would be like to have the courage to use only three of the four colors, because the red/yellow/black combination is often so much more fun than the realistic full-color rendition of your original photograph. But you shrug off that temptation.

Proofs show **color bars** along the bottom edge of the paper. These are standardized according to specifications set up by the Magazine Publishers Association and are references to the quality of the printing process in terms of the amounts of ink, trapping, and densities that are being produced.

How to correct color proofs

The character of a **transparency**, which depends on light shining through film, cannot possibly be duplicated by a printed version whose impression depends on light being reflected off a sheet of paper. They are two quite different mediums. You must, therefore, take this into account, compensate for it, examine the printed result on its own, and analyze it with respect to its own characteristics. Do you attempt to tell the technicians in technical terms what they ought to do (for instance, "+15 blue−5 mag, o.k. on Y & K*")? Of course not! You tell them as clearly and precisely as possible your reactions to the colors as interpretations of the story. It is the effect on your readers that matters. Is the effect created by the reproduction the effect that you, as editor, wish to have created? If not, then say so. If the object looks too green, write on the proof "Too green" and draw an arrow to the outline of the area that offends you. If the whole picture looks flat and dull, write "Too dull, make more contrasting." If you think there ought to be more sparkle, say "Emphasize highlights." Instructions such as these are qualitative criticisms that will be interpreted in technical terms by the technician. You tell them what you need done from your point of view. It is their expertise that will produce it for you.

But how can you be sure they will do it? If you have the time and

*K is shorthand for black to distinguish it from blue.

money, you can order a second set of proofs. That is rarely done, however, especially if your supplier is a respected house. You assume that your instructions will be followed and hope that the printed result (which will inevitably be somewhat different from the proof anyway) will be what you hope it to be. What happens in practice, of course, is that by the time the piece is printed you have forgotten the minutiae that irritated you about the proofs. You see the piece in its entirety from a totally different angle—as a complete object unto itself, the way the reader will see it—and those minuscule carpings somehow seem to matter much less than they did before.

Squinting through a 4" x 5" transparency into a 60-watt light bulb will make the colors look very different from the same image looked at against the bright blue sky. The industry has set up standards for viewing originals and printed versions in order to prevent misunderstanding between client and supplier. So if you use a great deal of color, it is wise to invest in a **light box** that has the controlled standardized lighting sources for viewing transparencies, and set up a space that is correctly lit for viewing proofs.

How to get more color for less investment

1. By **ganging up** or **common focus**. This means simply that several subjects are color-separated simultaneously as though they were a single unit, reducing the unit cost (although, obviously, you have to pay for a very large overall piece, plus a premium for every unit of which the entire piece is made). The limitations: all originals have to be either transparencies or **reflection copy**, because you can't mix them in one batch; all originals must be to the same focus for one single camera action; and all must have a similar density of color. You can't mix pale, overexposed pictures with dark, underexposed ones because the camera needs to be set for a median that will probably ruin both extremes. Lastly, you must clearly fit your material into the maximum size that the supplier's equipment can produce in one shot, both in maximum film size and in maximum **copyboard** size (the holder in which the originals are inserted for processing).

2. **Duping to size**. If your originals are not all reduced to the same focus and thus cannot be ganged up, you can have duplicate transparencies made to the correct size that you need. It is cheaper to copy a photograph before it is separated (duplicating or "duping" it) and gang it up for the separation than to have individual separations made.

3. **Page positioning**. If you are going to be duping anything, you might as well have the dupes composed so that they are mounted on acetate exactly as they will appear in print and are turned into separations that way. That dramatically reduces the stripping charges: every time you have a color picture, the printer must strip four individual pieces of film (one each for the red, yellow, blue, and black elements), and each strip costs a given price. If you have, say, four pictures on the page, you will be paying for 16 strip charges. But if you page-position them, you pay for only four stripping charges. The duping lab or prep house needs an accurate mechanical to indicate which photo goes where and at what focus and cropping.

12

What you need to know about paper

Paper has physical characteristics that affect the recipient's psychological reaction. Heavy, dull-coated, expensive-looking material is interpreted as carrying matter of greater value than newsprint might. Whatever is printed on newsprint is likely to have a very short shelf life—very few newspapers are filed away for future reference. Annual reports are something else again! Yet information in that newspaper may well be far more valuable than the pap usually found in the annual report. The perceived value is a direct result of the looks and, more importantly, the *feel* of the stock—the paper on which the material is printed.

Is it heavy or light? Stiff or floppy? Rough or smooth in texture? Crinkly or flabby? Handmade or machine made? Slick or pulp?

Your choice is probably going to have to be based on several criteria: appropriateness to the product and to the audience you are reaching; what is compatible with your printer's presses; what is available; what your designer suggests; and—what is probably going to sway your decision most—money. Paper costs have risen so much that they have absorbed a large proportion of the production budget, and you may well need to compromise on second best. However, the stock you use is crucial in persuading your reader of the value of your product, and that's why you should invest more in paper than you might otherwise think.

With that as a philosophy, how do you go about specifying what you want in paper? It is a dauntingly complicated and specialized area of knowledge, where common sense and observation can only serve you up to a point. There are technicalities you must know about in order to make confident decisions. Your printer will probably be your prime source of information and advice, and it is likely that you'll be using whatever stock he has available or recommends. That material is coordinated to the presses he is using by its size (sheet or rolls) and appropriateness or "runability." The printer buys it in bulk, keeps it in stock, and resells it to the customer at a markup, as part of the printing service. If you want special stock, you can ask the printer to order it for you, or you can buy it independently and supply it to the printer yourself. You might even save some money that way, but the aggravation and need for expertise may far outweigh such savings.

All paper manufacturers promote their products actively with printed samples, free dummies made to your specification on request, and promotional materials of all sorts, as well as sales representatives who will gladly come to discuss your needs and suggest solutions. Find them in the Yellow Pages under "Paper Distributors."

But before you start, you had better bone up on a few fundamentals to understand what paper dealers are talking about.

How big is a piece of paper?

It depends—and that's the problem. In paper everything depends! Most printing is done on sheets that are much larger than the final page size (except photocopying, which is done on the standard 8½″ x 11″ sheets;

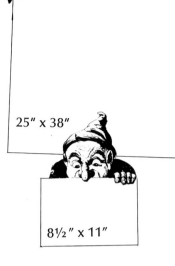

25" x 38"

8½" x 11"

8½" x 14" and 8½" x 17" may also be available). However, let us assume that your finished page size, the **trim size**, is 8½" x 11". It is likely that it will be run on a sheet of paper that measures 11" x 17" and thus will yield a four-page signature, printing two pages to each side. A sheet of 17" x 22" paper yields an eight-page signature. A 16-page signature fits onto a 23" x 35" sheet (to see typical impositions, see page 96). Printing four pages on each side at a time is called "four up"; eight at a time is called "eight up"; 16 at a time is—brilliant!

In fact, the paper comes yet a little bigger, allowing a sliver of paper around the edges to be trimmed after the sheet has been printed and folded and is ready to be bound. The economics of printing and the cost of paper dictate that you work within the standardized size system. That is also why you should consider always printing in multiples of four pages and why you have to take waste into account in planning your impositions.

But the plot thickens: Paper sizes, even the standard ones, vary according to the grade of paper.

Bond paper, used for letters and business forms, comes in a standard 17" x 22" size.

Book paper, offset paper, and **coated paper**, each specifically made for their particular printing purposes, come in standard 25" x 38" sheets.

Newsprint comes in sheets that measure 24" x 36".

Text paper, used for booklets and brochures that warrant color and texture, comes in a 25" x 38" size.

Cover stock, often coordinated with text paper in color and texture but made to a much heavier weight, measures 20" x 26" as a standard size.

You need to know the kind of paper and thus the standard size of the sheet before discussing:

Basis weight

Briefly defined, it is the weight in pounds of a **ream** (500 sheets) in the size of that particular grade. If you have a "basis 80 text," you are actually talking about a stack of 500 sheets of text paper that would weigh 80 lbs., each sheet measuring 25" x 38". That same paper can also be referred to as "80-lb. text." So far, this is not difficult. What is frustrating is that in price and availability tables, paper manufacturers don't talk in terms of a ream of 500 sheets, but list everything in multiples of 1000 sheets, or two reams, or one "M." So that same 80-lb. text has to be seen in the tables as 25" x 38"—160 M.

To complicate your life somewhat further, the basic sizes mentioned here are only reference numbers used for defining basis weight. The paper can actually be purchased in all sorts of other sizes, and, needless to say, there are also all sorts of different basis weights made in the various paper grades.

Lest you should think that the complexities of paper nomenclature and cataloging have been fully explained, be of good cheer—they have not. Should you be talking about business paper, the kind you type or write on, a whole different system is used. Instead of basis weight, you talk about **substance weight**—a measurement of a ream (500 sheets) of paper measuring 17" x 22" from which ledger, bond, manifold, and mimeograph papers are cut. So in this area, your symbols are "Sub-16," "Sub-20," or "Sub-24."

Weight of stock may be an important consideration if you are mailing your publication. It is wise to ask the paper supplier to make a dummy of the piece in the stock you expect to use with the right number of pages in it and have it weighed at the post office. You may well have to retrench a little and go lighter. But that may not necessarily make your product feel cheaper or flimsier, because you have to consider the next attribute of paper, which is:

Bulking and thickness

This is a measure of the thickness of a single sheet of paper (referred to as **caliper** in the trade) in thousandths of an inch, or **mils**. You don't need to know that figure. What you do need to realize, however, is that it is perfectly possible for one piece of paper to measure fatter or thinner than another, yet both weigh the same. Thickness depends on the degree of squeezing that the paper underwent in the manufacturing process. So it is reasonable to have a piece of paper that weighs less, yet feels thicker than another. For a publication that consists of just a few pages, a thicker-feeling sheet will add bulk and apparent weight.

In papers used for manufacturing books, bulk is not measured in terms of the thickness of a single sheet, but rather in terms of number of **pages per inch** (ppi).

The whole archaic measuring system that has evolved over the centuries into the complexity we now have will, perforce, be converted to metric in due course. The period of transition is a time to contemplate with trepidation.

Show-through and opacity

If you can see the printing from one side through the other side of the paper, you have show-through. Clearly, the thickness of the paper has something to do with this: The thicker it is, the less show-through you are likely to have. But it may not necessarily be thickness alone, because opacity can be affected by chemicals in the paper. Adding mineral fillers can cut down on show-through even in a very thin sheet. And having a sheet that has a low basis weight and high bulk may give you a thick-feeling piece of paper, but the fibers may be so loosely packed that the ink gets sucked through to the other side.

You have to see printed samples to make an intelligent judgment on this problem. The question that really concerns you is this: How much show-through are you willing to live with? The less the paper costs, the greater the likelihood of show-through.

Brightness

Brightness is an important quality in paper because it affects the way pictures will appear. The brighter the piece of paper, the more sparkle and contrast you can expect to have in your black-and-white photos. Fluorescent brighteners can be added to the paper to create startling effects. But if you don't have many photos, or if they are not important to your publication, the brightness is not a quality you should need to pay a premium price for.

Shininess

Shininess is usually achieved by coating the paper with chemicals that close up the surface. The surface can appear dull or glossy, or any degree of shininess in between. But whatever that degree of shininess may be, the coated printing surface has been made to have better ink "hold-out" or resistance to absorption than uncoated stocks have. Why do you need it? To reproduce halftones better. Screens have better definition and better density on coated paper than you could expect on uncoated paper. That is why you can use much finer screens on coated paper—up to 150-line or even 200-line. On the other hand, the shinier the paper is, the more difficult it becomes to read the text because of the mirror effect caused by highlights on that paper. Readers see a greater value in "slick" publications than they do in "pulps," so you have that aspect of value judgment to consider in your decision making.

Finishes

These affect the smoothness of paper and are the result of the manufacturing process. As the sheet of paper passes through the various rollers in the papermaking machine, the number and texture of those rollers affects the final surface. Uncoated book papers may be produced in the following degrees of smoothness: antique (the roughest), eggshell, vellum, English finish, machine finish (the smoothest).* Further smoothness can be produced by coating. Textures can also be embossed on the sheet by passing it through yet another machine that produces patterns such as linen, tweed, pebble, and more.

Wove paper has a uniformly smooth surface. **Laid** paper has parallel lines within it. **Offset** papers have been coated with sizing to make the surface less porous and prevent the water in the ink from seeping into the fibers of the paper.

Colored stock

We are used to white paper. It yields the best results as far as contrast with black ink is concerned. Whether this is in fact the ideal is arguable: Some recent tests have shown that that very contrast may be detrimental to readership and that a gentler contrast, such as you get by printing black on light grey, might be much better. (Lessening the contrast has been found to be helpful in helping dyslexic children read.)

An unlimited palette of colors is available from various paper

---

*Antique paper is one whose surface has been neither polished (also called calendered) nor coated. Eggshell finishes give uncoated paper a nonglossy, soft effect and are frequently used for antique papers. Vellum finishes on paper result in smooth, somewhat waxlike feel and some translucency. A smooth paper that has been calendered but not glossed is called English finish, while machine finish signifies paper that has been smoothed by passing through several rolls of the calendering machine. These and other paper terms may be found in *The Bookman's Glossary*, Sixth Edition, edited by Jean Peters (New York: Bowker, 1983), and *Dictionary of Publishing* by David Brownstone and I. Franck (New York: Van Nostrand Reinhold, 1982).

manufacturers. Is it wise to use colored stock? Yes, why not—if it is used carefully and wisely, and if it is appropriate to the product at hand. Problems to look out for:

1. Printing halftones on colored stock usually makes them appear muddy and dingy. That's because the highlights (which we expect to appear "white") cannot be any lighter than the color of the paper on which they are printed. Color, however, is a question not merely of the **hue** (redness, blueness, etc.) but also of the **chroma** (the intensity of that redness or blueness), as well as the **value** (the darkness or lightness, i.e., the equivalent in black and white to grayness). If your colored paper has a dark value, the highlights cannot help but appear dark, dull, and lifeless.

2. Printing in colored ink atop colored stock is potentially very exciting as a trick to get attention or to give your publication its own special character. But it is playing with fire in terms of legibility and reader fatigue. Invest in a test run before committing yourself to a plunge of this nature. By all means, look at the promotion material put out by the paper companies. They delight the eye with such things, and make you wistful for their freedom and excitement, their quality and originality. But be aware of the fact that on those promotion pieces, the tricks depend on the most subtle uses of various kinds of inks—transparent and opaque—running colors in unexpected rotation (i.e., what gets printed on top of what) and so on. You had better know about these tricks. They are always spelled out in detail in the technical notes printed on the last page of those promotion pieces.

3. Be sure that the particular color will remain in stock for the foreseeable future, and that your next issue won't have to be printed on a different material. The color you choose ought to become one of your recognition symbols, just like the logo, the typography, and the shape of the piece overall. The paradox is, of course, that the more special your color is, the less likely is it to remain in stock for a long time. Its specialness prevents it from selling widely, and it is obviously the wide sellers that the paper companies keep in stock. Therefore, you are most likely to wind up with a fairly ordinary-looking color because of its dependable availability.

Newsprint

Anything that is printed on newsprint gains an aura of newsworthiness from the expectation that newsprint has built up in the recipient over a long tradition. This built-in advantage balances the negative perception of the cheapness and, therefore, the lack of permanent value of the piece that is printed on newsprint. That built-in newsiness needs to be supported and paralleled, however, by the styling of the rest of the product if its positive characteristic is to be turned to your advantage. Thus, the way the copy is written, the way the headlines are handled, the way the pictures are placed and chosen, the way the **cut lines** (captions) are written—all should add up to a well-thought-through package appropriate to the physical material.

A new, heavier version of newsprint is gaining wide acceptance. It runs color well, and its perceived value is greater than that of the regular light **ground wood stock** (a slang term for newsprint).

Envelopes

The most common envelope sizes:

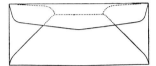

Commercial: # 9—3⅞″ x 8⅞″
            #10—4⅛″ x 9½″
            #11—4½″ x 10⅜″

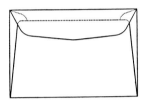

Booklet: 6″   x 9″
         6½″ x 9½″
         7″   x 10″
         7½″ x 10½″
         8¼″ x 11¼″
         9″   x 12″

In the planning of any publication, it is wise to take **distribution** into account. If that includes mailing, then it is merely common sense to coordinate the envelope with the contents so that they fit physically, as well as in terms of style. Chances are that standard-size envelopes are available in the same color and texture of paper that you are using inside, be it text or bond paper. Cheapest, of course, are the ready-made envelopes that come in all sorts of standard sizes. Large-size envelopes for bulky or heavy mailing use kraft papers—the brown stuff also generally available in white or gray.

Remember that envelopes also have a variety of features: the type of flap (square or pointed); the flap on the short or the long dimension; a variety of seam placements on the back of the envelope; with or without adhesive, button, string, clasp; with or without windows; and so on. Your printer can supply you with a chart showing the range of materials, sizes, and finishes available to choose from in the ready-made and custom-made envelopes.

13

What you absolutely must know about printing, folding, binding, and finishing

The way the piece will be printed and bound affects the way you prepare the copy, what you can do with it, how far you can go to embellish the product, what to expect in terms of quality of reproduction in your pictures, and the degree of excellence of the overall product that will reflect on you and your organization. The choice of reproduction technique depends on a number of interrelated factors:

1. The **print run** (how many copies you will need) and the frequency of publishing.

2. The availability of printing suppliers in your vicinity.

3. The kind of service they can supply (quick reproduction or full-scale commercial printing).

4. The availability of in-house equipment (photocopying or mimeo machinery in the basement or on your desk top).

5. The existence of printing contracts, if any.

6. The **scheduling** of your production (whether you need rush service while you wait, or whether you are so well organized you can spare a few days at the end).

7. The need for **color** (passing through the press once for each color can be a nuisance, but it is cheaper than printing on a multicolor press, whose cost is balanced by the simplicity and speed of production).

8. The distance from the office to the printer (the further away you are, the more difficult it becomes to make those inevitable last-minute changes).

9. Money, of course. Money isn't just a factor in the cost of the printing itself, but in other aspects of the production process—the comparative cost of the paper appropriate to the machinery to be used; the cost of your own time devoted to running it yourself, as compared to buying the service from professionals; and so forth.

Here is a list of the basic options in printing. No specific recommendations can be made since there are so many requirements, and individual situations have to be taken into account in any decision.

Stenciling it yourself

The most primitive reproduction method for runs of up to about 100 copies is the **spirit duplicator**—that rather smelly, smeary purple-inked product so reminiscent of school examinations. It is a dye carbon transfer process using two sheets of paper; the image is transferred onto the master from the back of the top sheet, which, like carbon paper, bears a coating of dye carbon. In turn, the printed copies pick up an image of that dye when they are passed over the master in the press. Naturally, the master gets weaker and paler and the type fuzzier as the run progresses.

Mimeographing

This is also a direct-stencil method of reproduction, which utilizes a **stencil** that used to have to be "cut" by the editor. The stencil is made of a thin, porous material coated with a waxy substance that is punctured by typewriter keys or any other sharp instrument. Ink passes through such breaks when the stencil is placed on a press between the ink roll and paper to be printed on. Although the term "mimeograph" was the name of a specific machine, it has become the generic term for this kind of reproduction, no matter whose machinery is actually used (like "frigidaire" for icebox and "escalator" for moving staircase). There are a number of manufacturers actively improving, promoting, selling, and servicing such equipment.

The image that a mimeographed publication has on the recipient is that of a homemade, comparatively inexpensive product. Thus, it can have all the advantages of intimate, in-group personalization. The image mimeographed publications produce in the mind of the editor is one of struggles with stencils, problems in making corrections, and time-consuming frustration. That used to be the case, but it is by no means so any more, now that **electronic stencils** can be made at comparatively low cost from copy prepared exactly the same way as for offset or photocopying. This enables you to use display type, drawings, and even photographs (screened to a rather coarse-looking 85-line screen, but better than nothing). A great advantage of mimeo is its moderate expense. The machinery is simple, so it costs less to buy or lease, and the paper you use needs to be porous, so cheaper stock is technically the correct kind to be using. (It also comes in a variety of pale colors.) Since the equipment is not difficult to use, it could make good sense to get a machine for doing it yourself, because that way you can also control it yourself. Such control has built-in advantages: convenience, cheapness, and precision. It also has disadvantages: messiness, the need for periodic maintenance, lots of space devoted only to its use, time required for upkeep, preparation, running, and washing off, as well as the problems that arise when it refuses to perform halfway through the run.

Photocopying and xerography

Electrostatic printing or xerography depends on electric charges to organize dry ink powder to fall on blank paper where marks on the original paper are sensed by the equipment. The ink particles hurtle into position like iron filings responding to a magnet and are permanently fused onto the paper by heat. The new machinery can print on both sides of the paper on a variety of sheet sizes up to 11" x 17", produce up to 150 copies a minute, and separate, collate, and even staple in the same pass. Needless to say, the per-copy cost is higher than mimeo; it is more economical than offset, however, if the number of copies needed is small but good quality is required.

One disadvantage of photocopying: It can only be done in black. Therefore, to make a more colorful product, you must either use colored stock or have your logo preprinted in color (on colored stock !) and imprint your text in a subsequent operation.

Letterpress

The method used by Gutenberg, who invented movable type, is still in some use, although the technology has been considerably improved since 1437! Letterpress is also called **relief printing** because the parts that are to print stand out above the nonprinting background; the ink is applied by rollers to those bumps and is, in turn, transferred to the paper in an impression that is made under considerable pressure, often damaging the original metal pieces. That is why exact duplicates, called **electroplates** or electros, are made. Halftones are etched on photo-sensitive copper sheets with acid and then attached to wooden blocks that are assembled on the stone together with the type. The type is made of **lead** (actually a specially formulated alloy) cast into line lengths on the **linotype** (line of type!) machine, after each line of text has been assembled as a sequence of individual letter molds.

Page makeup is copied from the layout, or dummy, that the editors have prepared from proofs of the type and the **cuts** (that's the old word for halftones, or illustrations of any kind). The type, by the way, is stored on long trays called **galleys** when it comes off the linotype machine; hence, the word "galley" for a long column of raw type.

Offset

Offset lithography, photo-offset, litho, sheet-fed offset, web offset—all are variations on the basic technology of **planography**, in which the printing is done from a flat surface. The principle on which it is based is simple: Oil and water don't mix. The surface of the printing plate is chemically treated in such a way that the areas that print attract ink and repel water, whereas the areas that do not print attract water and repel ink.

It is called **lithography**—stone printing—because Aloys Senefelder developed it around 1796 as a method of printing from slabs of limestone, on which he drew with greasy pencil and which he then covered with acid. The greasy parts were unaffected, but the clear parts later repelled the ink that adhered to the greasy parts. Paper pressed onto the stone picked up the ink, but not from the parts that were merely wet with water.

The reason why it is called **offset** is quite logical. Although fine artists continue using the old method of lithography for their special purposes, we no longer print from slabs of limestone in commercial printing. Instead, plates are made of metal or plastic and wrapped around cylinders or rollers on the press; then the ink is transferred—set off, or offset—from the printing plate onto a smooth rubber blanket on a second roller, which, in turn, prints the ink onto the sheet of paper passing beneath it.

Sheet-fed offset describes a process in which the press is fed precut sheets of paper. **Web offset** defines a press fed with paper from rolls; the paper is cut into signature-sized sheets after the printing has been done.

Plates or **masters** are made of aluminum, plastic, or treated paper. For short runs of perhaps five thousand copies that do not require too much fine detail in the halftones, usually paper plates are used. Halftone screens should not be finer than 100 lines. This kind of offset printing is produced by the fast-print shops, whether chain or individually owned, that typically occupy storefront premises in shopping centers. Such shops are probably restricted to a maximum of 11" x 17" paper size and have a limited stock of papers to choose from. The quality they produce can vary, depending on the equipment as well as the skill of the people involved, but it is usually remarkably good for the price.

Commercial printers are expected to deliver far better quality: finer halftones with better detail using up to 150-line screens; an unlimited variety of paper stock; far wider variety of folding capabilities; larger sheet sizes (17" x 22" or 8-page forms at the normal 8½" x 11" page size, or 23" x 35" or 16-page forms). The availability of such paper sizes is advantageous because it means shorter time on press to run off a job, and press time is a major cost factor in printing. Commercial printers also provide much more accurate registration, better color work, and certainly better stripping and **make-ready** (preparation of the press for running the job just so). They will supply you with a list of trade customs that spell out the printer's, as well as the customer's, obligations and expectations.

Gravure

It is unlikely that you will be using either letterpress or gravure, but it is mentioned here for the sake of completeness. Gravure or **intaglio** printing works in the opposite way from letterpress. Instead of the printing areas being raised above the nonprinting background, they are cut or incised into the printing plate by engraving or by etching with acid. These hollows, then, are filled with ink (the rest of the plate being cleaned off with a **doctor blade**). The paper to be printed on is then forced onto the plate under great pressure, and the paper sucks the ink out of the plate.

Rotogravure means that the press uses cylinders to which the plates are attached; **sheet-fed gravure** is a much slower flatbed process where the paper moves through the press one sheet at a time—and the highest quality of reproduction can be achieved. Rotogravure is faster, and many national magazines and newspaper color supplements are produced in this manner.

Can you tell the difference between offset, letterpress, and gravure?

Easily: Examine a single letter under a linen tester or 8×-power loupe. If the ink lies flat and smooth all over, it is offset. If there is a flare of ink around the edges, resulting from the metal being forced into the paper, it is letterpress. If the edges of the letter are zigzag, then it is gravure.

Why should you want to be able to tell the difference? To impress your friends and confound your enemies. But watch out! There are traps that need to be avoided. Some new typesetting machinery produces letters electronically and builds each letter up from tiny dots. The overall outline of such letters can resemble gravure under the enlarging glass, so don't bet more than you can afford to lose.

What happens after printing?

If your publication is printed on a single piece of paper distributed flat, then nothing in the rest of this chapter will interest you, and you may as well skip it. But if that publication is a bit more complex, then it is essential to bear in mind the last series of steps following the actual printing. They can cause problems and annoying delays unless they are understood and taken into account.

The printer is your best source of advice and information because folding, collating, binding, and finishing usually come under his contract—whether the actual work is subcontracted to a **bindery** or not. As in all other aspects of the print production process, it is wise to collect samples of printed pieces that you think are well done and use them for reference when discussing your needs with your suppliers. The trouble with such samples is that they are probably beautiful, flamboyant, and unusual pieces of high quality (or else you wouldn't have noticed them, would you?). That's why it is wise to remember White's observation of the facts of life: If you like it, it's too expensive.

Paper has grain that affects its proper utilization

As paper is made, the fibers of which the pulp consists tend to turn parallel to the direction of flow through the machine. That is what creates a **grain**, which in turn affects the utilization of the paper in two ways. First, folding the paper with the grain yields a smooth fold, whereas folding it against the grain cracks the surface and creates a rough edge. Second, the grain makes the paper stiffer in the direction of the grain; therefore, the grain should run parallel with the folded or binding edge of the publication because that helps the pages to turn more easily and lie flat. If this is the way the piece is planned, it is said to be **grain long**.

How various ways of folding the sheet can be useful

After a sheet of paper has been printed on both sides—no matter whether it is a small sheet (of four pages) or an enormous one (of 64 pages)—it is fed into a folding machine that buckles, creases, and folds it into a **signature** or booklet form. (The signature is made of multiples of four pages.) It is then passed on for **trimming**, where three guillotines slice off excess paper from the outside, head, and foot margins.

For stock that is too heavy or too thick to fold easily, **scoring** is a preliminary operation to folding. Scoring creases the sheet wherever a fold should fall and is somewhat tricky, for its purpose is to prevent the paper from cracking, and therefore it must be done right. It is best done on the press rather than on the folding machine because it can be more accurately controlled. In any case, though, it is essential to **emboss**, or raise a bump in, the paper, which should be facing into the inside of the fold.

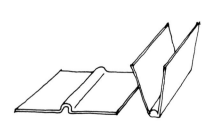

There are two basic **folds** possible on a machine: parallel and right-angle folds. Here are a few typical folder styles whose names you might find useful.

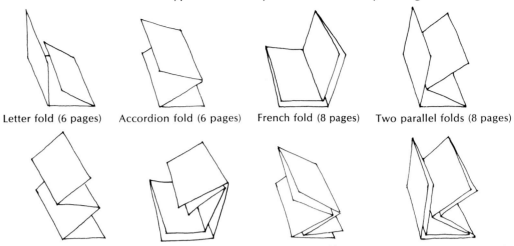

Letter fold (6 pages)	Accordion fold (6 pages)	French fold (8 pages)	Two parallel folds (8 pages)

Accordion fold (8 pages)	Regular fold (12 pages)	Accordion fold (12 pages)	One parallel, two right-angle folds (16 pages)

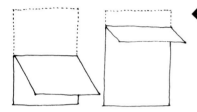

← If a piece is not folded in half, it is called a **short fold**.

These aspects of publication making are, admittedly, rather dull for people who only need to know about them as a means to an end. Once you absorb the technicalities and can utilize their potential, they can be important. Here are a few of these simple folds shown in uses that could give your product some surprising effects.*

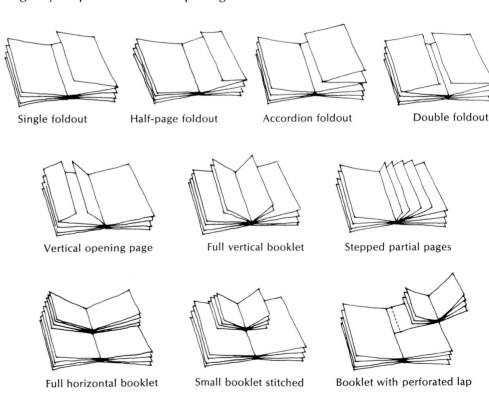

Single foldout	Half-page foldout	Accordion foldout	Double foldout

Vertical opening page	Full vertical booklet	Stepped partial pages

Full horizontal booklet	Small booklet stitched	Booklet with perforated lap

If there are a number of signatures to be assembled in proper sequence, the process, whether it be hand done or machine produced, is called **collating**.

---

*For more on this see Jan V. White, *Editing by Design,* Second Edition (New York: R. R. Bowker, 1982), p. 76.

Binding

There are seven basic methods of assembling pieces of paper.

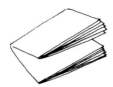

1. **Simple folding** to hold the sheets together without recourse to mechanical means. Newspapers are a typical example.

2. **Stapling**, whether by hand or machine, which is a satisfactory technique for simple publications using typewriter (or equivalent) typesetting and local reproduction processes (in other words, low-circulation, low-budget products). The top left-hand corner is the usual position for the staple—parallel to the left-hand edge or top edge or on the diagonal. If you need to attach more than three pages, it might be wise to explore the possibility of printing the piece as a four-page unit, thus avoiding stapling altogether.

3. **Saddle stitching**, which entails driving staples through the fold of the backbone or spine. The number of staples needed depends upon the number of pages: the more pages, the more staples. Most magazines are saddle stitched because it is the cheapest method of holding the pages together, and, more importantly, it allows the pages to lie flat when the piece is opened.

4. **Side-wire stitching**, which involves driving the staples through the face of the stack of signatures ¼″ from the backbone. Side-wire stitching is used for heavy-bulk products such as *National Geographic Magazine*, for instance. Its disadvantages: An extra-deep margin must be allowed at the gutter for the staples, and it is a struggle to keep the pages open, especially if the stock is heavy. Side-wire stitching also requires separate covers to be attached after the signatures have been stitched together.

5. **Perfect binding**, which holds the pages together by means of glue that remains flexible for a long time. When the signatures have been collated, the spines are scraped, leaving a roughened surface onto which adhesive is applied. As in side-wire stitching, a cover must be attached to the adhesive to make the product look neatly finished. The advantage of perfect binding is that pages lie flat. Disadvantage? The pages can fall out.

The advantage of both side-wire and perfect binding is that both give a **square back** to the publication. That allows for running the name, volume, and date on the **spine**. Furthermore, a square back gives the product an aura of value that saddle-stitched publications lack, so the recipient is likely to pay greater attention and keep the piece for a longer period of time, especially if the spine also lists the contents to facilitate reference.

6. **Smyth sewing** means sewing the signatures together by means of thread. This is used for **edition-binding** books (books in hard covers with end leaves, cloth covering, etc.; such books are also called **case bound**). The advantage of Smyth sewing is its permanence coupled with the fact that the pages can indeed lie flat in spite of the thickness of the overall volume. The disadvantage: expense.

7. **Mechanical binding**, in which plastic or wire doohickeys are inserted through a series of holes punched in the binding edge of the piece. Used for reports, notebooks, and so on, it offers the advantage that the pages lie flat. Among its disadvantages are expense, when a large number must be made; the need to have very deep gutter margins to accommodate the bindings; and the difficulty of stacking a number of mechanically bound units in neat stacks.

Diecutting

Diecutting is an attention-catching technique that depends on its unexpectedness for effect. But you had better know *why* you are using such trickery, and it had better be applied functionally to make a point or the expense may prove wasteful. Funny physical shapes are no substitute for the inner content of a story. As the poet says, "Form without substance casts no shadow."

Technically, diecutting is simply cutting the paper into an unexpected profile or punching a hole in it. It is done by attaching specially shaped knives (dies) to the appropriate machinery. The dies, made of extremely hard, sharp steel, are either straight steel rules or hollow, like cookie cutters. Standard shapes of various kinds are available, but custom shapes can be made if you want to invest the necessary fortune. Small holes, such as those found in paper for three-ring binders, are not diecut, but drilled.

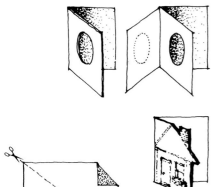

Diecutting holes acts on the reader's curiosity. The peek-a-boo or keyhole syndrome is hard to resist—as any ecdysiast will readily aver. The interrelationship of graphics and meaning, however, must be intimately worked out—and not just in the left-to-right direction, which is the one we usually think of, but backward too: the back side of the hole in relationship to the page that precedes it, or right to left.

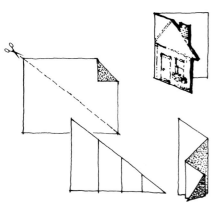

Diecutting the edges of paper can be used for two basically distinct purposes: to cut out a shape that may have meaning in and of itself, such as the outline of a house pictured on a page (a use commonly seen in greeting cards that can easily be applied to brochures and publications); or to cut a geometrical shape other than the expected rectangle with a view to its subsequent folding. Given such a situation, all sorts of rich effects can be achieved if one side of the sheet is run in one color and the other in another, and the piece is then folded to expose part of each. Just take a piece of ordinary typing paper, cut off one side at an angle and start folding it into an accordion fold—that's the only way to explain it.

Perforating

If a page, or part of a page, is to be detachable, the perforation is done by the bindery or folding machine. It can also be part of the diecutting operation. Trimming the piece can be done before or after the diecutting, depending on the kind of machinery being used.

Laminating

Although it is unlikely you'll be using this expensive process to enrich the effect of your cover, it is worthwhile at least knowing about its existence. Laminating consists of applying a layer of clear plastic material, such as mylar, to the outside of the cover. Lamination makes the colors sparkle and gives the covers greater durability.

A less expensive version yielding a similar effect can be produced as a last step in the printing process by using a coat of clear **varnish** on the last pass through the press. For special effect, the varnish can be restricted to just small areas, printing on the sheet the same way that halftones do. In that case, you would refer to the process as **spot varnishing**.

Mailing and distribution

Self-mailers and envelopes

The question of envelopes has already been discussed in the chapter on paper (see page 167). If you use a stock that is heavy enough, you may be able to dispense with the envelope altogether and send the piece out as a self-mailer. The paper must be stiff enough to resist scuffing and damage, but its increased cost will surely be lower than the cost of envelopes and stuffing. The postage will probably be about the same, although that could be a point critical enough to make it worth checking with the Post Office.

It is appropriate to touch on self-mailing pieces here because their success depends on understanding the folding process, assuming that the fundamental point of paper weight is understood: Obviously you can't send through the mail a flimsy, unprotected piece of paper that will get damaged by handling. But if the stock you are using is stiff enough, then you have solved that part of the problem, and all that remains is to think of what you can do to fold it interestingly, and how you will seal it so that it doesn't come open.

One 8½" x 11" page by itself is likely to need an envelope. The regular letter fold fits into a standard No. 10 envelope, and is the simplest, most direct means of sending out a letterlike piece. The four-page unit, however, allows for a variety of folds and self-mailers. Here are four basic shapes that an 11" x 17" page (i.e., two 8½" x 11" pages) can produce.

Sealing

You can seal the piece in the following ways:

1. With a staple: cheapest, but most annoying to the recipient because it results either in torn paper (if the staple isn't removed) or torn fingernails (if it is). After all, who has a staple remover near the mailbox?

2. With a sticky tab of some sort: It could be a gold seal or red legal seal that you can get at a stationery store, glued on by hand, or a peel-off seal made with adhesive on the back. Or it can be sealed with a small paper tab by machine. Cost and visual effect are the criteria on which to base your decision.

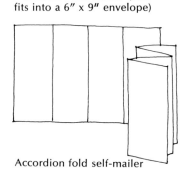

Full-page size

Accordion fold (fits a No. 10 envelope)

French fold self-mailer (also fits into a 6" x 9" envelope)

Accordion fold self-mailer

INDEX